Theology
in Turmoil

Theology in Turmoil

The Roots, Course and Significance
of the Conservative-Liberal Debate
in Modern Theology

Alan P. F. Sell

BAKER BOOK HOUSE
Grand Rapids, Michigan 49506

CONTENTS

PREFACE

'What is the Christian gospel?' This perennially important question was thrust to the fore in that debate between theological conservatives and liberals which was at its height between 1890 and 1930, and of which echoes may be heard to this day. In this book I seek to trace the roots of this debate, to outline its course, and to draw some lessons from it.

In the first half of the first chapter I take the considerable risk of saying a *few* words about Kant, Schleiermacher and Hegel. It is not too much to say that a great deal of modern theology comprises commentaries upon, or reactions against these thinkers. Moreover, their influence extends to quarters where it is not acknowledged or, in some cases, even noticed. They could not, then, reasonably be omitted. On the contrary, if we are to understand that immanentist-subjectivist thrust in modern theology which helped to fuel the conservative-liberal theological debate, their presence is essential. The first chapter concludes with an account of the advance of immanentist varieties of thought in the nineteenth century. Chapters on the rise and reception of modern biblical criticism, and on evolutionary thought follow; and it will become clear that, contrary to what might be suggested by my Table of Contents, these are by no means mutually exclusive topics. Albrecht Ritschl is a clear candidate for inclusion in this work because of his marked influence upon theological liberalism generally, and upon American Social Gospel thought in particular. An attempt to characterise (rather than precisely to define) theological conservatism and liberalism is followed by a discussion in which I make bold to suggest that possibilities of reducing the gospel obtain on either side of the argument. In a concluding section I enter a plea for theological balance.

I ought perhaps to explain the reason for my regular recourse to the views of older critics. It is not (as will become apparent) that I think that they always spoke the last word on the matters with which they dealt, though close acquaintance with them reveals how well many of their judgments have stood the test of time. Rather, I have sought to enter into the period through the eyes of contemporary writers. Thus, for example, I have not set out in chapter 4 to write a detailed critique of Ritschl's works, but to note the diversity of ways in which he was received by scholars as the conservative-liberal debate was gathering momentum, and to enter into discussion both with him and with them in relation to that debate.

My hope is that general readers and students will gain a bird's eye view of a fascinating period of shifting landmarks in theology, and that scholars may find it helpful to be reminded of the sources upon which I have drawn.

For more detailed discussions of the responses of individual British theologians to the tendencies here surveyed I may perhaps be permitted to refer to the following studies I have made in recent years: *Robert Mackintosh: Theologian of Integrity,* Bern: Peter Lang, 1977, 'Henry Rogers and the eclipse of faith', *The Journal of the United Reformed Church History Society*, II, 1980; 'An Englishman, an Irishman and a Scotsman', *The Scottish Journal of Theology*, XXXVIII, part 1, 1985. In a forthcoming book, *Defending and Declaring the Faith: Some Scottish Examples, 1860–1920* are chapters on John Kennedy, Robert Flint, John Caird, A. B. Bruce, James Iverach, James Orr, D. W. Forrest and James Denney.

A number of obliging editors have enabled me to test out much of the material in this book. The bulk of chapters 1, 3, 5 and 6 appeared in *Faith and Thought,* CIV, 1977–78, pp.119–45, 202–20, and CV, 1978, pp.62–118; chapter 2 was originally published in *The Evangelical Quarterly*, LII, 1980, pp.132–48; and an abbreviated version of chapter 4 appeared in *The Reformed Theological Review*, XXXIII, 1979, pp.33–41. The concluding paragraphs of chapter 1 contain material from 'Platonists (Ancient and Modern) and the Gospel', *The Irish Theological Quarterly*, XLIV, 1977, pp.153—74. I am most grateful for the cordial editorial responses to my requests for permission to reprint this material.

Alan P. F. Sell
Department of Theology
World Alliance of Reformed Churches
Geneva

CHAPTER ONE

IMMANENTISM AND THE GOSPEL

'From the time of Kant onwards', writes Professor Aiken, 'it is the thinking subject himself who establishes the standards of objectivity'.[1] Can there be any commerce between this standpoint and that which seeks to think God's thoughts after him? This question underlies much of the modern theological discussion of such issues as transcendence and immanence, the authority of the bible, evolutionary thought and ethical Christianity. The question is thrown into relief in the debate between theological conservatives and liberals. We hope to show how the question has arisen, and to consider the influence of the diverse answers given to it upon the statement of the Christian gospel.

I

We begin with Kant. It is a testimony at once to the genius and suggestiveness, but also to the elusiveness of Kant (1724–1804) that he has become not all things to all men, but very different things to very different men. His philosophical pilgrimage is well known. An enthusiastic disciple of Leibniz *via* Wolff, he never forsook the doctrine of innate ideas; the *a priori* ever weighed heavily with him. But empiricism awoke him, as he said, from his dogmatic slumbers[2] and, negatively, convinced him that Leibnizian talk about pre-established harmony and the like was so much dogmatism. Positively, Hume impelled Kant to seek a more excellent way than that of scepticism: Hume's empiricism could show us how things are, but it could never pronounce upon how they must be: 'it has hitherto been assumed that

our cognition must conform to the objects; but all attempts
to ascertain anything about these objects *a priori*, by means
of conceptions, and thus to extend the range of our knowledge, have been rendered abortive by this assumption. Let us
then make the experiment whether we may not be more
successful in metaphysics, if we assume that the objects
must conform to our cognition'.[3] Here is the essence of what
Kant called his Copernican revolution in philosophy. Far
from being *tabula rasa*, as Locke had (allegedly) maintained,
the mind is active in creating knowledge *out of what it
empirically presented to it.*[4] This it does by the application
of such *a priori* notions as space and time. Apart from this
logically prior, unificatory, work of the reason no meaning-
ful experience would be possible. Equally, were there no
sensory experience such categories as unity, plurality and
causality, applying as they do to phenomena only, would be
redundant. Professor Casserley has rightly said that for
Kant, 'The rationalist conception of innate ideas is, more
carefully and guardedly stated, a valid one, but rationalist
metaphysics are a delusion. The empiricist's distrust of
rationalist metaphysics is justified, but natural science
provides no clue to the mystery of the objective being of
nature'.[5] The point may be illustrated by reference to the
crucial category of causality.

Hume denied that the law of universal causation could
be known *a priori* to be true, and Kant agreed that the
rationalists had been mistaken in maintaining that such
supposed necessary truths are directly intuited. The statement 'every event has a cause' is not analytic, he argued.
He did not agree with Hume, however, that the category
of causation, being supplied by the mind, is inapplicable to
phenomena. He therefore sought a way of showing that
'every event has a cause' must be both synthetic and *a
priori*. Were it not *a priori,* and thus in some sense necessary,
we could have no assured knowledge of the world; were it
not synthetic, that is, open to empirical verification, we
should be imprisoned within ideas once more. Our knowledge
is thus of phenomena only as perceived by our mind. We do
not know the things in themselves, for these belong to the
noumenal realm. Likewise, although reason prompts us to

postulate such ideas as those of God, freedom and immortality we can have, strictly, no knowledge of these, for they are not phenomena. Are we then shut up to a scepticism as extreme as Hume's? Kant does not intend this result, for he considers that having clearly defined and limited the sphere of reason, he has left room for faith. Moreover, such faith is immune both to rationalistic demonstration and destruction. In all of this we have the seeds of an important bifurcation in post-Kantian thought; for on the one hand some came to rest in a Kant-inspired agnosticism, while on the other hand some, grateful for the way in which Kant had made room for faith, launched out upon a sea of transcendentalism, or set off on the quest of experientially-confirmed faith claims.

If the *Critique of Pure Reason* (1781, second edition 1787) leaves us with an idea of God which, though not intuited is not rationally justifiable, the *Critique of Practical Reason* (1788) employs the concepts of God, freedom and immortality as postulates — that is, as conditions, and not simply as presuppositions, of thought. Man's will, the practical reason, is subject to a self-imposed moral demand, the categorical imperative; man knows that he cannot refuse to acknowledge this demand; it is directly given in his experience, and is autonomous. As Professor Pringle-Pattison put it, 'Man as noumenon, or purely rational being, gives the law; man as phenomenon receives it'.[6] Hence, morality does not depend upon religion: if it did, morality would be heteronomous — a possibility which Kant shunned as undermining his belief that that is moral which is done for its own sake. However, by way of guaranteeing an eternal order in which the due apportionment of virtue and reward, evil and punishment will be competently achieved, we may, not irrationally, postulate God, freedom and immortality. This last train of thought is more fully elaborated in the *Critique of Judgment* (1790). But man remains his own lawgiver; his autonomy is firmly entrenched. Robert Mackintosh, as so often, encapsulates most of the difficulties in Kant in a few sentences:

'On one side, the world we know by valid processes of thinking cannot, we are told, be the real world. Or, beginning from the other side; neither the reality which ideal thought reaches after, nor yet the reality which our conscience postulates, is the valid world of orderly thinking. The great critic of scepticism has diverged from idealism towards scepticism again, or has given his idealism a sceptical colour, mitigated — but only mitigated - by faith in the moral consciousness.'[7]

Needless to say, this faith is remarkably different from biblical faith in a knowable (truly though not, of course, exhaustively) personal God who has revealed himself supremely in Christ. Yet not a few later liberal theologians, rejoicing that Kant, by separating reason from faith, had once and for all demolished the old grounds of natural theology, came to believe that 'doctrines whose validity thought failed to substantiate might be justified by religious faith'.[8] The words of Professor Van Til are scarcely too harsh: 'the primacy of the practical reason as over against the theoretical reason . . . leads to the postulation of the wholly unknown God and of his manifestation through Christ in the world. And this Christ is also both wholly known and wholly unknown. As such it is that he is supposed to help man who has in the first place constructed him.'[9] Lest the last sentence here seem too severe, let us attend to Kant's own words: 'Though it does indeed sound dangerous, it is in no way reprehensible to say that every man *creates a God* for himself . . . For in whatever manner a being has been made known to him . . . he must first of all compare this representation with his ideal in order to judge whether he is entitled to regard it and to honour it as a divinity.'[10] Theologically, this overlooks the word of God the Holy Spirit. Philosophically, it places autonomous man above God. Psychologically — did not P. T. Forsyth somewhere say that the religious man does not review God's claims and then admit him as he is satisfied? *Isaiah* 6 is more to the point.

Kant appears to think exclusively in terms of a natural religion. The question as to whether or not there is a word from the Lord seldom seems to occur to him. Indeed he has great respect for the person of Christ, though he really finds him no more than an exemplar; and for Kant's 'Son of God' we may read 'moral ideal'. For all his criticism of the rationalists, he ends up in a practical deism. Nor is that all. He is religiously unsatisfying because of his tendency to 'use' God.

Religion's real purpose is as a support for morality, and here God is very useful — but he is a *deus ex machina* no less than the deist's God.[11] Read Kant as we may, we find ourselves unable to resist H. R. Mackintosh's conclusion that 'God is introduced with deep reverence, yet not for His own sake, but rather as a necessary presupposition of the moral system. He enters to effect a reconciliation between duty and happiness, becoming, in Herder's felicitous phrase, "a nail to hold together a morality that was falling to pieces".'[12]

In view of all this it comes as no surprise to find that the note of the gospel is decidely muffled by Kant. An inherently unknowable God, who is the projection of autonomous man's reason is not the holy creator before whom man stands as sinner. Hence the exemplar Christ will suffice; and in the result the Christian life is not a joyous life of fellowship with the risen Christ and his people, but rather a lonely attempt to attend to one's duties understood as divine commands. We do not say that Kant has no understanding of evil. On the contrary he speaks of 'man's natural propensity' to it, and he opposes the Aufklarung's 'easy-going Optimism which is repugnant to the very genius of religion'.[13] It is on the remedy that he is so weak. Yet, as Brunner pointed out, had Kant moved from the view of evil as the breach of an impersonal law to an understanding of sin as the wilful spurning of a holy, loving God, he would have forsaken the rational standpoint of the philosopher for that of the believer.[14] To Kant religion remained the determination to 'look upon God as the lawgiver universally to be honoured'.[15] This is Kant's greatest utterance on the matter; but since the religious man's experience is not so much 'I ought therefore I can' as 'I ought but I cannot — who will deliver me?', it is also his most tragic. It is not difficult to see why some have felt that we do not in Kant find an attenuated gospel: we find law without grace, and that is no gospel at all.[16]

II

Schleiermacher (1768–1834) appears to us to be both attractive and disturbing. He opposed that rationalistic

theological aridity which did not take account of pious
feeling — to him it was 'a badly stitched patchwork of
metaphysics and ethics'. He opposed those detractors of
religion whose attacks upon the 'evidences' of religion left
true religion intact. As for Kant's God who is 'brought back
through the back door of ethics', he is no God at all, and
the cultured despisers of religion are right to reject him.
Unlike some theologians who 'outgrow' the generality of
the faithful, Schleiermacher maintained pastoral contact
with the Church — Kantian individualism was not for him.
He sought to combine 'both religious interest and scientific
spirit in the highest degree and in the best possible balance
for theory and practice alike'.[17] With this objective we are
in entire accord, and it is worth underlining in passing that
his oft-mentioned romanticism notwithstanding, Schleiermacher stoutly opposed sloppiness of thought wherever he
found it. Above all, in face of Christian scholasticism, Catholic and Protestant alike, he set Christ as Redeemer at the
heart of his theology, so that we can at least understand why
A. M. Fairbairn should have commended him for having
saved religion 'from friends and enemies alike'.[18] Yet it is
hard not to believe that Schleiermacher leaves us with a
reduced Christianity, and that some of theology's subsequent
weaknesses originate from him.

   In 1799 Schleiermacher published his *On Religion:
Speeches to its Cultured Despisers,* and on the basis of the
understanding of religion there set forth he brought out his
The Christian Faith in 1821, and a second edition of it ten
years later. Central to his understanding of religion, and of
Christianity as the highest expression of it, is the pious feeling. Eschewing both innate ideas and sensation, he contends
that apart from this feeling there is no real religion. He carefully describes the nature of this feeling. It has nothing to do
either with unconscious states, or with those moments of
self-reflection in which we contemplatively view ourselves as
quasi objects. Though not entirely divorced from knowing
and doing, feeling is to be distinguished from them; certainly
it is not derived from them — it is immediate. The character-
istically religious feeling is one of absolute dependence, and it
is designated by the word 'God'. Thus, 'in the first instance

God signifies for us simply that which is the co-determinant in this feeling, and to which we trace our being in such a state; and any further content of the idea must be evolved out of this fundamental import assigned to it'.[19] When a person recognises that the feeling of absolute dependence is indeed the consciousness of God, we may properly speak of revelation, though not in the sense in which God is given, or intervenes, from without.

We should grievously misunderstand Schleiermacher were we to suppose that his 'feeling' is individualistic. Far from it: his doctrine of the Church, and of the new humanity in Christ entails the collective nature of the experience. It is, moreover, at least in intention, an experience of the *historic* Christ, apart from whom, in Schleiermacher's view, there would be no Christianity at all. Schleiermacher's centre is ever this Jesus, the proper man, as he is known in the individual's self-consciousness; in union with him man finds true life. (Schleiermacher never makes it entirely clear why the feeling of absolute dependence requires the historic Christ; perhaps the truth is that Schleiermacher's faith cannot proceed without him.)

Even from this summary description we see the justice of W. A. Brown's claim that 'the original feature in Schleiermacher's definition of Christianity is the combination of the speculative and the historic';[20] but, to reiterate, he does not deal in the old rationalist speculations. Just as he waged war on the older rationalism, so in turn he has been charged with psychologism. That is, it has been denied that the analysis of one's feelings is informative of anything (least of all, of God) other than of one's emotional states. It would not be difficult to find passages in Schleiermacher's works which would, in isolation, justify this charge. We consider, however, that on balance H. R. Mackintosh has correctly assessed the situation when he concludes that Schleiermacher's over-all intention was to regard feeling as 'a mode of objective apprehension, a species of emotional perception or awareness of spiritual things', and to view God 'as confronting the soul in His real and infinite causality'.[21]

This most favourable interpretation does not, as far as we can see, get Schleiermacher out of the wood. To us it seems that his difference with the Enlightenment rationalists and with the deists is still, like Kant's, a family difference only. Whether reason or the pious feeling is to the fore, man remains the key to the system. The starting-point is variously my own reason, my own grasp of the moral law, or my own feeling of absolute dependence; and we question these starting points, not least because from them flow those modifications or reductions of Christianity which we detect at several points in the work of those who espouse them. Let us then indicate those points in Schleiermacher's position which bear with particular force upon the question of the nature and relations of God and man.

Schleiermacher's work is pervaded, as we have implied, by anti-supernaturalism. The God who intervenes from without; still more, the God who remains without in ultra-deistic fashion, is not God at all. In harmony with this conviction is Schleiermacher's understanding of miracle. He contends that the traditional apologetic had erred in utilising the supposedly evidential properties of miracles conceived as divine breaches of the natural law. In fact piety requires no such miracles. On the contrary, since God is immanent in all things, the distinction between natural and supernatural occurrences no longer holds; 'Miracle is simply the religious name for event. Every event, even the most natural and usual, becomes a miracle, as soon as the religious view of it can be the dominant. To me all is miracle.'[22] In the interests of both science and religion 'we should abandon the idea of the absolutely supernatural because no single instance of it can be known by us, and we are nowhere required to recognise it'.[23] We do not wish here to defend the old understanding of miracle, nor to discuss Schleiermacher's alternative in detail. We simply outline his position as illustrative of his blurring of the creator-creature distinction. For what he says concerning miracles is a function of his general position which called forth G. P. Fisher's adverse, yet just, comment, 'In the conception of God at the outset [of Schleiermacher's system] His transcendence is sacrificed and absorbed in His immanence'.[24]

Does this mean that Schleiermacher is a pantheist? Just as it is difficult to make the charge of subjectivism hold against him in an unqualified way, so with the charge of pantheism. We do not believe that Schleiermacher intended to advocate pantheism — for all his admiration for Spinoza, for example, he dissociated himself from the latter's idea that there could be no reciprocity of relations or emotions between the deity and the individual. On the other hand, his way of equating all causation, including human, with divine providence made it difficult if not impossible for him to allow adequate freedom either to God or to man. It is as if he seeks both to dispense with supernaturalism and yet, even while asserting immanence, to transcend the temporal. The mystical impetus in this latter direction is nowhere more clearly indicated than when he says that since 'the reason is completely one with the divine Spirit, the divine Spirit can itself be conceived as the highest enhancement of the human reason, so that the difference between the two is made to disappear. But further . . . whatever opposes the movements of the divine Spirit is the same as what conflicts with human reason; for otherwise there could not exist in man (as there does), before the entry of those divine influences, a consciousness of the need of redemption, which these very influences set at rest'.[25] This blurring of the creator-creature distinction has called forth Professor Bloesch's comment, 'In mysticism the eternal God calls to the eternal within man. In the Christian faith the eternal becomes man'.[26] Moreover it results in that anabaptism whereby 'revelation' comes to mean 'human discovery',[27] and Christian proclamation becomes not a proximate (human) cause of, but rather the way of describing, the emotional disturbance of salvation.[28]

With a doctrine of God which, despite his best intentions, verges upon pantheism; with God conceived as cause or power, it is not surprising that Schleiermacher does not understand sin as wilful rebellion against a holy, righteous, loving Father. In the wake of Spinoza, who regarded sin as a defect whereby the sensual affections overcome man's reason, Schleiermacher conceives of a war within man between higher and lower states of consciousness. Of this war Adam is the first exemplar, and Christ is redeemer in so far as in him God-consciousness reached its highest expression. Union with him, elevation by him — these are the redemptive steps, and second-century understandings of *recapitulatio* come to mind. Far from being a state of radical alienation from God, 'sin in general exists only in so far as there is a consciousness of it'; far from describing broken inter-personal relationships, sin 'manifests itself only in con-nexion with and by means of already existent good, and what it obstructs is future good'.[29] In Schleiermacher's emphasis upon man's freedom to will ever more God-consciousness with a view to emulating Jesus, we have a rather more than incipient Pelagianism, and a corresponding weakness on the nature and redemptive necessity of divine grace. Redemption is a process rather than an act.

We thus come to the realisation that for all his emphasis upon the historic Christ, Schleiermacher's Jesus is so bound up with the relativities of history that his uniqueness is not established, though it is inconsistently adhered to. We might almost say that Schleiermacher's Christ is an incarnate idea rather than an incarnate person; certainly he by-passes much New Testament teaching concerning Jesus's life, and he will not allow the possibility that Jesus was tempted.[30] Small wonder that Dr. Lovell Cocks said of Schleiermacher's Jesus that he 'stimulates our God-consciousness, but is not Himself the Word, being indeed no more than the "occasion" of the emergence of something that is not a "Word of God" at all, but the secret treasure of our human reason. Neither in its rationalistic not its romanticist form has humanism been able to exhibit the Gospel as "news" and Christ as the unique Mediator of salvation'.[31]

Concerning Schleiermacher's system as a whole, H. R. Mackintosh prophesied that 'more and more it will impress rather by its contrast than by its likeness to the faith of Prophets and Apostles'.[32] Not all have concurred, however, and it cannot be said that the question as to whether in theo-logy we should begin "from below" or "from above" has yet decisively been settled.[33]

III

We turn now to Schleiermacher's contemporary Hegel

(1770–1831)[34] who, although he started from the rationalistic side of Kant rather than from the psychological interests
of Schleiermacher nevertheless promoted an immanentism
which was as reductive of the gospel as was Schleiermacher's.
Hegel set his face against that Romanticism represented by
Schleiermacher, Jacobi and others. To him it seemed to make
for conceptual weakness concerning the Absolute; it exalted
intuition; and it fostered a truth-obscuring relativism.[35] He
was no less opposed to that dualism between thought and the
thing-in-itself which Kant had bequeathed to philosophy. Nor
was Hegel alone in this; indeed his indebtedness to Fichte
(1762–1814) and Schelling (1775–1854), though by no
means complete, is clear. Fichte developed a naturalistic
pantheism in which the material world is held to be the construct of man the thinker — man whose thought is yet held to
be derived from God's thought; and Schelling, anxious to give
the material universe a real life of its own, so to speak, pro-
pounded the idea that nature is a never-absolutely-objective
organism whose ultimate meaning is gained as it achieves
consciousness in the thinking self. They both attempted to
correct what they, and Edward Caird after them, took to be
Kant's oversight, namely, that the phenomenal and noumenal
realms 'are essentially relative to each other, so that either,
taken apart from the other, becomes an empty abstraction'.[36] For his part Hegel suggested that Kant's doctrinal
affirmation that we have no knowledge save of phenomena
could be turned against him, for the assertion is presumed to
give us knowledge, yet it has nothing to do with phenomena.
Hegel would allow no barriers in the quest of knowledge, and
more than once rebuked Kant for attempting to learn to
swim without entering the water.

Schelling's idea of movement, evolution, was vigorously
pursued by Hegel. His Absolute was not a static object or
substance susceptible to immediate apprehension, but a
spirit — God even — which encompasses all phenomena.
The phenomena remain real and are not absorbed by the
Absolute; rather they are embraced by it in an eternal flux of
immanent, evolutionary activity. The plasticity of the system
is such that there could not be absorption of subject by
object or *vice versa;* nor, as with Spinoza, do subject and ob-

ject continue as individuals within a static substance; nor
again, as with Schelling, is there a convergence upon a common abstract identity of nature and spirit. Above all we do
not have in Hegel, contrary to what some have supposed, an
aloof Absolute which transcends and is for ever apart from
the phenomenal world. So concerned was Hegel with the real
world that we may agree that he was 'a man . . . possessed of
an eye for the concrete only second to Aristotle's'.[37] Hegel's
Spirit acts immanently to gather up consciousness and
nature within its own complete, yet ever mobile self-consciousness. (The somewhat strange conjunction of adjectives
must be pardoned: it has been well said that with Hegel one
must first attempt to grasp the system, or see the vision, and
only then examine the parts).

From the human side, the hard way of rational thinking,
rather than the softer mystic or intuitionist options represented respectively by Boehme and Jacobi, is the way by
which man attains the truth; the route takes man through art,
religion and philosophy — themselves the thesis, antithesis
and synthesis of Absolute Spirit. There is no escaping rationality, for 'that which is rational is real, and that which is real
is rational'. Thought and being, though in mutual contradictory opposition, are one, since there cannot be the one
without the other. The Absolute resolves all antitheses with
which our experience confronts us; indeed our own selves are
real only as they are caught up by the Absolute. This is not
to say that there is no distinction between man and God. The
distinction is, however, within man's 'unhappy consciousness';
it pains man and God, and its resolution, though assured, is
not yet. Meanwhile the dialectic proceeds as antithesis suc-
ceeds, yet never cancels or replaces, thesis, and as synthesis is
ever more nearly approached. As G. R. G. Mure has it, 'The
triadic formula writ large is the total manifestation of absolute spirit alienating itself and returning upon itself through
(and as) Nature and man'.[38] In other words, in the dialectic
process contradictions are resolved, not by being swept aside
or explained away; nor, as with Fichte, by being regarded as
apparent only; but by being caught up into a higher unity.
It is not that Hegel deliberately set out to sabotage the law of
contradiction as ordinarily understood by perversely main-

taining contradictories. Rather, he sought a way of accommodating the *real* contradictoriness of human experience within a system which properly recognised the world as it is.[39] His theory must both accept the world as it is and at the same time, since the world is rationally grounded, deny that there can be any absolute and final contradictions. As Caird acknowledges,

> 'The thought that there is a unity which lies beneath all opposition, and that, therefore, all opposition is capable of reconciliation, is unfamiliar to our ordinary consciousness for reasons that may easily be explained. That unity is not usually an object of consciousness, just because it is the presupposition of all consciousness . . . It is the unity itself which gives its bitter meaning to the difference, while at the same time it contains the pledge that the difference can and even must be reconciled.'[40]

It follows that both a proof and a disproof of the principle presuppose the principle itself. Hegel's contradictoriness is not, as with Aristotle, a static matter of logic. It is dynamic; it is, as has been said, the fuel of his system.

How does all of this bear upon the question of the God-man relation? We first underline the point that Hegel who 'lived, apparently, for no other purpose than that of playing secretary to the Absolute'[41] adopts a thoroughly immanentist stance. Moreover, like Bultmann after him, he adopts the Enlightenment's God who cannot work visibly on the world.[42] Accordingly, we endorse the verdict of Dr. De-Wolf that 'Hegel . . . is, par excellence, *the* philosopher of continuity, by reason of the fact that he shows so explicitly how thoroughly he means to resolve all the apparently conflicting elements of experience and being in the one unbroken life of the all-inclusive Process, the Spirit which is the Absolute'.[43] The eternal Spirit unfolds itself in the universe — indeed, the universe *is* that unfolding, and the Absolute is the totality of things. Such a view cannot but do violence to the concept of the personality of God, and nowhere is this more clearly seen than in connection with the Hegelian Trinity, which H. R. Mackintosh concisely stated, and pertinently criticised as follows:

'As pure abstract idea God is Father; as going forth eternally into finite being, the element of change and variety,
God is Son; as once more sublating or cancelling this distinction, and turning again home enriched by this outgoing
in so-called self-manifestation or incarnation, God is Holy
Spirit. Such a Trinity, clearly, represents that which is in
no sense eternal but only coming to be; it has no meaning,
or even existence, apart from the finite world. It is a
dialectical triad, not Father, Son and Spirit in any sense
in which Christian faith has ever pronounced the three-fold
Name.'[44]

(We recall that the latter-day idealist F. H. Bradley denied
that the Absolute was personal, moral, beautiful or true).[45]

In Hegel's idea of a God of becoming, who is inseparable
from, though not identical with, his creation, we have the
genesis of that notion, sentimentalised by some later liberal
theologians, that God needs us as much as we need him. The
tendency of Arminianism thus finds metaphysical justification; and some of Hegel's left wing successors upheld a
position which 'does away with the self-existence and independent reality of the Deity, identifies God with man's
thoughts about Him, and makes the communion of man
with God to be nothing but man's communion with himself
or with the progressive spirit of the race'.[46] In this way, and
for all his concern with history, Hegel leaves us with an un-
historically rooted, idealised Christianity in which, not
surprisingly, the God-man as an historic person has little
place. This despite phrases which appear to tell in an opposite direction: '*Christ has appeared;* a Man who is God; God
who is Man, and thereby peace and reconciliation have
accrued to the World'.[47] Here is Hegel, the true Lutheran, at
his most final. But he was not ever thus, and G. R. G. Mure
has well said that 'Jesus was in fact for him much less real in
Nazareth and Jerusalem than he was in Martin Luther's inner
consciousness'.[48] Christianity's main role, as far as Hegel is
concerned, is to provide a fund of doctrines symbolic of that
relation between the finite and the infinite which it is philosophy's business to delineate.

Anyone who begins from as close and *total* a kinship
between God and man as Hegel posits will almost inevitably

be in difficulties over the doctrines of sin, grace and redemption. Hegel does not indeed under-estimate sin. He takes it very seriously, though not, we feel with that moral urgency which can flow only from a real grasp of God's holy otherness over against the (genuine) individual. He does not grasp the tragedy of alienation, for his evolutionary theory encourages an optimism which regardes sin as a necessary step towards self-determined moral goodness. As a later prominent Hegelian wrote, 'there is nothing in evil which cannot be absorbed in good and contributory to it; and it springs from the same source as good and value'.[49] It was this kind of remark which prompted Reinhold Niebuhr to speak of the almost unanimous 'easy conscience of modern culture'[50] — though as Professor Pingle-Pattison noted, Hegel himself spoke much of the *labour* of the Spirit, whose ultimate triumph, though a foregone conclusion, is not *easily* won.[51]

Given this understanding of sin the atonement can be only a further testimony to the rhythmic unity of God and man. It is the means whereby God as Absolute Spirit reconciles himself to himself by the death of Christ understood as symbolic of the resurrection of Spirit. Again we see the result of the lack of genuine individuality in either God or man. There is truth in the charge that Hegelianism has no room for Hegel — hence Kierkegaard's protest against it. Nor does there seem to be any room in Hegelianism for God apart from Hegel. Here we have the consummation of that humanistic, rationalistic-immanentist thrust which from the Renaissance onwards had been gathering increasing momentum. It is one thing to regard union with God as a sharing of his nature; it is quite another to regard it as a pantheistic absorption into his being. Many will feel that the latter is too high a price to pay for salvation from deism; and many Christian thinkers may well find themselves in unusual agreement with McTaggart, who opined that as far as Christianity is concerned Hegelianism is 'an enemy in disguise — the least evident but the most dangerous'.[52] The danger is at its height in the bland disregard in Hegelianism of anything resembling God's regenerating grace.

With Kantian agnosticism concerning the noumenal realm, with Schleiermacher's emphasis upon the religious consciousness, and with Hegel's version of idealism, the scene was set for a far-reaching and diverse immanentist movement of thought, the force of which is as yet by no means spent.

IV

If one were to write a history of nineteenth century western Christianity under some such title as 'The Ramifications of Immanentism', a surprisingly comprehensive account could result. We use the term 'Christianity' advisedly, for, whether positively or negatively, immanentism influenced both thought and practice. Thus, to take some random examples: Professor Horton Davies finds a link between immanentism and the preference of most nineteenth-century Free Church theologians and ministers for Zwinglian, memorialist, views of the Lord's Supper, rather than for the High Calvinist doctrine; and again, between immanentism and that embarrassment to certain liturgiologists, the Harvest Festival.[53] For some ecclesiological implications of immanentism we might turn to H. B. Wilson's article on 'The National Church' in *Essays and Reviews* (1860). He suggested that since the old dogmatic standpoints of the Church of England were ripe for supersession, a new Church should be envisaged, built, in undogmatic fashion, upon the moral consciousness of the nation. In the field of scientific advance immanentist theory and investigatory zeal acted as mutual stimuli upon one another, as we shall see in chapter 3. Finally, as he reflected upon the missionary situation at the beginning of the twentieth century, Dr. A. E. Garvie expressed concern lest the concept of God as already immanent in man should undermine the missionary enterprise by reducing the importance of the historic Christ, and by minimising the tragedy of sin and, in consequence, the need of a Saviour.[54]

Returning to more strictly intellectual matters we find that immanentism inspired no one variety of philosophy. We have already seen that the immanentist tendency was shared by men in other ways so different as Schleiermacher and Hegel; but in the nineteenth century the proliferation of immanentism is even more remarkable, and inspires both kindred and diametrically opposed philosophies. Over some of these we need not delay,[55] for they were so clearly out of accord with Christian thought that few theologians, if any, thought of expressing their views in terms of them. Thus, there were positivistic and agnostic varieties of immanentism which, since they ruled out a transcendent object, whilst deeming such an object the *sine qua non* of religion, had no use for religion at all — except, in some cases, as an emotional crutch for the weak-minded. There was materialism (as equally immanentist as its opposite, absolutism), whose high priest Ludwig Feuerbach (1804–72),[56] with *quasi*-discipular dialectic licence, turned Hegelianism on its head, made actual matter rather than mind his fundamental principle, equated God with man's nature, and resolved theology into anthropology. There was August Comte (1798–1857),[57] whose positivism, whilst denying the transcendent, allowed for a religion of humanity wherein inter-personal relations were accorded divine status. Dr. Elliott-Binns notes Frederic Harrison, E. S. Beesly and J. H. Bridges as being among Englishmen who took Comtism seriously. That not all were thus inclined is evidenced by the wag who alleged that at their Fetter Lane meetings for the worship of humanity there were three persons and no God.[58] Professor William A. McKeever of the University of Kansas was among Americans who exalted man: 'Man is my best expression of Deity', he wrote, 'and so I bow reverently at this shrine'.[59] It was left to Professor R. W. Sellars and others to make the point that man is not fit object of worship, and therefore that 'the very best attitude and implications of worship must be relinquished'.[60] The pragmatists, of whom F. C. S. Schiller (1864–1937) was a prominent British example, tended to agree.

Other varieties of immanentism made a considerably greater appeal to Christian thinkers, and hence the perils of reductionism were correspondingly greater. We continue to speak of *varieties* of immanentism, for some have written as if monism alone appealed to theologians. The monistic tendency of all forms of immanentism cannot be denied, but it is only proper to note how earnestly some sought to resist it. Of these some were moved by a romanticism which made for a decidely immanentist transcendentalism (a paradox shortly

to be resolved); others, making the Incarnation the foundation of their theology, were at least as indebted to the
Alexandrian theologians as they were to Hegel. It goes without saying that the continuing Platonist insistence upon the
God-man continuity, though by no means exclusively immanentist, had clear immanentist features.[61] But, yet again, a
cautionary word: to think too much in terms of groups or
schools would suggest a degree of tidiness, and a series of
master-disciple relationships, which do not always appear.
We shall follow the relatively safe chronological path, making
our points as we go.

Dr. Vernon F. Storr listed the following distinctive features of Romanticism:[62] (1) The belief that man is not simply
an intellectual being, and that reason, far from being merely
the logical faculty, is 'a creating and unifying factor'. (2) The
awakening of the spirit of wonder. (3) The high place accorded to the imagination. (4) An emphasis upon the sympathy
between man and the natural order. These, taken all together,
make for a profounder study of man's psychology than had
ever before been undertaken; and made possible a new apologetic which would no longer rely upon external evidences
(which were being increasingly called into question with the
growth of biblical criticism), but which would appeal to the
religious man's spiritual experience.

Such an atmosphere was one in which Coleridge (1772–
1834)[63] revelled. While acknowledging his debt to the Cambridge Platonists, and to More and Smith in particular, he
went further than they in understanding the continuity
between God and man to be moral and spiritual, and not
intellectual only: 'God in His wholeness, and therefore
chiefly in His holiness, not merely God's *mind* in man's *mind*
— that was the note; with the necessary consequent, that
Christian truth was at the same time an affirmation of this
immanence and a means of intensifying it still more'.[64] To
Coleridge man is essentially a spiritual being, but he by no
means endorsed monism. On the contrary, from Kant he
inherits a transcendentalism, though not one which leads him
either to Kant's scepticism or to the deist's absentee deity. In
a very important footnote Professor Welch draws his readers'
attention to three factors in Coleridge's experience which

modified his indebtedness to the Platonists, to Kant and to others. They are 'the quality of personal religion, in which prayer and the struggle of sin and redemption were at the centre . . . Second, a deep sense of social need and a hope for the revitalization of English society and the church — a cause which he wanted to serve . . . Third, Coleridge's religious thinking developed from a position within the historical Christian faith. He had little interest in religiousness in general'.[65]

It was, indeed, Coleridge's profound sense of the reality of moral evil, together with his high view of conscience, which proved the greatest bulwark against the pantheistic tendencies in his thought. For him sin could never be anything other than sin, and redemption was required. This conviction coloured his attitude towards the older rationalism which, he thought, did not really get to grips with the whole man at all; and it prompted his quest of a theory of rationality which should both make good this deficiency by permitting genuine apprehensions of divine reality; but which would set its face against simple emotionalism whether pietistic or evangelical. Further, he sought an understanding of reason which appreciated reason's bounds and was not afraid to pause before the ineradicable mystery which lay at the heart of things. He was thus led to distinguish between the understanding and the reason. The former provided us with experimental knowledge *via* sensation, while by means of the latter we intuitively apprehend spiritual truth which is not amenable to empirical verification.[66]

Coleridge's distinction was employed by the American transcendentalists from about 1830,[67] though Dr. Buell has made it clear that their definition of reason varied from one to another:

'Those who recognised such a faculty sometimes called it by different names, such as "Spirit", "Mind", "Soul", and they also differed in the claims they made for it. For some Transcendentalists it was simply an inner light or conscience; for others it was the voice of God; for still others it was literally God himself immanent in man. Some regarded the informing spirit primarily as an impersonal cosmic force; others continued to think of it in traditional anthropormorphic terms.'[68]

As with Coleridge then, their transcendentalism was immanently anchored, so to speak. They opposed pantheism, but were equally averse in spirit to external evidences of religion. Instead, like their fellow-Unitarian, the Englishman Martineau (1805—1900), they made conscience the seat of authority in religion, and were to that extent at one with the immanentist spirit of the times. They had the example of Channing (1780—1842), by whose assertion of the dignity of man they had been much impressed, and with whose criticisms of what was regarded as a degrading Calvinism they were in utter sympathy. Dr. McLachlan informs us that the monument to Channing in Boston bears the legend, 'He breathed into theology a humane Spirit and proclaimed a new divinity of man'.[69]

Supreme among the transcendentalists was Emerson (1803—82) for whom man was equally in harmony with nature as with God. Theodore Parker (1810—60) evinces the difficulty to which we saw that Hegelianism could tend, namely, he is reluctant to ascribe personality (and, for that matter, impersonality) to God on the grounds that to do so 'seems to me a vain attempt to fathom the abyss of the Godhead, and report the soundings'.[70] Loyal to the Congregationalist family (out of which American Unitarianism had sprung) was Horace Bushnell (1802—76), whose New Theology opposed tritheism and the governmental theory of the atonement; upheld the divinity of man, and sought to show that the fundamental truths of religion are hindered rather than helped by the older apologetic methods of shoring them up.

Meanwhile in Britain the general immanentist tendency was being fostered by Erskine of Linlathen (1788—1870), and by his friend John McLeod Campbell (1800—72), whose book *The Nature of the Atonement* (1856) played down the penal aspects of the atonement, and whose belief that Christ's saving work had been done for all and not for the elect only caused such heart-searching in conservative Scottish circles.[71] Another Scot, Carlyle (1795—1881)[72] exercised a wide influence upon theological thought, not so much because he erected a persuasive system, which he did not, but because he seemed to strike certain chords which, as many thought, would have to appear in any adequate theological score. Among these were his anti-materialistic immanentism, inspired by Goethe, and his strong sense of the moral law — inherited from a Calvinism with which, as with institutional Christianity generally, he was in other respects profoundly disenchanted.

Among those of the Church of England who were most receptive to new ideas we note Connop Thirlwall (1797–1875) — a student of Schleiermacher — and Julius Hare (1795–1855). The latter carried forward the main emphases of Coleridge, utilising the doctrine of the Holy Spirit in relation to such themes as progress and development, which were shortly to become theological talking-points of the first importance. Supreme among the Anglicans influenced by Coleridge, however, was F. D. Maurice (1805–72).[73] Like his mentor, Maurice stood firmly for the trustworthiness of spiritual experience. God does not have to be sought as if he were afar off. He is immanent in man and our seeking of him is itself a response to his prior presence. Against High Calvinism and High Anglicanism alike Maurice maintained the essential divinity of man, uring that the essence of sin is refusal to acknowledge that fact; salvation is the glad recognition of it. For his denial of the eternity of punishment Maurice was deposed from his Chair at King's College, London, in 1854 — he would lose his position rather than have the God-man continuity immorally disrupted. His immanentist-transcendentalism found its chief expression as he developed his 'Greek' Logos theology of the Incarnation. To him the supreme meaning of the Incarnation was that the world, far from being fallen, is *already* redeemed. Not surprisingly, Maurice's use of older soteriologies is relatively slight.

Other more adventurous Anglicans included the contributors to *Essays and Reviews* (1860).[74] Eschewing external religious evidences, they sought to do some theological ground-clearing and, in the process, to prise open the minds of their readers. Conscience and reason were, for them, the joint arbiters of valid doctrine, and both conscience and reason were helped rather than hindered by the scholarly advances in science and biblical criticism that were being made. A generation later *Lux Mundi* (1889) was more positively 'Greek' and incarnational. Among its illustrious contributors was J. R. Illingworth (1848–1915) who, for all his indebtedness to the post-Hegelianism of T. H. Green, had no intention of blurring the creator-creature distinction, as may be seen from one of his later works, *Divine Transcendence* (1911). In this he was at one with Charles Gore, the editor of *Lux Mundi,* who was later to criticise the Modern Churchmen's Union in such a way as to draw the following response from one of the Union's distinguished members: 'Dr. Gore is correct in affirming that we believe that . . . the difference between Deity and Humanity is one of degree. The distinction between Creator and creature, upon which Dr. Gore and the older theologians place so much emphasis, seems to us to be a minor distinction'.[75] It is a large part of our purpose to present a cumulative case against this view on the ground that those who entertain it are in real danger of vitiating the gospel.

We come full circle to the professional philosophers, and we note Edward Caird (1835–1908) and T. H. Green (1836–92)[76] as being more or less faithful disciples of Hegel. The qualification is important, since while, for example, Green endorsed Hegel's criticisms of Kant, he nevertheless felt that Hegel's own system was over-ambitious and on one occasion declared, 'It must all be done over again'.[77] For Green mind is constitutive of the relations which make up the world; there is no possibility of isolating phenomena and of considering them in abstraction from mind. With all of this Caird agreed and so, in broad terms, did the younger absolutists, F. H. Bradley (1846–1924) and Bernard Bosanquet (1848–1923). C. C. J. Webb properly observed, however, that these last were even more strongly immanentist than their older contemporaries, and that they did not subscribe to the doctrine of immortality, which inspired the teleology of both Caird and Green.[78] Neither would they, like Caird, have invoked the Incarnation of Christ as signifying the truth of the claim that God was immanent in all men. Both Bradley and Bosanquet denied personality to God and regarded their Absolute as superseding the God of religion altogether. By the time we come to McTaggart (1866—1925) God is entirely redundant.

Not surprisingly, the tendency of post-Hegelian immanentism to exclude the truly personal identity of both God and man gave rise to some influential thinkers who came to be known as the personal idealists. Of these one of the earliest and greatest was Professor A. S. Pringle-Pattison (1856—1931) whose criticisms of Hegel are to be found in his *Hegelianism and Personality* (1887). One of the best summaries, and most gracious criticisms, of his position is that by his pupil H. R. Mackintosh.[79] Pringle-Pattison's main platform is that 'in the conditions of the highest human life we have access, as nowhere else, to the inmost nature of the divine'.[80] Mackintosh welcomes this, but questions how far his teacher's identification of God with the Absolute allows for the fatherhood of God. He is also hesitant conerning the notion of the mutual reciprocity of relations between God and man, for this may lead to the false suggestion that 'God needs man for existence just as man needs God'.[81]

How shall we assess the immanentist thrust in nineteenth-century thought? First, immanentists of all kinds are to be applauded for having set their faces so firmly against deism; and immanentists of certain kinds are further to be praised for their staunch opposition to naturalism; for with neither deism nor naturalism can Christian theology happily trade. Secondly, the generosity of spirit and openness of vision which characterises the best of the immanentists is a welcome relief from the more arid patches of earlier rationalism, whether philosophical or theological.

Having allowed all this, we cannot overlook the fact that all types of immanentism really look to man — to his reason, his conscience or his religious experience — as the arbiter of truth. This makes them part of that very broadly rationalistic post-Renaissance humanistic family which includes Descartes, Locke, Schleiermacher and Hegel, all of whose members sat more or less lightly to certain aspects of the Christian message. Having noted this all-embracing tendency, we now note certain difficulties which arise in connection with particular varieties of immanentism.

Professor A. C. McGiffert once questioned whether theo-

logy needed the doctrine of immanence at all. He quoted
McLeod Campbell as saying that 'The one great word of the
New Theology is unity — the unity of the individual with the
race, and of the race with God', and commented, 'Much that
the conception of divine immanence conserves is taught by
the Christ of the synoptists — the nearness of God, the kinship of man and God, the value of the present life — but all
this might be taught also by one whose philosophy was of
another sort'.[82] This is a fair judgement as applying to monism, but not all nineteenth-century immanentists took that
line, as we have seen. In particular, the 'Greek' incarnational
line represented by Maurice and the *Lux Mundi* group upheld
the transcendent, maintained the creator-creature distinction,
and met pantheism head on. That the monists should be in
greater peril at this point was almost inevitable, and their
danger was one inherited, however unconsciously, from
Spinoza as much as from Hegel. As A. E. Garvie was to say,
'In the new theology the distinction between God and man,
which morality and religion alike demand, is confused, if not
altogether denied'.[83]

Although Coleridge never minimised sin, many of the
monists could not give a due account of it. Hence H. R.
Mackintosh's complaint concerning the 'sophistical manipu-
lation of moral evil'[84] which characterises all absolutisms:
evil, for them, can only be a stage on the way to good.
Similarly, Professor L. Hodgson urged against William Temple
that 'if all creation, including myself, be God fulfilling Himself in His historical self-expression, then I, even the sinful I
when engaged in sinning, am in the last analysis a mode of
God's self-expression'.[85]

Again, the immanentist was frequently in difficulties with
the historical. As Strauss said, giving the game away, 'It is not
the fashion of the Idea to pour its fulness in a single life'.[86]
Certainly the general tendency has been for immanentists of
the monistic kind to be more than a little embarrassed by the
Jesus of history; and those Logos immanentists who made so
much of the Incarnation tended to do so on principles which
made redemption much more of a symbolic idea than an
historically accomplished fact: man was already divine, and
hence a *relatively* radical atonement would suffice.

The perils of immanentism were thrown into relief by the work of R. J. Campbell (1867–1956), whose book *The New Theology* (1907) was the most sensational if not the most scholarly product of the hey-day of theological liberalism.[87] Campbell was appalled by authoritarian biblicism and ecclesiasticism, and in his work we find echoes of Platonism and of eastern theology, together with a heavy coating of post-Hegelian immanentism. He opposed transcendentalism and criticised that practical dualism which, he said, caused men to 'think of God as above and apart from His world instead of expressing Himself through His world'.[88] He regarded the New Theology as 'an untrammelled return to the Christian sources in the light of modern thought. Its starting-point is a re-emphasis of the Christian belief in the Divine immanence in the universe and in mankind'.[89] But what kind of 'Divine' is here envisaged? By 'God' Campbell means 'the one reality I cannot get away from, for, whatever else it may be, it is myself'.[90] He proceeded to smooth the corners of those theologians who sought to preserve the creator-creature distinction, to emphasise the uniqueness of Christ, and to maintain the radically disruptive effects of sin. He ascribed uniqueness to Christ in the sense that no other was so possessed by, or so able to display, divine love; but for *agape* as atoning grace he had little place. Again, while many were prepared to agree that there was need of a protest against that demeaning of man to which some varieties of Calvinism had led, they considered that Campbell's way of speaking of the Christhood of every man was quite unhelpful. And when Campbell said such things as 'What we succeed in doing some of the time Jesus did all the time; when all men are able to do it all the time the Atonement will have become complete, and love Divine shall be all in all'.[91] large numbers felt that enough was enough. Finally, when Campbell declared that 'the whole cosmic process is one long incarnation and up-rising of the being of God from itself to itself'[92] he caused consternation not only among Platonists who lamented the loss of the transcendent dimension, but amongst an even greater number who felt that Platonist and neo-Hegelian alike were prevented by their presuppositions from paying due heed to the *historic* incarnation of Christ.

The stir which Campbell's book caused prompted Charles Gore (1853–1932) to enter the lists against him; and Gore, the main inspiration of *Lux Mundi* was neither an ultra-conservative biblicist nor an anti-Platonist.[93] He clearly grasped, however, the point we are concerned to make, and expressed it thus:

> 'We may say . . . without any risk of mistake, that the tendency of the New Theology is to bring into exclusive emphasis the idea of the immanent God, of God in nature. Nature is one, and one universal Spirit pervades it: this is God. Nature is His expression; and man's soul is a conscious spark of the universal God.
>
> Now it is not too much to say that this is not new theology, but very old theology. When Christianity came into the world it found the civilized world full of a religious philosophy, in part Platonic, in part Stoic, which held a doctrine substantially identical with that of the New Theology.'[94]

The significance of this statement as coming from one who belonged to a party anxious to *revive* the Greek Fathers' notion of the ever-immanent Logos is clear.

We shudder to think what Gore would have made of the remark of the celebrated liberal Baptist preacher, Harry Emerson Fosdick, to the effect that he believed both in the divinity of Christ, and in that of his own mother. To such sentimentality, which merges God with man, or makes man a dimension of God, the positive tendency of the negative theology provides a salutary rebuke: provided always that we remember that the mysteriousness of God is mysterious to us only; there is no scriptural warrant for the doctrine of ultimate unintelligibility. Another Baptist may atone for Fosdick's lapse. John Clifford (1836–1923), who was second to none in his quest of theological relevance, and who welcomed the fact that immanentist thought had brought God closer to men, yet saw that 'our peril is our loss of the great truth that whilst God is in all and through all, He is also over all, and above all'.[95] The real or imagined loss of that great truth had more than a little to do with the conservative case against theological liberalism, as we shall see. Meanwhile we shall consider in turn the rise of modern biblical criticism, evolutionary thought, and Ritschlianism. These developments took root in soil fertilised by immanentism, and each played its part in the conservative-liberal debate in theology.

CHAPTER TWO

THE RISE AND RECEPTION OF
MODERN BIBLICAL CRITICISM

In 1878, Julius Wellhausen (1844–1918) published his view of the dating of the Pentateuchal documents in a work entitled *Die Geschichte Israels.*[1] He thereby advanced the cause of that 'higher criticism' of the Bible in which some Christians took such delight, and over which others poured so much scorn. However much they may have modified or departed from his views, the descendants of those in the former group would admit that Wellhausen was a pioneer who to this day cannot entirely be ignored. Nor have some of the descendants of those in the latter group creased to honour the German with their adverse criticisms. It is not our purpose, however, to examine Wellhausen's theories or their derivatives in detail. Rather, by means of a chronicle of the advent and reception of the modern understanding of the Bible, we shall seek to show that the presuppositions of the critics were diverse. Some, under Hegelian influence, sat lightly to history and verged upon pantheism; others, under naturalistic inspiration, focussed upon historical, observable events, to the detriment of the supernatural; and yet others — including the majority of British critics — sought to pay heed to the problems posed by historical criticism whilst retaining belief in the supernatural and in the divinity of Christ.

The story of the interpretation of the Bible is both fascinating and complicated. Marcion's 'pruning', Origen's allegorizing, and Luther's uncomplimentary (and often decontextualized) reference to *James* as being 'an epistle of straw' are among the better known, not to say more notorious,

landmarks. The very different contemporaries Spinoza
(1632–77) and Locke (1632–1704) both held opinions
concerning the Bible which were to be woven into the fabric
of later theories. The former considered that while the historical record of revelation may be true, God is accessible without it;[2] the latter's procedure of taking the over-all sense of
the biblical books was an earnest of exegetical things to
come.[3] But with the suggestion of the French physician
Astruc (1684–1766) that since in the Pentateuch the
names Jehovah and Elohim are both used of God we are
dealing with a composite work, we have an even more definite fortaste of 'modern' things to come. Astruc's younger
contemporary, Wolff's pupil Hermann Samuel Reimarus
(1694–1768), was meanwhile bringing a deistical attitude to
bear upon the scriptures. In his unpublished work *Apologie
oder Schutzschrift fur die vernunftigen Verehrer Gottes* he
rejected the miraculous, noted contradictions in the Bible,
and pronounced the biblical writers fraudulent. Lessing
(1729–81) published seven extracts of this work under the
title *The Wolfenbuttel Fragments* (1744–8), and further
portions were published by C. A. E. Schmidt (pseud.) in
1787, and by W. Klose between 1850–52.[4] Though not
himself a deist — he was a child of Enlightenment immanentism — Lessing would have found Reimarus in sympathy
with his view that 'the accidental truths of history can never
become the proof of necessary truths of reason'.

Among others in the line of Reimarus was Heinrich Eber-
hard Gottlob Paulus (1761–1851), whose position may be
understood as a stage on the route from Reimarus to D. F.
Strauss (1808–74), and whose deathbed testimony, 'I am
justified in the sight of God by my desire of that which is
good' was not calculated to impress the orthodox. Paulus's
predecessor at Jena, J. G. Eichhorn (1752–1827) seems to
have been the first to speak of the 'higher criticism' — an
approach which he adopted in relation both to pentateuchal
criticism and to the synoptic problem. Also in the field was
Schleiermacher's colleague W. M. L. De Wette (1780–1849)
who moved from rationalism to a more experience-based
view of the kind espoused by Jacobi. He thereby earned the
disapproval both of his erstwhile rationalist friends, and also

of the more conservative of the pietists to whom his mythological interpretation of Christ's birth, resurrection and
ascension was anathema. Against rationalism he protested
that 'Christianity must become life and deed', a sentiment
which was later to be reaffirmed by certain liberal theologians who felt decidely uneasy in the presence of more
than a modicum of doctrine. It is not without interest that
De Wette's pupil, Friedrich Bleek (1793—1859) became one
of the foremost *conservative* biblical critics of his day. E. W.
Hengstenberg (1802—69) and H. A. C. Havernich (1805—46)
were among others of like spirit.

Meanwhile in eighteenth century England, and especially
among the rationalistic Arminians, biblical and related investigations had become increasingly adventurous. Thus John
Taylor (1694—1761), tutor at Warrington Academy from
1757—61, whose *Scripture Doctrine of Original Sin* (1740)
was a challenge to the Calvinists, also wrote a *Scheme of
Scripture Divinity*. Having himself 'discovered that many
points of theological doctrine, which were universally accepted, were not to be found in Scripture', he exhorted his
readers 'To suspect or reject any principle or sentiment
advanced by him which afterwards upon careful examination should appear doubtful or false; and . . . to keep their
minds always open to fresh truth, to banish prejudice, and
steadily to assert and fully to allow to others the inalienable
right of judgment and conscience'.[5] Joseph Priestley (1733—
1804) likewise was quite disinclined to affirm anything simply because an apostle had taught it. On the contrary, he rejected the doctrine of the Virgin Birth on historical grounds,
and presented a Christ who was less than infallible. At the
same time, he held to the evidential value of the biblical
miracles, and was conservative on the questions of the
authorship and dating of the scriptural texts. For his part
Edward Evanson (1731—1805), who had already publicly
tampered with the more doctrinal portions of the *Book of
Common Prayer*, relinquished his Anglican living in 1788 on
publishing his unitarian views; and in his *The Dissonance of
the Four Generally Received Evangelists* (1792) he denied
the apostolic authorship of the Fourth gospel, and accepted
Luke alone as authentic. To all of which Thomas Falconer

replied in his Bampton Lectures, *Certain Principles in Evan-son's Dissonance . . . Examined* (1810). Finally there was Thomas Belsham (1750–1829), who acknowledged his debt to Astruc, Eichhorn and others and who, in 1807, ascribed the Pentateuch to more than one hand. By 1821 he felt able to declare that the *Genesis* creation narratives were incompatible with scientific knowledge, and his general advice was that the individual should 'read the Scriptures of the Old and New Testaments with the same thirst after knowledge, and with the same liberal and candid spirit with which he would read any other ancient volume'. Dr. McLachlan bids us observe that 'this was said nearly forty years before Benjamin Jowett, in *Essays and Reviews,* pleaded that the Bible should "be interpreted like any other book, by the same rules of evidence and the same canons of criticism" '.[6] Which remark brings us to the Anglicans.

Herbert Marsh (1757–1839), one of the most prominent Anglicans of his day, had studied under J. D. Michaelis (1717–91) in Germany. Such was the esteem in which he held his teacher that he translated Michaelis's *Introduction to the New Testament* into English (4 vols. 1793–1801). Marsh was the first in England to apply the techniques of modern historical criticism to the synoptic problem, and he presented his findings in his *History of Sacred Criticism* (1809). By this time he had aroused the hostility of conservatives – and that not only because of his 'advanced' critical views, but because of a series of sermons delivered in 1805 in which he attacked distinctively Calvinistic tenets. Unlike most who engaged in the latter increasingly popular pursuit, Marsh was in a position to take practical steps against the sons of Calvin. Thus for a time after his translation to the Bishopric of Llandaff in 1816 he refused to grant licences to Calvinistic clergy.

Of even more theological significance than Marsh were the members of the early Oriel school, the Noetics.[7] In his Bampton Lectures on *The Use and Abuse of Party Feeling in Matters of Religion* (1822) the acute mind of Richard Whately (1787–1863) recognised the place of a proper agnosticism in religious matters, and took strong exception to that biblical scholasticism upon which so much theology had lately rested. In 1827 there appeared Whately's *Essays on Some of the Difficulties in the Writings of St. Paul,* a work in which, as harbinger of the historico-grammatical exegetical method, he advocated the need to understand the mileu of the biblical writings. R. D. Hampden (1793–1868) continued to maintain the supreme authority of the Bible, though in his Bampton Lectures on *The Scholastic Philosophy in Relation to Christian Theology* (1832) he adopted a liberal stance *vis a vis* received dogma; and Thomas Arnold (1795–1842) sought to understand inspiration in a way which would take due account of the constraints of historical circumstance. But nothing did so much to forward the serious pursuit of historico-grammatical biblical criticism as the publication of Thirlwall and Hare's translation of the *History of Rome* (1827) by B. G. Niebuhr (1776–1831), and Milman's *History of Latin Christianity* (6 vols., 1854–6). Contemporaneously, interest in archaeology was awakening, and those, such as Arthur Evans and Flinders Petrie, who had the time, the inclination and the money, were vastly to increase man's knowledge of time and place as they turned the sod of civilisation. As Archdeacon Storr reflected, the claim of the new historical method 'to interpret history causally and genetically implies the abandonment of the customary antithesis between the natural and the supernatural'.[8] In other words, the new biblical criticism found prepared soil in that immanentism which had come down from Spinoza and Kant.[9]

In 1835 two considerable boulders were dropped into the pond of continental criticism. J. K. W. Vatke (1806–1882), an Hegelian, published his *The Religion of the Old Testament,* in which he applied the idea of development to the Pentateuch and concluded that the sacrificial regulations therein were post-exilic. In this as in other respects he was a forerunner of Wellhausen, and he was sufficiently before his time to be refused a full professorship. Immensely more significant, however, was *The Life of Jesus* by D. F. Strauss. He worked with that peculiarly Hegelian understanding of history which had the effect of *removing* individual personality from history, and almost demanded the thoroughly earthbound response of Ludwig Fuerbach's *The Essence of Christianity* (1841). We shall delay further mention of Strauss's *Life* for a moment, because although it was trans-

lated into English by 'George Eliot' in 1846, it was known
only to the cognoscenti until the popular edition appeared
in 1864.

The traditionally orthodox English Congregationalists
provide us with some of the earliest and most interesting
responses to increasingly liberal criticism. In 1843, despite
the fact that he enjoyed the support of his Principal, Walter
Scott, William Benton Clulow (1802–1882)[10] resigned his
teaching post at Airedale Independent College, Bradford,
because his approach to the Bible, though by no means
radical, did not commend itself to the College Committee.
In 1846 Edward White's *Life of Christ* appeared, and in it
he opposed the doctrine of the eternity of punishment,
preferring to maintain the destruction of the ungodly.[11]
What is particularly noticeable, as an indication of the speed
of intellectual change in an erstwhile conservative body, is
the fact that although White's work was deemed to be a
'dangerous heresy',[12] and notwithstanding his rejection of
infant baptism in 1850, he was called to the Chair of the
Congregational Union in 1887.[13] Again, that 'thoughtful,
godly and very retiring Independent minister'[14] Thomas Toke
Lynch (1818–71)[15] was at the bottom of the Rivulet controversy, so called after his *Hymns for Heart and Voice. The
Rivulet* (1855). Though welcomed by *The Eclectic Review,*
this volume was held by James Grant, editor of *The Morning
Advertiser,* to contain 'not one particle of vital religion or
evangelical piety', and to be such that it 'might have been
written by a Deist, and a very large portion might be sung
by a congregation of Freethinkers . . .'[16] That the *Morning
Advertiser* could warn its readers against the 'German error'
as represented by Lynch (of all people) betokens an almost
megalomanic desire to guard the Ark. This same spirit helps
to explain the case of Samuel Davidson (1806–1898) of
Lancashire Independent College.[17] Davidson contributed to
the tenth edition of T. H. Horne's *Introduction to the Critical Study and Knowledge of the Holy Scriptures* (1856). As
with Clulow, so with Davidson: the College Committee dis-
approved. It appears that although Davidson was (justly)
accused of denying the Mosaic authorship of the Pentateuch,
it was his naturalistically framed view of inspiration, together

with his apparent duplicity in publishing an 'explanation' which most of the Committee regarded as grossly inadequate, which really incensed his critics. Davidson resigned on 29th June 1857, thereby provoking ambiguous feelings on the part of those who on the one hand — and for reasons not altogether unconnected with finance — could not afford to offend the faithful, and on the other hand did not wish to admit that they had harboured a 'rationalist' for so long. Within a month Principal Robert Vaughan (1795—1868) tendered his resignation also.[18]

The year 1860 saw the publication of *Essays and Reviews,* to which reference has already been made. W. E. Gladstone (1809—98) detected a threat to supernatural authority in the collection, and responded indirectly with his *The Impregnable Rock of Holy Scripture* (1890), a work which had originated in a series of articles in *Good Words.* J. W. Burgon (1813—88), an older-style Tractarian, and Bishop Samuel Wilberforce (1805—73) likewise opposed the work. So ardent was the debate that recourse was had to the courts, where the resulting judgement gave the Church of England freedom to pursue critical questions. Meanwhile the first Bishop of Natal, John William Colenso (1814—83), had caused strife with his commentary on *Romans* (1861) in which he denied the eternity of punishment, and undermined other cherished dogmas. His subsequent work, *The Pentateuch and the Book of Joshua Critically Examined* (in parts 1862—79), led ultimately to his excommunication.[19]

The 1860's brought further investigations of the life of Jesus to the attention of the British. There was Renan's sentimental Life of Jesus (1863) and Seeley's anonymous, non-supernaturalist *Ecce Homo* (1866), both of which caused some consternation in conservative circles, though the devotional sincerity of the books was generally granted. But above all there was the popular edition of Strauss's *Life of Jesus.* In true Hegelian fashion, and notwithstanding his desire to strengthen Hegel precisely at this point, Strauss sat lightly to actual historical events. He sought to distinguish between mythological expressions of the Christian Idea and the facts of history, and to this end he determined that 'in the person and acts of Jesus no supernaturalism shall be

suffered to remain'.[20] Thus, for example, for Strauss the
meaning of the Cross-Resurrection event was that humanity
dies and rises again, and that Christ is the paradigm case of
this process. Not surprisingly, A. M. Fairbairn had stern
words to say of this book: 'It professed to be critical, but was
throughout a pure creation of the philosophical imagination
. . . its exegetical method was applied, to work out a foregone
conclusion . . . The man was a speculative, constructive
thinker, blind to probabilities, forcing history to become the
vehicle of an *a priori* system . . . he is no critical historian,
but a dogmatic controversialist . . . The work was thus least
scientific where most negative, and positive only where speculative . . . Hegel meant his philosophy to explain what had
been and is; Strauss used it to determine what must be or
have been. The eternal process became the immanent God
realising himself in the invariable and necessary order of
nature. Deity was impersonal, miracle impossible, and so the
supernatural incredible.'[21] Among other better informed
reactions to Strauss's work was a lecture by William Dinwiddie. It was one of a series of 'Lectures to Young Men'
delivered at the English Presbyterian College, London, under
the general title, *Disputed Questions of Belief.* As far as
Dinwiddie is concerned, Strauss's theory 'has one value' —
it teaches us, with painful vividness, the helplessness of the
most powerful intellect in presence of the great problems of
life when the light of a Divine revelation has been aban-
doned; how, like a rudderless ship, it will run wild on the
chartless waste of speculation, and cast away from it under
the exigencies of its course every precious thing, until, at last,
stript and lone, without God and hope in the world, it is
lost in the shadows of a gloomy nihilism'.[22]

   The members of the Tubingen school — notably its founder F. C. Baur (1792–1860), an Hegelian influenced by
Schleiermacher — reacted against his pupil Strauss's prostitu-
tion of the idea of history, and prosecuted a policy of exact
analysis of the biblical texts in their historical contexts.
However, in making the faith of the early Church, rather than
the life and work of Christ, determinative, Baur set a fashion
which was to result in the driving of that most unfortunate
wedge between the Jesus of history and the Christ of faith.

What has been called Baur's Hegelianism emerged in his early work, *Untersuchungen uber die sogenannten Pastoralbriefe des Apostels Paulus* (1835), in which he argued that Paul represented the antithesis to the earlier apostles' thesis, and that the resultant Church constituted the synthesis. We should note however, with Mr. Morgan, that biblical exegesis and an acute historical sense contributed as much to Baur's case as overt loyalty to Hegel.[23] This same combination of factors eventually led Baur to sceptical conclusions concerning the authenticity of all the Pauline epistles except *Romans, Corinthians* and *Galatians,* as may be seen in his *Paulus* (E.T. 1873–5).

A more empirical approach to biblical study was adopted by G. H. A. von Ewald (1803–75). He utilised archaeological findings, and his massive *History of Israel* was translated into English (1869–83) by the Broad Churchman A. P. Stanley (1815–81). Stanley himself had published a *History of the Jewish Church* (1863–76). In the line of Vatke, Graf brought out his *The Historical Books of the Old Testament* (1866), and his source-critical approach was carried further by Wellhausen, whose *History of Israel* was dedicated to Ewald, the author's 'unforgotten master'. Many felt that the effect of Wellhausen's method was to reduce the Bible to a collection of unco-ordinated fragments. The Wellhausen school, thought Dr. James Orr, 'really subverts the basis of a reasonable faith in the Bible, and of a revelation of God contained in it, altogether'.[24] Conservatives who sought *comfort* in Germany tended to look towards F. A. G. Tholuck (1799–1877) and F. J. Delitzsch (1813–90).

The mention of the polymathic Dr. Orr directs our attention to Scotland. In the first quarter of the nineteenth century there had been a controversy surrounding the British and Foreign Bible Society. In 1813 the Society had, at its own expense, published the Apocrypha with a view to facilitating the distribution of the scriptures in Greek, Roman and Lutheran areas. This action raised the question of the status of the canon, and occasioned a vociferous conservative protest. The flames of the bitter dispute were fanned by the recollection that the Council of Trent had accorded like status to the Old and New Testaments and to the Apocrypha.

Robert Haldane (1764–1842) wrote many pamphlets against 'that dreadful abomination the Apocrypha', while Ralph Wardlaw (1799–1853) took the opposing view. Among others who sided with Haldane were Andrew Thompson (1779–1831) of St. George's, Edinburgh, and Edward Irving (1792–1834). In the event the Society continued to circulate the Old and New Testaments only, and that 'without note or comment'. The Apocrypha Controversy was, in Dr. MacLeod's opinion, 'the first token of the working of an unbelieving leaven as to Holy Writ in Evangelical circles in Scotland'.[25]

The supreme critical challenge in Scotland, however, came with William Robertson Smith (1846–94), who was appointed to the Old Testament Chair in the Free Church College, Aberdeen, in 1870. A. B. Davidson (1831–1902), of New College, Edinburgh, had, in the early 1870's, begun to introduce students to higher critical views, but when in 1875 Smith's articles appeared in the ninth edition of *Encyclopaedia Britannica* the storm broke. Smith's admiration for his teacher, Wellhausen, stood him in no good stead with many of his fellow churchmen, who suspected him (as Samuel Davidson had been suspected thirty years earlier) of undermining the doctrine of inspiration. Smith's view was that the Bible contained the Word of God, but that its words were not synonymous with that Word. On the other hand, Smith was not an anti-supernaturalist, rationalising scholar, and he had attacked the liberalism of the established churchman John Tulloch (1823–86). For all that he was deposed from his Chair in 1881, though not expelled from the ministry. In 1883 he proceeded to Cambridge where he continued his researches until his early death.[26]

When attempts to convict A. B. Bruce (1831–99) and Marcus Dods (1834–1909) of heresy also failed, it became clear that widespread accommodation to critical views had occurred in Scotland — at least among ministers and leaders of the Free Church; and if there, then how much more elsewhere? Many endorsed the verdict delivered in regard to eighteenth-century Arianism by the Irish Professor Thomas Witherow: 'Heresy in the pulpit may slay her thousands, but heresy from the rostrum slays its tens of thousands'.[27]

Perhaps the comment of the American Calvinist B. B. Warfield both indicates the true position of the Scots referred to in this paragraph, and also shows the distance between them and the members of the Princeton school. In a review of Dods' *The Bible, Its Origin and Nature* Warfield complained of the author's superficiality and said, 'We rejoice that Dr. Dods would preserve to us at least a supernatural Redeemer, even if he draws back before too supernatural a Bible'.[28] But the tide was already turning against Warfield in his own country. As early as 1891 Dr. Lewis F. Stearns said of the higher criticism that 'Some of our ablest scholars have accepted, to a greater or less extent, the new views'. But he was also able to add that 'our ministers and intelligent laymen . . . are more cautious . . .'[29] In churches more confessionally conscious than Stearn's Congregational fold there was even more caution. As late as 1922 Ralph Janssen was deposed from his Chair at Calvin Theological Seminary because of concessions he had made to higher critical views of the Old Testament.[30] Between Stearns and Janssen there appeared in America The Fundamentals, that series of twelve pamphlets (1910–15) by sixty-four authors, including James Orr, whose purpose was to advocate doctrines deemed central to the faith; to defend the Bible against higher critical assaults; and to publish reasoned critiques of such sectaries as the Mormons. Not all the contributors were equally opposed to criticism or to (the other bogey-man) evolution, and some considered Orr too liberal in both areas. Some contributors were millenarians, others were not; indeed we might also say that seldom had such a wide variety of conservatives united in support of a doctrinal platform from which few contemporary Roman Catholics would have dissented.[31] But change was coming even in the latter communion. Pope Leo XIII's encyclical *Providentissimus Deus* (1893), which declared the Bible to be inerrant in its entirety, appeared in the same year in which Alfred Loisy (1857–1940)[32] was removed from his Paris professorship because of his espousal of modern critical views. In 1894 the editor of *The British Weekly* concluded that the Princetonians Green and Warfield were 'the only *respectable* defenders of verbal inspiration' left.[33]

However 'unrespectable', there was opposition, however —

even in England. Among the Congregationalists Henry Rogers
(1806?–1877) in his *The Superhuman Origin of the Bible*
(1873) and Alfred Cave (1847–1900)[34] in his *The Inspiration
of the Old Testament Inductively Considered* (1888) sought
to stem the advancing tide. Supremely, there was C. H.
Spurgeon (1834–92), whose part in the Down-grade controversy was inspired both by the realisation that old scriptural
landmarks were being removed, and also by what he was sure
would be the consequence of doctrinal laxity within the Baptist Union. The controversy opened with the publication in
March and April 1887 of two articles in Spurgeon's magazine
Sword and Trowel; they were entitled 'The Down Grade',
and though anonymous they were in fact by Robert Shindler,
an erstwhile student at Spurgeon's Pastors' College. In the
same journal in August Spurgeon published his own list of
errors to be combatted: 'The Atonement is scouted, the
inspiration of Scripture is derided, the Holy Spirit is degraded
into an influence, the punishment of sin is turned into a
fiction, and the resurrection into a myth, and yet these enemies of our faith expect us to call them brethren, and maintain
a confederacy with them'.[35] Events moved fast, and notwithstanding the mutual esteem in which Spurgeon and Jonn
Clifford (1836–1923) held each other, Spurgeon resigned
from the Baptist Union on 28th October 1887. Clifford's
subsequent affirmation that 'Systems of doctrine are trifles
light as air to souls that see God face to face in immediate
fellowship with the Eternal Spirit'[36] was, to put it mildly,
not of a kind to commend itself to Spurgeon and his followers.

Although there was truth in R. W. Dale's remark in 1879
that 'Mr. Spurgeon stands alone among the modern leaders of
Evangelical Nonconformists in his fidelity to the older Calvinistic creed';[37] despite the fact that modern biblical scholarship was to some 'an exhilarating emancipation';[38] notwithstanding the High Church blessing accorded by Charles Gore
to the view that Christianity, though it brought with it 'a
doctrine of the inspiration of Holy Scripture . . . is not based
upon it';[39] the fact remained that as to that very doctrine 'we
are all at sixes and sevens'.[40] In such an environment of un-
certainty popular opposition could flourish. In this con-

nection the notable preacher Joseph Parker (1830–1902) was one of the bigger guns. The following is a typical statement of his (and one which, frankly, begs most of the questions at issue): 'The Bible proves its own authenticity by its knowledge of human nature, its moral sublimity, and its infinite anxiety for the good of mankind'.[41] Then there was that numerous company of penny tractarians who, with considerable frequency, extolled A. H. Sayce (1845–1933) for his defence, in *The 'Higher Criticism' and the Verdict of the Monuments* (1894), of the Mosaic authorship of the Pentateuch. In one of his tracts G. Campbell Morgan (1863–1945) declared, 'My own ministry is based upon the conviction that the Bible is the Infallible Word of God';[42] and the evangelical Anglican Bishop J. C. Ryle (1816–1900) averred, 'Whether we like it or not we cannot shut higher criticism out. Like frogs in the plague of Egypt, it creeps in everywhere . . . The result is a general *shakiness* in many minds about the Old Testament . . . I stand firmly by the old faith of the Church, and refuse to give it up until I can find a better'.[43] That some of the *defenders* of the inspiration of the Bible were by now taking a dangerously subjectivist stance emerges in an account of the argument of Mr. Hancox, a Primitive Methodist minister, published by his Unitarian contemporary, Peter Dean, in the latter's polemical monthly, *The Religious Reformer*: 'if anyone puzzled them with questions as to the inspiration of the Bible, they were to act as some man who said: "I cannot answer, but placing his hand on his heart) the secret lies here". Acting in this way, what superstition may not be held? . . . Men have no business holding beliefs they cannot give sensible reasons for; and it is precisely because sensible reasons for the infalibility [*sic*] of the Bible cannot be given, that Bibliolaters – like Mr. Hancox – have to advise such childish expedients'.[44]

Despite all the opposition a considerable distance (non-evaluative term!) was travelled during the nineteenth century. One way of measuring the distance is to place comments by William Van Mildert and James Drummond side by side. In his 1814 Bampton Lectures the former asserted with regard to the Bible that 'it is impossible even to imagine a failure, either in judgment or in integrity'.[45] Eighty years later the

latter, in his Hibbert Lectures, waxed lyrically eucharistic
thus: 'Thanks . . . to the despised critics, and to the general
advance of knowledge, the night is passing away, and the
dawn is shedding its orient beams upon the world'.[46] Somewhat more soberly Dr. Fairbairn summarised three misconceived policies as follows:

> 'The common premiss is: Criticism has affected the author-
> ity of the Bible in matters of religion, — *therefore,* says the
> rationalist, since criticism is true, the authority is at end;
> *therefore,* says the conservative, since the authority must
> be maintained, criticism must be resisted and its decisions
> rejected; *therefore,* says the neo-Catholic, since, keeping as
> regards the Bible an open mind, we must confess the diffi-
> culties created by criticism, let us rest in the authority of
> the Church.'[47]

The fact that Fairbairn's own preferred alternative — that of
recognising that 'Criticism has, by binding the book and the
people together, and then connecting both with the providen-
tial order of the world, given us back the idea of the God
who lives in history through His people, and a people who
live for Him through His word'[48] — was so painlessly adopted
by the vast majority of British theologians, is in large measure
due to the careful and unsensationalist work of such
Anglicans as B. F. Westcott (1825–1901), F. J. A. Hort
(1828–92) and J. B. Lightfoot (1828–89); and to such Free
Churchmen as R. W. Dale (1829–95) and Fairbairn (1838–
1912) himself.[49] Their successors included, notably, the
Primitive Methodist A. S. Peake (1865–1929). To the
Manchester Guardian Peake's greatest service to 'the whole
religious life of England [was] that he helped to save us from
a fundamental controversy such as that which had devastated
large sections of the Church in America'.[50] What we have
found most surprising about Peake in his role of midwife-to-
criticism is that in a popular work designed to reassure the
godly he denied that criticism was due to rationalism, to the
rejection of Christianity, or to the entertainment by critics of
Hegelian or evolutionary presuppositions; on the contrary, he
claimed that the 'generally accepted results of criticism . . .
rest on a number of phenomena actually present in the docu-

ments themselves . . .'[51] We grant his affirmation, but his denials are too extreme. No scholar came to the biblical books with his mind a *tabula rasa,* and we have discovered an assortment of naturalists, empiricists, subjectivists and post-Hegelian idealists among the critics.

So successful were the British critics that by 1932 T. R. Glover, who had himself done much to acquaint his fellow Baptists with the positive results of criticism, was able to claim that 'Today if you want a real old obscurantist college, you have to found one'.[52] In similar vein the Methodist A. W. Harrison wrote a letter to *The Times* in which he stated that 'Today, in all the seven English theological colleges of the Methodist Church the point of view known in America as Fundamentalist is not represented at all'.[53] Latter-day fundamentalists may well discern a causal link between such a state of affairs and the subsequent closure or amalgamation of so many Anglican, Methodist and Congregationalist theological colleges! And an impartial non-fundamentalist must note that Britain's only confessionally Reformed college, that of the Free Church of Scotland, continues to this day; and that of a number of evangelical colleges and Bible institutes which have been founded *since* 1932 the London Bible College enjoys probably the highest academic reputation.[54]

On 11th May 1869 — nearly ten years before Wellhausen's *History* was published — R. W. Dale addressed the Congregational Union of England and Wales. He granted what Peake later seemed reluctant to grant, namely, that the analytical work of the higher criticism was something to which men were impelled 'by the whole spirit and temper of our times'[55] — and it was an anti-supernaturalist temper. Dale proceeded to enumerate some of the chief areas of controversy, and then he said this: 'it becomes plainer every year that the real questions in debate are far different from these. The storm has moved round the whole horizon; but it is rapidly concentrating its strength and fury above one sacred Head. This, this is the real issue of the fight — Is Christendom to believe in Christ any longer or no?'[56] This was the question which lay behind the contrary positions of Harnack and Schweitzer at the beginning of the twentieth century. This was the question which fuelled the conservative reaction to the higher criticism, and which prompted the affirmation of Martin Kahler (1835–1912) that the Jesus of history *is* the Christ of faith. The same question lay behind much of the uneasiness concerning evolution, to which theme we now turn.

CHAPTER THREE

EVOLUTION: THEORY AND THEME

Whatever truth may lie behind the suspicion that the ultra-conservative no less than the ultra-liberal *needs* an Aunt Sally, the fact is that Charles Darwin (1809–1882)[1] has been regarded as an appropriate target by many in the former category. To him has been attributed a slide into scepticism of gigantic proportions; an increase of moral laxity fired by the belief that humans are but animals — and so on. It will not be our purpose to examine the detailed scientific arguments which Darwin and others proposed, nor the counter arguments which other scientists urged against them. Rather, we shall attempt to put evolution into its proper perspective as an influential motif within nineteenth century thought, and we shall be especially concerned with the use theologians made of it. We shall suggest that Darwin himself, far from being an originator, was in debt both to that immanentist tendency whose origins we have uncovered in Kant and German romanticism,[2] and to that increasingly popular understanding of history which sought to explain the present as being a development of the past.[3] We shall show that Darwin's distinctive scientific contribution, the hypothesis of natural selection, far from holding any real terrors for the more thoughtful theologians, was quite often ignored by them in their positive constructions: the evolutionary theme rather than specific theories was what appealed to them, not least because it harmonised so well with what, on other grounds, they wished to believe in any case. We shall observe in passing that the generalisation to the effect that large tracts of the world of nineteenth century thought were caught up in a wave of evolution-based optimism to which only the First World War could give the lie is open to ques-

tion. That there *were* such optimists we shall not deny (and
the further they were from the theatre of war the more of
them there seem to have been); but some had a properly
sober understanding of sin before the War, while others
managed to retain their optimism *after* it. Whatever nineteenth century theologians might think of evolution, they
could not ignore it: not indeed that they were always very
clear about what it was that they were not ignoring! As one
commentator put it, 'Evolution has, since Darwin's time, become invested with an omnipotence which, it may safely be
affirmed, belongs to it only through a haze in the ideas of
those who so exalt it'.[4]

The liberal preacher T. Rhondda Williams was typical of
many popularisers in his pragmatic approach to the matter:
'Evolution is still a hypothesis, but it is *the* hypothesis which
is now used in every department of investigation, and, quite
apart from the question of its ultimate validity, the use made
of it at present is such that no man who wishes to serve his
age in the interests of the Kingdom of God can afford to
ignore it'.[5] To the extent that Williams is accurate here — and
undeniably evolutionary thought did permeate many fields of
enquiry — we have impressive testimony to the rapidity with
which the concept of evolution took root in the minds of
men; for as A. J. Balfour said, even 'men of science did not
habitually think in terms of evolution till well into the second half of the Victorian epoch'.[6] That they bagan so to
think at all is as much owing to the work of geologists as it is
to workers in any other field of science.

The researches of Charles Lyell (1797–1875), which were
written up in his *Principles of Geology* (first volume 1830),
had two main effects. First, they demolished the approach of
Archbishop James Ussher (1581–1656) to biblical chron-
ology. Ussher, it will be recalled, had calculated that the
world was created in 4004 B.C. Lyell showed that the rocks
gave evidence that the earth was much older than had once
been thought. Secondly, Lyell's findings suggested that uniformitarianism rather than catastrophism was the more tenable hypothesis in respect of the development of the universe. Lyell thus threw down the gauntlet not only to natural
theologians in the line of Paley (1743–1805), who *required*

God's dramatic creative intervention to shore up their version of orthodoxy, but also to such a pioneer *geologist* as Adam Sedgwick (1785–1873), who by no means relished the possibility that science might undermine the scriptures. Dr. Young has put the terms of the debate in a nutshell thus: 'If Sedgwick was concerned that *without* creative interference there might be no God, then Lyell was concerned that *with* creative interference there would be no science'.[7]

At least three kinds of response were open to Christians confronted by the work of Lyell and his fellows. They could argue, as Dr. Pye Smith did in his Congregational Lecture for 1839, that theologians had erred in the chronological deductions they had made from scripture, and that uniformitarianism more accurately reflected biblical teaching than did catastrophism.[8] They could be deeply troubled, as was John Ruskin who, as early as 1851 wrote, 'If only the Geologists would let me alone, I could do very well, but those dreadful hammers! I hear the clink of them at the end of every cadence of the Bible verses'.[9] Thirdly, there was the somewhat later response to the effect that science can do the Bible no harm because each seeks answers to *different* questions. This approach is typified by R. W. Dale's comment that 'ordinary Christian people . . . have frankly accepted all that the geologists have ascertained in relation to the antiquity of the earth and the antiquity of man; but their faith in Christ is undisturbed'.[10]

It was when Robert Chambers (1802–71) published his *Vestiges of the Natural History of Creation* (1844) that the transition was made in the popular mind from concern with rocks to concern with man; for Chambers scandalised some by maintaining that Lyell's uniformitarian principle ought to be applied not only to the physical creation, but also to man and his mind.[11] On this very problem Darwin was hard at work. Not indeed that he was without predecessors in the field. Certainly the notions of development and progress were well known in the ancient world. To take examples almost at random: Anaximander (611–547), Anaximenes (588–544), Xenophanes (576–480) and Empedocles (495–435) all entertained, in however *a priori* a fashion, the notion of the evolution of man from lower orders of creation. Again,

Heraclitus (c. 500) is famed for his doctrine of flux. Still more definite affirmations (we use the term advisedly) concerning the origin and development of living things are to be found in the writings of Aristotle (384–322). He supposed that life originated from the inorganic, and that there was movement through successive stages from plants, which neither feel nor think, through animals, which feel and have elementary powers of thought, to man, who both feels and engages in abstract thought. The whole depends upon the Pure Form, said Aristotle, though what exactly he meant by this, and what kind of dependence he had in mind, is not altogether clear. Although Aristotle thus thinks in terms of successive stages of development, he does not employ the idea of evolution; indeed, he could not, for to him both species and genera are eternal. From Platonism, and especially from Neoplatonism, came the impetus to think of spiritual growth towards the divine; and the New Testament, with its teleological emphasis (growing up into Christ; the consummation) could be summoned in support. We find intimations of evolution in Leibniz; Lessing, Schelling and Hegel applied the evolutionary principle to history (though Hegel could well manage without a *scientific* hypothesis!); and J. G. Herder (1744–1803) regarded evolution as the vehicle of the divine providence. Ideas of development, progress, evolution, were thus not new when Darwin came on the scene, and indeed the implications of such ideas for social reform had already been indicated by Comte (1798–1857). It remained for modern scientists, by the production of evidence, to anchor these concepts empirically and, above all, to posit an explanatory hypothesis which would answer the 'how' question.

Whereas Linnaeus (1707–78) in his monumental *Systema Naturae* did not raise the question as to how the species which he so diligently classified had come to be differentiated from one another, Georges Buffon (1707–88) was not so inhibited. It was one of his speculations which Erasmus Darwin (1731–1802), Chevalier de Lamarck (1744–1829) and Geoffroy de St. Hilaire (1771–1844) exploited — namely, that change occurred as a species progressively adapted itself to its environment. Both the contemporary scientific and theological orthodoxies were implacably opposed to any such suggestion, and it was not until Lyell's results were known that the modern evolutionists found much extrinsic support. Even then the evolutionist blaze was slow to kindle, not so much because of the opposition already mentioned, as because of a feeling that the crucial clue had yet to be produced. What Charles Darwin and Alfred Russel Wallace (1823—1913) independently arrived at was the principle of natural selection — or what Herbert Spencer (1820—1903) was to call the principle of 'the survival of the fittest'.[12] Justice prompts the comment that not even here were Darwin and Wallace the first in the field. The idea of natural selection had been mooted by W. C. Wells (1757—1817) in 1813 and by Matthew in 1831; but Darwin and Wallace were the men of the hour and, moreover, they had the *evidence* with which to support their hypothesis.

Both Darwin and Wallace had been influenced by Malthus's *Essay on the Principle of Population* (1798), which showed that when the human population outgrew the available sources of food an inevitable struggle ensued. They drew the analogy and applied it to all forms of organic life, thereby providing the world with an explanatory hypothesis to account for that change and development which many agreed was too well documented to be gainsaid. Once the secret was out — and *The Origin of Species* appeared in 1859 — Huxley remarked, 'How extremely stupid not to have thought of that!'. Principal Griffith-Jones was only echoing those of an earlier generation when he expressed his opinion that Darwin had formulated 'one of the most revolutionary generalisations ever attempted by the human mind'.[13] In working out his theory Darwin was able to use the insights of his grandfather and of Lamarck concerning environmental factors in the production of change; and the special significance of Wallace from the theological point of view is his denial that distinctively human qualities could result from natural selection — for these a unique 'special influx' was required.

It was only to be expected that Darwin's work should prompt jubilation in some quarters and consternation in others. The numerous debates and pamphlets often engendered more heat than light, and for this very reason it is

especially important to record the fact that Darwin himself
was the humblest of men, and that unlike some scientists
before and since he was reluctant to pronounce upon matters outside his field of specialised knowledge. He did not
regard himself as doing more than advance a biological hypothesis: it was not until his *Descent of Man* (1871) that he
extended his interests specifically to man. An agnostic himself (though he defined himself thus only very hesitantly),
he had no wish to upset the faith of others. He did recognise, however, that 'the old argument from design in nature,
as given by Paley, which formerly seemed to me so conclu-
sive, fails, now that the law of natural selection has been
discovered'.[14] Even so, Darwin truthfully declared that he
had never 'published a word directly against religion or the
clergy'.[15] Some of the latter found no difficulty in thinking
otherwise. Thus Bishop Samuel Wilberforce (1805–73)
attacked Darwinism in the *Quarterly Review,* and spoke
against the new teaching at the Oxford meeting of the
British Association in 1860; while from the ranks of the
laity the statesman W. E. Gladstone (1809–1898) rose to
the defence of *The Impregnable Rock of Holy Scripture*
(1890). Among the numerous complaints were the following: that what was presumed to be the biblical teaching
concerning the fixity of species was being undermined; that,
despite Wallace's concession, man, as now naturalistically
understood, could no longer be regarded as God's special
creation;[16] that there was something morally offensive in the
idea that survival depended upon an individual's being sufficiently aggressive; that the tendency of evolutionists to
observe results rather than seek causes left little room for the
idea of purpose – as Huxley declared, evolution dealt the
death blow to teleology;[17] and, as we have noted earlier, that
apologetics had been undermined. For all of these reasons,
and others, some, including the judicious James Orr, were
persuaded that Darwinism 'asks us to believe that accident
and fortuity have done the work of mind.[18] Such scholars
took little comfort from Darwin's own testimony that 'The
birth both of the species and of the individual are equally
parts of that grand sequence of events which our minds refuse to accept as the result of blind chance';[19] indeed, given

his presuppositions, they were hard put to understand how he could say such a thing at all.

Few Christians gave evolution so cordial a welcome as did Baden Powell, F.R.S., in his paper in *Essays and Reviews* (1860). Rather more felt that the Ark was being assailed. Two types of development assisted thinking men and women towards a more balanced view. In the first place, a number of scientists began to fault Darwin's detailed case. More importantly, some, including the highly respected Lord Kelvin, affirmed that science required rather than destroyed the concept of a creative power: still others began to reach the conclusion bluntly expressed by Sir F. G. Hopkins, President of the British Association in 1933, that 'all we know is that we know nothing of life's origin.[20] Secondly, such views as T. H. Huxley's that 'it is not true that evolution necessarily presupposes natural selection'[21] came to be regarded as providing theologians with a convenient escape from naturalism. This accorded well with their twin desires to shun a doctrine which 'estimates a man solely by his worth to the community, and is proud of him only as he has the strength that can be victorious in the struggle',[22] while exalting the ideas of progress and of ethical development.[23] *A fortiori* it armed them against 'the sanctified competitiveness of a Social Darwinianism in which, as Bishop Gore said, "it is a case of each for himself as the elephant said when it danced among the chickens" '.[24] So it transpired that R. W. Dale could sound in no way untypical in arguing that whereas Christians had for too long, in deistic fashion, employed God as a necessary hypothesis, 'It will be something if science enables us to recover a firmer hold of the ancient faith, and enables us to see for ourselves the present activity of God'.[25]

The very fact, however, that theologians could be as sanguine as this confirms our claim that *Darwin's* views had been so modified as to be almost unrecognisable. Dean Inge was not wide of the mark in asserting that 'In reality, human progress is the primary assumption, which the scientific theory of development was brought in to support. A popular religion is a superstition which has enslaved a philosophy. In this case the superstition was belief in the perfectibility of the species; the philosophy was a misreading of the biology of Darwin'.[26] If we overlook the fact that we are confronted by a *variety* of interpretations of evolution, and that evolution is pressed into the service of a number of different and sometimes contradictory presuppositions, we shall be in danger of making those very generalisations which it is part of our purpose to question. Thus, for example, Professor H. G. Wood reminded us that while Marx read revolution out of evolution, the Fabians contented themselves with gradualism.[27] Again, whereas A. N. Whitehead thought that Victorian Christians were ill advised not to give evolution a more cordial welcome since, by virtue of its anti-materialistic organic principle and its underlying necessary activity, it facilitated the very kind of teleological interpretation in which they might have been expected to be interested,[28] Huxley, as we have seen, thought that evolution destroyed teleology. This latter view was reaffirmed by Otto to whom Darwin was the Newton of biology because of the 'radical opposition' of his doctrine of natural selection to teleology.[29] Some Christians knew only too well that if they were to purge evolutionary theory of its less congenial aspects they would have to *spurn* Darwin's gift of *natural* selection. Even Baden Powell, "advanced" as he was, was under this necessity, for he invoked 'a Supreme Moral Cause, *distinct from and above nature'*.[30] Whatever the precise terms of his personal ideology may have been, Darwin's biological hypothesis left little room for this. But if Powell trimmed evolutionary thought in the direction of deism, as the words we have just italicised suggest, others employed the notion in quite different ways.

In the first place, there were the naturalists. Few subjected them to such searching criticism as A. J. Balfour (whatever we may think of his own alternative), and it will suffice us to hear him:

> 'this is a position which is essentially incoherent. Its conclusions discredit its premises. The doctrines in which we believe throw doubts upon the truth-producing value of the process by which we have to come to believe them. For we remember that these reasons are without exception not only reasons but effects. As effects they owe nothing

in the last resort to reason or purpose. If snatches of reason and gleams of purpose occasionally emerge in the latest stage of the evolutionary process, this is but an accident among accidents . . . Everything we believe, we believe because in the order of causation blind matter and undirected energy happened to be distributed in a particular manner countless aeons before man made his earliest entry on the cosmic stage. From this senseless stock, and from this alone, has sprung, according to naturalism, all that there is, or ever can be, of knowledge, practical or speculative, earthly or divine — including, of course, the naturalistic theory itself! How then can we treat it with respect?'[31]

Next, there was the ambivalent and delightfully eclectic Herbert Spencer (1820–1903), whose writings had considerable vogue, and who was the butt of many a theologian's jibe. He was, moreover, in the evolutionary field before Darwin's *Origin* appeared. As early as 1850 he had published his *Social Statics,* and in 1855 there appeared his *Principles of Psychology.* From 1862–93 he was found publishing the several parts of his synthetic philosophy. Spencer's evolutionary stance, and in particular its ethical implications, earned him the attention of numerous theologians. Turning his back upon the older intuitionism, Spencer held that our ethical notions are inherited from our ancestors, and that our present mental and moral capacities are as they are by virtue of the evolutionary process which must continue. The empiricism here places Spencer in the line of Hume; the implied relativism he, together with Hamilton (1788–1856), explicitly affirmed; and his agnosticism emerges in his declaration, following Kant, that the Absolute is unknowable. We might therefore have expected to find consistent naturalism or materialism in Spencer, but we do not. His ambivalence emerges in that so long as evolutionary process is allowed he seems to fluctuate between cashing the doctrine variously in idealistic or materialistic terms. Thus he can allow that there is a Power behind the universe, though when he declared that 'the Power which the Universe manifests to us is utterly inscrutable'[32] he provoked not a little incredulity among such competent theologians as Dr. Iverach: 'He speaks of knowl-

edge and its manifestations, and does not see that if the
Unknowable is manifested, so far as it is manifested it can be
known'.[33] Iverach and others were equally baffled by Spencer's insistence on explaining the higher in terms of the lower: 'One has sympathy with those who labour at an impossible task. It is hard on one who has undertaken to explain
evolution in terms of the distribution of matter and motion
to arrive at a stage where matter fails, and then to be com-
pelled to deal with super-organic matter . . . We can but express our sympathy, and pass on to the conviction that the
source of explanation lies not where they are seeking it'.[34]
Many theologians appealed to naturalists to 'come clean' on
these two points, and H. R. Mackintosh was subsequently to
feel that 'The one fact which has given Materialism its otherwise inexplicable fascination for the less instructed modern
mind is, we can scarcely doubt, its wholly illegitimate alliance
with the doctrine of Evolution'.[35]

Turning once more to the theists we find that many of
them absorbed evolutionary theory (though not Darwinism)
into their systems by the expedient of assuming God to be
immanent in the evolutionary process. (The refrain of the
jingle comes to mind: 'Some call it evolution; others call it
God'.) On this basis even the cautious Dr. Orr could envisage
the possibility that evolution 'may become a new and height-
ened form of the theistic argument'.[36] A. E. Garvie went further in maintaining that the notion of cosmic evolution
demands an immanent, dynamic God, and declared that since
God works out his purposes in history, the understanding of
religion as 'the flight of the alone to the Alone' is no longer
tenable.[37] Garvie further held that evolution indicated the
method by which the immanent God made himself known —
that is, gradually and progressively, rather than catastrophi-
cally.[38] Edward Caird (1835–1908) and Henry Jones (1852–
1922) were among those who followed a similar line from the
side of philosophy. It cannot be maintained, however, that
the immanentists gave an entirely satisfactory account of the
divine transcendence. They tended, perhaps in partial reaction against both the older natural theology and deism, to
leave the concept on one side, and certainly Kingsley's early
attempt to solve the difficulty by redefining all *natural* events

as miracles did not find universal acclaim.[39] Again, some theologians were alive to the fact that certain forms of teleological idealism, in which the end was determined from the beginning were, as William James said, but the 'reverse side of mechanism';[40] while Professor Emmet, viewing the debate from a more distant vantage point, noted the evolutionary idealisms tended to get into difficulties over the empirical, and that the supreme deductive idealist, McTaggart, was forced to recognise that apart from the empirical premise that 'something exists' his system could never have got under way.[41]

If some varieties of evolutionary idealism were as inimical to theologians as the various kinds of naturalism and materialism, there were other developments of evolutionary thought which promised them more encouragement by reason of their 'spiritual' approach to matters. Thus James Ward (1843–1925) in his *The Realm of Ends* (1911), and Bergson (1859–1941) in his numerous writings, spoke respectively of epigenesis and of the *elan vital*.[42] According to both, evolution was the datum, but in opposition to materialism they held that the more recent was not merely educed from the earlier, but that there was novelty attaching to it. The process is dynamic, vital, creative – not merely reproductive. The appeal which such teaching could have to the more homiletic popularisers is plain, though such men had perforce to sit rather loosely to such empirical factors as disease and pain – in theological terms, the problem of evil – which tended to militate against it. Dean Inge had his own, characteristic way of expressing his dissatisfaction:

> 'Bergson and his followers naturally advocate the Lamarckian *elan vital*, an inner impulse towards change, in opposition to the merely mechanical doctrine of Darwin, which does not admit of qualitative alteration. It must, however, be admitted that for a metaphysician a minimal change is as great a problem as a mutation. We cannot admit the excuse of the girl who palliated the appearance of her baby by saying that it was a very small one.'[43]

In the twentieth century we find a development in the direction of emergent evolution. According to this theory the Creator himself is subject to change, and reality is identified

with process. This doctrine is variously associated with the
names of C. Lloyd Morgan (1852–1936), Samuel Alexander
(1859–1938) and A. N. Whitehead (1861–1947), and some
theologians felt, with Donald Baillie, that they were too
ignorant to pass judgement upon it.[44]. Others felt that their
understanding of God could be neither helped nor harmed by
the more esoteric speculations of their philosophical contemporaries, Lloyd Morgan's talk of 'Spiritual Agency'[45] notwithstanding. It is only much nearer to our own time that Charles
Hartshorne, Schubert Ogden, John Cobb and others have
developed process theologies out of Whitehead's later metaphysics; and into these we cannot at present enquire.

We turn instead to the doctrinal implications of the earlier
theological utilisation of evolutionary theory. Concerning the
doctrine of creation, the realisation that Darwinism was not a
theory of causes, but rather an account of causal methods,
gave considerable comfort to theologians:

> 'All these terms — Evolution, Natural Selection, the Sur-
> vival of the Fittest, and the like — are descriptions of a
> method, or of a result, and not a definition of a cause. Yet
> to mistake a result, a method, or a description for a reason
> and a cause is the failing of the common talk of many
> Evolutionists, a mistake from which Darwin, at least in his
> circumspect moments, kept himself entirely free.'[46]

Theologians thus felt justified in understanding evolution as
being God's way of revelation. Dr. Garvie said as much:
'Evolution is God's method of creation of the world and
man, and it is no less the method of His revelation, for a
communication beyond the capacity of man to receive and
respond would be idle and vain. We may say that human development is by divine education.'[47] (It is interesting to note
in passing that a not dissimilar stance was adopted by those
who were working within the Roman Catholic fold for a
revival of Thomism. They urged evolution as the *modus
operandi* whereby universals were realised in the actual
world). Garvie and others like him were quite convinced that
evolutionary theory could and should coexist with supernaturalism:

> 'The recognition of evolution, and of progress in evolution,

removes an objection to the admission of the supernatural which was rooted in the static view of the world. If the world were thought of as a finished article . . . any fresh departure must seem incredible. But admit the conception of progress, then no stage can be regarded as so finally and adequately expressing the whole mind and will of God that any new expression would appear incredible.'[48]

As far as man is concerned, it is by a gradually evolving process that he increasingly co-operates in God's advancing purpose;[49] evolution inspires us onward in the struggle against evil;[50] indeed, 'in the whole long story of evolution pain is the condition of progress'[51] and of this the Cross is the supreme illustration.

Thus it was that some theologians, not to mention many preachers, adopted an optimistic attitude towards the world and man's place in it. One might have thought that Spencer's declaration concerning the inevitability of both the disappearance of evil and immortality, and of the perfection of man, would have given them pause. But the appeal of the idea in the air was too much for some. We can understand this — after all, it really did seem that science and the new technologies held the promise of a better life than most had ever dreamed of. As early as 4th January 1851 *The Economist* had roundly declared that 'All who have read, and can think, must now have full confidence that the "endless progression" ever increasing in rapidity, of which the poet sung, is the destined lot of the human race'.[52] Even the sober Martineau, having examined regress, stoicism and progress, could affirm that the last alone 'is the most accordant with the divine interpretation of the world . . . neither of these two modern discoveries, namely, the immense extension of the universe in space, and its unlimited development in time, has any effect on the theistic faith, except to glorify it';[53] and Garvie, even *after* the First World War could still declare that God 'is completing the evolution of the world and of mankind in the progressive manifestation of the sons of God'.[54]

Commentators have sometimes generalised from such statements in an unacceptable way. There was optimism, but it was not universal — as the works of von Hartmann (1842—

1906), for example, show — and it was not always unthinking. Many of those theologians who wished to make most of progress, development, aspiration, sought also to take due account of sin, and of the actuality of moral stagnation and decadence. In this connection Dr. Garvie comes to mind once more.[55] Others were even more reserved concerning the inevitability of progress. Of Croce's words 'The plant dreams of the animal, the animal of man, and man of superman . . .' Inge confessed, 'I can see nothing in his hymn to progress except delerious nonsense'.[56] And with even more direct implications for the theological utilisation of the evolutionary principle the poet James Thompson averred,

'I find no hint throughout the Universe
Of good or ill, of blessing or of curse.'

In his Romanes Lecture for 1893 Huxley warned that the theory of evolution 'encourages no millenial expectations'. Those who overlooked such warnings may have felt that they were in good company, for near the end of *The Origin of Species* Darwin had said that 'as natural selection works solely by and for the good of each being, all corporeal and mental endowments will tend to progress towards perfection'.[57] Thus if he had wished, Dr. L. F. Stearns, the American Congregationalist, could have claimed *quasi*-apostolic authority for his jubilant statement, 'We have seen the scientific theory of evolution turned from an enemy to a friend of religion'.[58] It was but a short step to Social Gospel theory.

Dr. Iverach, by contrast, was by no means so persuaded of the unqualified benefits of evolutionism. While he was prepared to accept a version of theistic evolution according to which evolution was the method of God's working, he did not wish to minimise the importance of sin, or the need of grace. He could not regard evolutionary progress as automatic: 'Many hindrances there are on Christ's view to the communication of God to His creation; but the main hindrance is that men are not pure in heart'.[59] The Anglican Scott Holland complained that the doctrine of evolution 'yields no Categorical Imperative';[60] John Dickie argued that whereas evolution may at best be able to tell us why we do what we do, it could not explain why 'our moral sense condemns some of our actions as *sinful*:'[61] and, above all, James Orr attacked those who would replace the doctrine of the Fall with the view that sin is a necessary part of man's ascent rather than 'the voluntary defection of a creature who had the power to remain sinless'.[62] and who overlooked the fact that 'Sin is that which ought not to be *at all*. It has throughout the Bible a volitional and *catastrophic* character.'[63] Orr may sum up for us the adverse bearings of an uncritically accepted doctrine of evolution on the heart of the gospel:

> 'Man, on the new reading, is not a fallen being, but is in process of ascent; he deserves, not blame, but, on the whole, praise, that he has done so marvellously well, considering the disadvantageous circumstances in which he started; the doctrines of redemption associated with the older view — atonement, regeneration, justification, sanctification, resurrection — have no longer any place, or change their meaning . . . Unfortunately, the elements it is proposed to dispense with — the sense of sin and guilt, the pain of spiritual bondage, the war between flesh and spirit, recognised as *evil* in the shame and self-condemnation that attend it, the craving for atonement, the felt need of regeneration, the consciousness of forgiveness and renewal — are not simply so interwoven with the texture of Scripture that to part with them is virtually to give up *Christian* theology altogether, but are parts of an actual human *experience* that cannot be blotted out of existence, or dismissed from consideration, even to suit the requirements of a modern scientific hypothesis.'[64]

We believe that in adverting to the bearing of evolutionary theory upon the doctrines of sin and salvation we have reached the crux of the matter. This is not to deny that evolution impinged on other aspects of theological thought. We have already referred to the doctrine of creation; but in addition to that evolutionary theory fertilised the doctrine of development beloved of Catholic Modernists; it undergirded the work of the new breed of comparative religionists, some of whom profoundly disturbed the faithful because of the relativism to which their position tended, and in which some of them rejoiced;[65] and Dr. Gill has pointed out that evolutionary assumptions persist in sociology down to our own day — 'even within the sociology of religion'.[66] It is not difficult to echo E. C. Moore's sigh, 'This elaboration and reiteration of the doctrine of evolution sometimes wearies us'![67] But *we* need elaborate no further, for we have provided enough evidence for our case, and may now present our summary conclusion.

We have seen that Darwinism was a debtor both to an agelong idea of progress, and to that modern immanentist thrust which derived from Kant and the German Romantics, and which found one of its expressions in the modern understanding of history. We have emphasised the fact that Darwin himself did not set out to destroy the faith, and that his particular offering of natural selection was by-passed by the majority of theologians.[68] Some theologians, of whom Orr was a prominent example, entertained serious reservations concerning evolution; others, like Dale, saw advantages in the theory provided that the rights of conscience and morality were not submerged under naturalism.[69] The upshot is that even when the more competent theologians utilised the evolutionary principle they were not entirely uncritical of it, and many of them retained a sufficiently strong sense of the exceeding sinfulness of sin. On the other hand some were bowled over by an optimism in man which could hardly be described as scriptural. That last word prompts the reflection that those who took most readily to evolution were, on the whole, those who were most open to the findings of the newer biblical criticism. There have ever been those who have set their faces against that criticism, and Professor Floyd E. Hamilton may be taken as representing their view:

> 'Whatever prejudice theologians have against evolution is due to the fact that they have independent proof that the Bible and Christianity are true, so they feel that a theory which denies the truth of both is false and should be rejected . . . We have, it is true, certain presuppositions . . . A man may have assumptions and yet be fair in his examination of evidence and arguments. His very prejudice may enable him to see flaws in the evidence that would escape the advocate of the theory.'[70]

But this was a minority view. Most would have endorsed the following typical statements: 'Physical Science may render service to Religious Faith; but first of all Religious Faith must render a greater service to Science by teaching her that Nature is not God, and that although the Heavens declare His glory, and the earth is full of His goodness, in Nature God is not seen at His highest and best'.[71] Again, 'in Jesus Christ, and in Him alone, we have the pledge of the human world's fulfilling its destiny, of the vanquishing of all the obstacles than can arise, of the great career's reaching, at last, that

one far-off divine event
To which the whole creation moves'.[72]

Here we see clearly the qualified use of the evolutionary idea. Undeniably Darwinism created a climate of thought in which such affirmations could gain wide acceptance among Christians. But upon Darwin's distinctive biological hypothesis such affirmations do not depend in the slightest degree. To those theologians who got most mileage out of it, evolution was more a theme than a theory.

CHAPTER FOUR

THE CONTRIBUTION OF ALBRECHT RITSCHL

'The Ritschlian theology had an enormous success. Its consequences were worked out in all sorts of ways: in lives of Christ which exhibited Him as the Revealer of God's Fatherhood and the example of self-sacrificing Love; in books on the Social Gospel and Christian ethics; and in a general liberalising of Christian thought, which was satisfied that, if the husk of ancient dogma had been stripped off, the kernel of Christianity remained intact.'[1]

R. S. Franks wrote these words in 1945, by which time Barth was well established upon the theological scene. Of *his* theology Franks's contemporary, A. E. Garvie, wrote that it was 'a minor evil product of the war'.[2] Perhaps the least generous estimate of Barthianism would nowadays rate it more highly than that! When Franks wrote Ritschlianism was on the wane, and Ritschl himself had been one of the main inspirations of that theological liberalism against which Barth rebelled. Such are the swings of the theological pendulum that today Barth is, in some quarters, under a cloud. Since it is all too easy to go too far too fast, a reappraisal of Ritschl will not only serve our main purpose of illuminating the conservative-liberal debate in theology, but will also suggest items of importance for today's theological agenda.

Albrecht Ritschl (1822–1889)[3] impinged somewhat tardily upon the British theological consciousness. As Garvie said in 1899, (it is only within the last five or six years that the Ritschlian Theology has attracted much attention in this country'[4] — the publication in 1870 of the English translation of the first volume of *Justification and Reconciliation* notwithstanding. Mr. J. K. Mozley attributed the time-lag to the Englishman's general suspicion of German theological

scepticism; to the fact that Anglicans could not easily take to
one who appeared to sit so lightly to the creeds; and to the
fact that English Free Churchmen had become attuned to the
historico-critical foundation on which Ritschl built even
more recently than the Anglicans.[5] The bulk of the early
work of introducing Ritschl to Britain was done not by
Englishmen but by Scots who all happened to be graduates
of, or teachers in, Glasgow: by the Presbyterians Orr and
Denney; by the Congregationalist Garvie; and by the Congregationalist (*ex* Free Church of Scotland) Robert Mackintosh.

Numerous questions gather about Ritschl's head: was he
really anti-metaphysics, or was he a metaphysician manqué?
Was he, or was he not, a subjectivist? Does he, or does he not
so 'refine' the gospels as to leave us with a Jesus who is little
improvement upon the exemplary Jesus of the older rational-
isms? Theologians took up sides. While A. T. Swing felt that
'Ritschl has probably done more than any other theologian
to prepare the way for a fundamental and yet conservative
reconstruction of the theology of the Church,[6] Orr lamented
that Ritschlianism 'has no doctrine of objective Atonement,
but only one of subjective reconciliation. Other great doctrines of Scripture are either absent, or have a large part of
their meaning taken from them';[7] and there have been not a
few theologians who have described Ritschl as — and some
conservative scholars who have castigated him for being —
the father of modern liberal theology. After allowing for the
influence of the commentators' diverse presuppositions, it is
hard to resist the feeling that these ambivalent responses
mirror a measure of inconsistency in Ritschl himself. For
example, it seems that on the one hand Ritschl was in reaction against a scien*tism* (not against science — Ritschl
thought he was being very scientific) which would undermine
the believer's religious security; yet he reacted in such a neo-
Kantian manner that he *appeared* to exalt man's subjectivity
at the expense of God's objectivity — and that in a way
which places him in the line of humanists from the Renaissance onwards.

Of Ritschl's system H. R. Mackintosh wrote, 'One might
almost say that it was thought out by a sincere believer in the
truth of religion, with his back to the wall and his face to the

advancing forces of materialistic science'.[8] It is certainly true to say that confronted by materialism, naturalism and positivism, and convinced of the barrenness of Hegelianism, Ritschl sought to provide an independent basis for theology which would guarantee to spirit 'its pre-eminence over the entire world of nature'.[9] It would be a grievous mistake, however, to read either pietism or mysticism into those words, for Ritschl staunchly opposed both. This emerges most clearly in his *Geschichte des Pietismus* (3 vols. 1880–86) in which he represents pietism as a serious departure from Lutheranism in that it diverted attention from the roots of faith to the attainment of its fruits. As for mysticism, its danger was, as Ritschl's disciple Herrmann put it, that it can 'lead the soul away from Christ' in its attempt to go beyond the humanity of the historic Christ.[10] Dr. Garvie correctly perceived that in opposition to mysticism Ritschl desires 'to show that the genuinely Christian experience is dependent on the historical revelation in Christ. He is not defining general laws about the relation of God and the soul; he is describing particular facts of the Christian experience.'[11]

With the introduction of the term 'experience' we come to Ritschl's 'love-hate' relationship with Schleiermacher. Thus, in *Theologie und Metaphysik* (1882, second edition 1887) he can declare of Schleiermacher that 'He is, in respect of method, my predecessor'; whereas in a letter to Diestel written in 1869 he had been equally clear that 'I have never had sympathy with Schleiermacher's theological method'.[12] If we view Ritschl's position in its entirety it is possible to make some sense of both statements. Thus, he was at one with Schleiermacher in his opposition to rationalism, and in his espousal of what we may roughly designate the inward way. He approved of Schleiermacher's view of religion as having to do with the sense of the wholeness of things. He was in thorough accord with Schleiermacher's emphasis upon the concept of fellowship – indeed his view of his work was that as a dogmatician he needs must live in the community of the faithful and announce (rather than write apologies for, or seek by theistic arguments to prove[13] its faith. Again, Ritschl capitalised upon the model of vocation – in preference to penal categories – as applying to Christ's redemptive work.

There were, however, significant differences between the two. For his part, Schleiermacher interpreted reconciliation as being a consequence of redemption, but Ritschl, as we shall see, reversed this order. But what more immediately concerns us, especially in view of the charges of subjectivism which have been levelled against Ritschl, is that it was in part his *anti*-subjectivist intentions which prompted him to eschew, at least ostensibly (a cryptologism to be explained shortly), Schleiermacher's way of relying upon the deliverances of the pious self-consciousness. In place of feeling, and in accord with his intensely practical bent, he put the value judgement; and when he was at his most careful he always made it plain that this was a verdict passed upon a series of actual historical events.

Before pursuing the value judgement further it will be convenient to explore the nature of Ritschl's opposition to that metaphysics in reaction against which his positive contribution was developed. We say 'that metaphysics', for on his own admission Ritschl intended to oppose only some types of metaphysical undertaking. In any case, there is more of the metaphysician about him than at first meets the eye, even granted the likelihood that he advanced his epistemological views in a half-hearted attempt to justify and defend the dogmatic position he had reached by another route.[14]

After early sympathy with Hegel and Baur, Ritschl broke decisively with their methodology. He came to see that if metaphysics meant the investigation, by *quasi*-scientific means, of an extra-spatio-temporal realm with a view to the aquisition of knowledge, then it was a forlorn enterprise indeed. He thus set about the task of eliminating idealistic metaphysics from theology, whilst at the same time opposing positivism and materialism. But, as he said, 'It is an unthinking and incredible contention that I exclude all metaphysics from theology'.[15] It seems therefore that Professor Pringle-Pattison misconceived Ritschl's purpose when he complained that 'Unless the objects of religious faith are real, theology is entirely in the air; and if they are real it is impossible to treat the world of religious belief and the world of fact, as science and philosophy handle it, as if they were two non-communicating spheres'.[16] That way lies the pitfall of the double truth, as Pringle-Pattison rightly saw; but Ritschl was alive to the fact, and avoided the trap by nowhere maintaining that since scientific and religious facts were of fundamentally different kinds it followed that a proposition could be true in religion and false in science, and *vice versa*.[17] Again, while Emil Brunner rightly saw that Ritschl forsook Hegelian ontological speculations he is perhaps over-hasty in saying that 'he did not perceive that his whole theological system was simply a well-constructed system of ethical metaphysics . . . '[18] Ritschl was almost certainly more aware of this than Brunner allows.

More positively, Ritschl embraced an epistemology and identified it with a metaphysic. He thereby courted Dr. Garvie's disapproval on the ground that human intelligence and universal existence may not be assumed to be identical.[19] On the other hand, Dr. Orr[20] and others have pointed out that one's adoption of an epistemology is rationally undertaken on metaphysical principles. Be that as it may, Ritschl returned to Kant, but as Barth pointed out, to 'Kant quite definitely interpreted as an anti-metaphysical moralist, by means of whom he thought he could understand Christianity as that which grandly and inevitably made possible, or realized, a practical ideal of life'.[21] In Ritschl's own words, the dogmatician must prove 'the Christian thought of reconciliation by the thought of the moral Kingdom of God, in which Kant, in a purely philosophic way, recognises the final end of the world'.[22]

Ritschl believed that by limiting human knowledge to knowledge of phenomena Kant had laid the foundation of a moral basis for dogmatic truth which would meet the needs of Christianity.[23] Man could acquire no knowledge of the noumenal realm, but by the exercise of his practical reason he could achieve full assurance of faith. To this Kantian insight Ritschl added the Lotzian refinement (and in the process, according to some, partially misconstrued Lotze) that while remaining ignorant of things in themselves (Kant) we can actually know not simply appearances, but things in appearances (Lotze *sic*). Ritschl thus declared, in *Theologie und Metaphysik*, that he was a Lotzian in epistemology.[24] We may not, however, conclude that Ritschl was a neo-

Kantian pure and simple; for his emphasis upon phenomena was such that Garvie went so far as to brand him a vulgar realist in that by declaring knowing and being to be identical he evades rather than solves the epistemological problem.[25] For all that it is debatable whether Ritschl's evasion is as serious as that evasion of history against which he so justifiably protested — an evasion which left men not with a personal Christ, but with a Christ who was but the illustration of an abiding principle. We recall that Ritschl was writing at a time when the quest of the Jesus of history was among the most fashionable of theological pursuits, and Professor Orr well said that Ritschlianism's attractiveness lay in this, that

> 'in its distinctive watchwords it strikes chords which are already vibrating in the intellectual and spiritual atmosphere around us, — that, addressing itself to an age profoundly distrustful of reason in its metaphysical flights, enamoured of the methods of the positive sciences, yet craving a ground of religious certainty which neither philosophy nor science can give, it mirrors back to that age with unerring fidelity its own dissatisfactions and desires. . . . The religious instinct, refusing to be stilled, yearned for a satisfaction in a region where reason could not intrude with its questionings, nor science enter with its doubts. The Ritschlian teaching could not but powerfully appeal to all who, consciously or unconsciously, had come under these influences of the time-spirit.'[26]

According to Ritschl the believer's certainty rests upon his consciousness of value; and the believer's faith is faith in the object (mark the word) of that consciousness. In thus making the value-judgement (*Werthurtheile*) foundational Ritschl does not intend to suggest that God does not exist unless or until he is valued by someone; but rather that the believer is confronted by the reality of God as he evaluates the benefits God confers upon him.[27] In Ritschl's opinion, 'We know the being of God only within His value for us'.[28] Here Ritschl significantly modifies Kant, who had spoken of an absolute distinction between fact and value. For his part Ritschl saw that evaluation is involved in the very perceiving of facts — as has been said in a different connection, 'There is no "IS" without an "OUGHT" in the offing'.[29] However, while 'Value-judgements . . . are determinative in the case of all connected knowledge of the world, even when carried out in the most objective fashion . . . Religious knowledge moves in independent value-judgements . . .'[30] These latter have reference not to the perceived facts of science, but to the ideal order of things conceived under the category of personality.

Undeniably Ritschl's position bristles with difficulties. There is the unresolved question of the *nature* of the religious value-judgement, and in particular of the way in which it differs from moral and aesthetic evaluations.[31] There is the fact, constantly reiterated by Orr, that for all his objectivist intentions Ritschl's theory prevents us from proceeding from the will to the nature of Christ. A similar point is made by Professor Paterson in connection with the God-man relation: 'There is a curious prejudice in the view of the relation of God and man which heartily recognises the influence of His Spirit upon the will, but regards with repugnance the idea that it should ever have illuminated and enriched the intellect'.[32] Then there is the fact that, for all his repudiation of Schleiermacher at this point Ritschl made the feeling of pleasure or pain determinative of the worth of ideas.[33] Just as surprising is the way in which *quasi*-Ritschlian terminology began to enter the writings of the most unlikely authors. Thus Dr. Garvie was able to quote with approval the words of the personal idealist J. R. Illingworth who declared that 'what affects me personally, and thereby becomes part of myself, is real for me; while what affects me most persistently and most powerfully is most real'.[34] We can no longer delay facing up to Ritschl's alleged subjectivism.

The slipperiness of this issue cannot be gainsaid — at least if we may judge by what appear to be contradictory assessments of the matter within the writings of one scholar. Thus W. Adams Brown finds in one place that 'It has one of the merits of Ritschl that, in his emphasis upon the historic in Christianity, he has called attention, in contrast to the purely subjective method of Schleiermacher, to the objective basis of the Christian faith'.[35] Elsewhere Professor Brown admits that 'the charge of subjectivism brought against the theology

of Ritschl is not without a certain justification in fact'.[36]
Dr. Orr was not so ambivalent. He detected in Ritschl a
'dangerous subjectivity' in which experience is substituted
for facts;[37] and he pointed to pure subjectivism as being the
only logical outcome of Ritschl's method — an outcome fully
realised in the work of Bender of Bonn.[38] Further, Ritschl's
'exaggerated subjectiveness' is said by Dr. Alexander to contain 'the seeds of much that is unsatisfactory in the later
tendencies of German theology';[39] while Pringle-Pattison
thought it led Ritschl to an unsatisfactory blend of idealsm
and agnosticism.[40] On the other hand Professor Swing found
Ritschl emphasising 'the objective history of revelation as it
is hardly emphasised by any other theologian';[41] and J. K.
Mozley, though recognising Ritschl's subjectivist tendencies,
thought that Orr erred in failing to allow sufficiently for the
fact that in his doctrine of the value-judgement Ritschl was
more concerned with *how* we know, while not denying that
there was a reality there to be known.[42] Our own conclusion
is that despite his objectivist intentions, Ritschl failed to
ground religious faith adequately. His failure lay primarily in
his inadequate grasp of the truth that if the evaluative norm
is objective it cannot be defined by reference to feeling
alone. Here we are in entire accord with H. R. Mackintosh,
and we make his words our own: 'Revelation cannot com-
municate objectivity to the value-judgments of faith in
general, if a value-judgment is the source of its own cogency
. . . so long as feeling is the supreme court of appeal, religious
belief is condemned to imprisonment in the dungeon of
subjectivity . . . we must look to *thought* for the self, and for
objects, and for the value which the one finds in the others
. . . Otherwise theology is left where Schleiermacher left
it . . . bereft of a genuinely scientific foundation'.[43]

   We have now to see how Ritschl's incipient subjectivism
led him to pay much more attention to some Christian facts
than to others — a circumstance which has resulted in the
charge levelled by conservative theologians from his day to
ours that Ritschl has only a seriously attenuated gospel to
offer. By way of setting the matter in context we first quote
Ritschl's own statement of the essence of Christianity:

   'Christianity, then, is the monotheistic, completely spiritual, and ethical religion, which, based on the life of its Author as Redeemer and as Founder of the Kingdom of God, consists in the freedom of the children of God, involves the impulse to conduct from the motive of love, aims at the moral organisation of mankind, and grounds blessedness on the relation of sonship to God, as well as on the Kingdom of God.'[44]

This affirmation is consistent with Ritschl's celebrated dictum to the effect that 'Christianity . . . resembles not a circle described from a single centre, but an ellipse which is determined by two *foci* (*i.e.* the religious conception of redemption, and the ethical conception of the Kingdom of God)'.[45] As we consider the foci in relation to each other we shall see the force of Garvie's contention that the latter takes precedence over the former — which is, after all, in keeping with Ritschl's understanding of the Kingdom as the means to the end, and with his belief in 'the teleological character of Christianity'.[46]

For Ritschl 'Christ's design is the Kingdom of God, regarded, as Kant expresses it, as a fellowship of men regulated by laws of virtue'.[47] Further clues as to the nature of the Kingdom are imported from Kant: the fact of the Kingdom as being man's moral end, and the notion of a communal progression towards that end which vanquishes evil *en passant*. In his exposition of this teleological theme Ritschl reverses the traditional order of justification and reconciliation by making the latter the *ultimate* consequence of the former. Reconciliation is for him the religious community's goal, and the achievement of it is synonymous with the realisation in the temporal sphere of the Kingdom of God. Clearly this idea was quite consistent with that evolutionary optimism which so many adopted in the later nineteenth century — though some Ritschlians, notably Kaftan, regarded the Kingdom's realisation as a matter for the *next* world. Nor are the nearly-Pelagian phrases which Ritschl sometimes used (while denying that he was a Pelagian) out of accord with that variety of popular religion, expressed in hymns and sermons of the day, which regarded God's Kingdom not so much as his gift, but rather as man's achievement: 'In Christianity the religious motive of ethical action lies here, that the Kingdom of God,

which it is our task to realize, represents also the highest
good which God destines for us as our extramundane goal'.[48]
This apparent Pelagianism is a function of Ritschl's concen-
tration upon the phenomenal realm; he cannot easily accom-
modate the eschatological, biblical idea that the Kingdom
which is here and yet to come comes only as the gift of God's
grace. On the other hand, the way in which this anti-ontolo-
gist moves by 'deductions' from the personality of God to
the love of God and thence to humanity *qua* the Kingdom of
God is more than a little surprising.[49]

How does Ritschl's regulative principle of the Kingdom
influence his understanding of other Christian doctrines?
In the first place he would have us believe, against the biblical
testimony, that the justification of the community precedes
that of the individual believer.[50] To this Robert Mackintosh
objected:

> 'Ritschl does indeed protest that the soul's relation to God
> or Christ is not through the Church, but in the Church.
> And that is well said. But so long as Ritschl brands as
> "unhistorical mysticism" all recognition of God's working
> in grace additional to what is seen in history or in psycho-
> logical law, for so long he practically makes the Church
> not the sphere but the substitute for personal piety. And
> those who prize Ritschl's protest against individualism,
> just because they value his social doctrine, regret that he
> should discredit and degrade it by an inadequate philo-
> sophy of the religious life.'[51]

Indeed, Brunner found a tendency in Ritschl so to magnify
the community as almost to divinise it.[52]

Ritschl's understanding of the Kingdom in turn affects his
conception of sin, of God and of redemption. Sin, he says, is
the result of ignorance and is pardonable. When God pardons
a man God experiences no attitudinal change towards the
erstwhile sinner; rather, the latter's guilty fears are removed.
While retaining the ideas of the fact of, and of man's awareness of guilt, Ritschl dispenses with the notion of original sin.
He pays little heed to the biblical doctrine of law; and wrath
is reserved by him for those who finally oppose the Kingdom.
The essence of sin lies in the opposition which the Kingdom

of Sin offers to the Kingdom of God. In that battle God's Kingdom must be victorious, for love must be triumphant. This may be so, but we wonder whether Ritschl sufficiently qualifies the idea of love by the idea of holiness. If God's love is holy love, love in whose presence sin cannot stand; and if man is a sinner, then his case is somewhat more tragic, and his upward march somewhat less inevitable than Ritschl seems to suppose.[53] Nowhere is Ritschl more in danger of contradicting the biblical witness,[54] and here, however unintentionally, he paves the way for that sentimentality concerning God's love which was to be the bane of so much subsequent liberal theology. Although he valued the idea that God forgives sinners for the sake of the Kingdom, Professor Paterson thought that 'much weight must be given to the fact that this seems an inadequate ground of acceptance to those who have undergone the experience of repentance in its classic form, realised the unspeakable heinousness of sin, and known the wrath of God to be one of the most assured of facts of the spiritual world'.[55] So it is that at crucial points Ritschl's understanding of the Kingdom prevents him from honouring to the full his intention of being true to the believer's religious experience.

We detect similar attenuations of the gospel, and for the same reason, in connection with Ritschl's view of the person and work of Christ. Part of the difficulty here is that to Ritschl the person of Christ is the noumenon, and therefore it cannot properly be discussed, the work of Christ is the phenomenon, and is therefore open to investigation. On this basis Ritschl sits lightly to the doctrine of the pre-existence of Christ — except that he does allow that since for God there can be no separation of decree and act, Christ in that sense existed eternally; he rejects the Chalcedonian two-nature doctrine of the person of Christ, and the doctrine of the Trinity as so much metaphysical speculation; and he is hard put to account for all that Christ has meant to the believer. He focusses attention upon Christ's role as the founder and exemplar of the Kingdom. Jesus is the King-dom's prototype.[56] He is the prophet who as covenant Head represents man before God in everything he does. But what is his real status? Some have wondered whether Ritschl improves upon the older rationalism's exemplary Christ, and they have found little comfort in such words as these: 'What in the historically complete figure of Christ we recognise to be the real worth of His existence, gains for ourselves the worth of an abiding rule; since we at the same time discover that only through the impulse and direction we receive from Him is it possible for us to enter into His relation to God and to the world'.[57]

We should be the last to deny that a proper agnosticism attaches to every expression of humble Christian faith. There are many matters concerning the mystery of the Godhead, the person of Christ, and so on, upon which those who see only "puzzling reflections in a mirror" must be reticent. In Ritschl's case, however, his agnosticism[58] was intellectually rather than religiously inspired. That is, it resulted from his horror of ontological metaphysics on the one hand, and his inclination towards naturalistic biblical criticism on the other. Were it otherwise he could hardly have 'bracketed' the Incarnation so easily as he did, or have held that we know nothing of the relation of eternity to time.[59] All of which caused a flutter in the theological dove cotes. Dr. Orr said that Christ's humanity may, for Ritschl, 'be a "God-filled" humanity; still a God-filled man is one thing, and God become man is another'.[60] Professor Paterson concurred, and found Ritschl's Christ 'lower in the scale of being than the Arian Son' who was at least 'conceived to be the godlike instrument of creation and providence'.[61] Finally, Canon Quick observed that the logical terminus of Ritschl's conception of the person of Christ was either Unitarianism or 'mere Jesuolatry'.[62] On the other hand A. E. Garvie, followed by J. K. Mozley, affirmed that the assumption of the adverse critics that to Ritschl 'Christ may have the *worth* of God for us without *being* God . . . is one of those logical subtleties for which they alone can claim the credit, for the Ritschlian school is quite innocent of it'.[63] There is justice in this remark, but it does not follow that Ritschl gave an adequate account of Christ's divinity — not least because Ritschl's understanding of Christ's nature is severely handicapped by his inadequate account of Christ's work.

Ritschl contends that Jesus 'bears God's moral lordship

over men'[64] and realises his own vocation in the utter service of God.[65] Because of this we may properly ascribe divinity to him. Further, Jesus progressively draws men into harmony with the purpose of God, and that, as we have seen, is the realisation of the Kingdom. There is little in all this of the traditional doctrine of atonement for sin; rather we are said to be assured of our victory as Christ was granted his.[66] Gone is the juristic element in Christ's work, and as P. T. Forsyth remarked, 'The chief defect of the great revolution which began in Schleiermacher and ended in Ritschl has been that it allowed no place to that side of Christ's work'.[67] Thus, at the crucial point concerning Christ's redemptive *activity* Ritschl, in his use of his 'Founder of the Kingdom' motif, seems to be appealing to an unhistorical Christ *idea* no less than did the post-Hegelian immanentists against whom he rebelled. As Professor Torrance wrote in relation to Ritschlian and post-Ritschlian developments, 'when atonement itself is not rooted ontologically in Christ or in God Himself, then it becomes what the Germans call *Ereignis-theologie,* a theology of events. Thus the saving benefits of Christ in which we rejoice, becoming detached from His personal Being, rapidly degenerate into timeless events with no essential relation to history.'[68] For all that, and at the risk of repetition, we should not deny that in calling Christ divine Ritschl does so because he believes that Christ is supremely at one with God's purpose, and because he regards Christ as doing God's work in incorporating men into the Kingdom. The difficulty is that what is necessary to be done — atonement — is not readily accommodated under Ritschl's rubric. While he sees Christ's divinity in his actions, Ritschl's Christ does not do enough: 'what he predicates of the exalted Lord is principally His power over the world through patience and suffering. Christ reconciles men to God by enabling them to know that He provides the solution to the problem of the self's involvement with the world ... The vicarious character of Christ's own work tends to be subordinated to priority of the present fact of evaluation occurring within the self appropriating the *beneficia Christi*'.[69]

Again, while we should be grateful for Ritschl's emphasis upon the corporate nature of Christian experience, his horror of mysticism precludes him from giving adequate place to the individual believer's abiding in Christ. Once again the Kingdom idea is employed as a sanction in a context in which conjunctive rather than disjunctive considerations should prevail; and, moreover, at this point Ritschl appears to introduce an obstacle to his normative idea of value. The upshot is that 'Whatever deductions may have to be made from [Ritschl's] thought as a whole, the fundamental religious principles on which he built are sound. Christianity rests on the historic Christ, and, in the redeemed experience, sonship by grace is the central and organising fact. These things are beyond challenge. What will rightly be challenged is the special and detailed application he has made of ideas so vital.'[70] Ritschl sought to ground on religious experience, yet the leaning towards subjectivism is undeniable. His intention was to adopt a biblical position, yet the presuppositions with which he approached the Bible — and particularly his understanding of the Kingdom — prompted Garvie's reflection, 'there seems to be much more to be got out of this treasure-house than he has found in it'.[71] His aversion to some forms of metaphysics, though understandable, prompted the later Ritschlian disjunction of fact and value — a disjunction which Alan Richardson regarded as 'a veritable *hereditas damnosa* in subsequent theological discussion'.[72] As Robert Mackintosh poignantly inquired, 'What have we done to advance the study of the religious consciousness by identifying it with judgments of value, if every body of human ideas is also a thing of value judgments . . . and if there is no such thing in existence as direct study of facts or the vision of abstract truth?'.[73] Again, Ritschl sought to give men something to do towards the advance of the Kingdom, though ethical humanism is not far from some of his statements, and, when associated with his evolutionary stance, the undernourishing Social Gospel is one possible outcome. Perhaps most serious of all was the way in which Ritschl's regulative concept of the Kingdom was employed is such a way as to blunt the edge of some of the profoundest affirmations which genuine Christian faith and *experience* desires to make. Every pitfall we have noted was to be detected in late nineteenth century liberal theology. But at one point in particular Ritschl differed from some of his liberal sons. Where many of them resisted authority in the name of faith, he manfully strove ever to hold the two in balance. He did not seem to realise how difficult his value-judgement made this task. Not surprisingly many who came after him went in one of two directions: towards rationalism or towards relativism.

Ritschl, as we said at the outset, was a major inspiration of those theological liberals against whom Barth reacted. To what extent are those now in reaction against Barth Ritschlians *manque* or (what is less justifiable *academically*) 'Ritschlians' who know not Ritschl? One way of approaching an answer to this question would be to enquire whether P. T. Forsyth's verdict upon Ritschl's *Werthurtheile* has any more recent applications: 'The idea of a God who is chiefly a God of value rather than of right and rule really canonises Humanity. He is a "God for man". God is made to serve. We are not provided with a power over us but only in us . . . Humanity tends to think itself indispensable to God's holy purpose, whereas it is God's holy purpose that is indispensable to Humanity.'[74]

However the contemporary question is to be answered, Ritschl's influence upon the theological liberalism of the late nineteenth-century cannot be gainsaid. To the issues between that liberalism and its conservative opposition we now turn, bracing ourselves to view a confused, and sometimes a confusing, tapestry in which immanentist, higher critical, evolutionary and Ritschlian strands all have their parts to play.

CHAPTER FIVE

CONSERVATIVES AND LIBERALS
IN THEOLOGY

To those who have been brought up to regard the late nineteenth century as the hey-day of preaching — which, at least in some Anglican and nonconformist circles, it was — it comes as a surprise to discover that the prevailing homiletic assurance was set against a background of shifting landmarks, and of a degree of theological fluidity, the like of which had seldom if ever been known before. From the Renaissance onwards man had increasingly come to the fore. His autonomy, real or imagined, was extolled by many; to his possible achievements in scientific and other realms there seemed to be no limit. The attack upon the transcendent and the supernatural, and the rise of immanentist thought had provided soil in which modern biblical criticism could take root, and in which evolutionary thought could flourish. The concern with history and the idea of progress; the increasingly fashionable agnosticism and naturalism; the optimism of many, the pessimism of a few; the virtual demise of the old Calvinist-Arminian debate which, for all its discourtesies, had kept alive the question of the heart of the gospel — all these were factors which contributed to the nineteenth century ferment of thought. Anyone who, like Ritschl, sought to establish theological bearings could hardly avoid a measure of ambivalence, and could certainly expect fully to satisy nobody.

Nor was it in the case of theologians as W. S. Gilbert said it was with boys and girls: that they were 'either a little liberal, or else a little conservative'. Theology produced no such tidy disjunctions. On the contrary, the terms 'liberal'

and 'conservative' are so highly ambiguous that any attempt
at stipulative definition is hazardous in the extreme.[1] We
might, for example, wish to designate Ritschl a liberal; but
the term requires immediate qualification, and its relativity
becomes plain, as soon as we find Ritschlianism dividing,
inconveniently, in a *threefold* right, left and centre manner,
represented respectively by T. Haering (1848–1928), A.
Harnack (1851–1930) and W. Herrmann (1846–1922).
When we further consider the way in which Ritschlianism
was more widely assimilated — by those, for example, who
welcomed the emphasis upon God's Fatherhood as an anti-
dote to what they understood as Calvinism's capricious deity;
and by those Americans who extracted thence a theology of
progress which seemed to undergird the 'American dream' —
it becomes clear that all manner of nuances are detectable in
the Ritschlian phenomenon, and that many motives are at
work.

We are not here dealing with doctrine alone. Thus, the
liberal W. P. Merrill explained, 'The liberal can never hope to
state his views with the sharp definiteness that marks the
theology of the older school. For he is dealing, or attempting
to deal, with life, not with the forms it takes; with reality,
not with theories about it.'[2] (Though the Anglicans of the
Churchman's Union, founded in 1898 and renamed the
Modern Churchman's Union in 1928, were often more than
a little intellectualist!) Lest anyone should think that by contrast *all* conservatives have ever been exclusively concerned
with doctrine, we would draw attention to the political
dealings of the anti-Marxist American 'fundamentalists of
the far right'.[3] Confusion is worse confounded by the fact
that some have variously allied themselves with both conservatives *and* liberals. Thus, with reference to three Anglicans;
the self-styled Liberal Catholic Charles Gore, the protestant-
evangelical H. C. G. Moule, and the liberal Broad Churchman
Hastings Rashdall, Dr. J. K. Mozley wrote, 'On the subject of
the value to be attached to the miraculous in Christianity,
Gore and Moule are near to one another, as neither of them is
to Rashdall; in their general view of the nature and results of
the inspiration of the Bible Gore and Rashdall adopt a position which Moule would not entertain; while in regard to

their conception of the Church, the ministry and the sacraments, Moule and Rashdall, in their affirmations and denials, stand over against Gore'.[4]

Again, there is the kind of complication represented by the fact that the liberal Dr. E. W. Barnes's definition of *evangelicalism* — 'It is Christianity in its most simple and purest form, free from accretions, marvellously alive because it has escaped from the clutch of the dead hand of the past'[5] — would be taken by many as an excellent definition of *liberalism*! As if all this were not enough, there are the manifold qualifications required by historical time-lags, and concerning geographical origins. Fundamentalism, for example, never made the orchestrated impact upon Britain that it did upon America; nor was the millenarian impetus as great in the former nation as in the latter; and within America itself the Mennonites, the Calvinists of the Christian Reformed Church, and the Lutherans of the Missouri Synod — all theologically conservative — were not shaken by the fundamentalist-liberal convulsions of the nineteen twenties and thirties to anything like the degree that the larger of the Baptist and Presbyterian Churches were.[6] Our final cautionary point has already been alluded to in our reference to Dr. Barnes: we shall not be surprised to find those who claim the name 'evangelical' within both of the blurred-edged tendencies ('groups' is too tidy a word) of which we speak. It remains only to add that some, during the heat of battle adopted the attitude, 'A plague on both your houses!'. Thus Bernard Manning declared, 'It is a scandal that controversialists, degrading words like "evangelical" and "catholic", have given them the fustiness of party banners'.[7] Certainly it was not lack of personal conviction which prompted Dr. A. E. Garvie to say, 'I disown any party labels for myself altogether'.[8] But such men could usually be pigeon-holed fairly easily — at least by others. Our contention is that liberal and conservative were locked in combat over the fundamental question, 'What is the heart of the Christian gospel?'. Since that question is of perennial importance, their disputes, however hoary, are of more than passing interest, and may even — especially since pendulum-swings are not unknown in theology — hold warnings for their successors.

I

We shall first note some who were more or less conservative whilst decidely evangelical (liberal evangelicals will engage our attention later). At once we come face to face with the disputed question, what are the characteristics of conservative evangelicalism? D. R. Davies argued that 'Evangelicalism affirms that regeneration is an indispensable condition of the Christian experience of redemption and forgiveness . . . No redemption without second birth — this is the irreducible essence of Evangelicalism'.[9] In similar vein P. T. Forsyth writes, 'By an evangelical theology I mean any theology which does full justice to the one creative principle of grace'.[10] On this definition Luther, Calvin, Edwards, Whitefield, Wesley, would be numbered among evangelicals, though perhaps the 'Pelagianising' C. G. Finney would not. On the other hand, if we take Finney as a pioneer modern revivalist, whose evangelistic methodology comes down through Billy Graham to the present day, then evangelicalism seems to be a more recent phenomenon, and Finney is its fountain head.[11] Again, to the material principle of regeneration, Dr. K. Kantzer would add the formal principle of biblical authority.[12] With this Dr. Gordon Clark would agree — indeed apart from the latter principle, he thinks, the Reformers could not have challenged the Romanists.[13] Then, in true Reformed fashion, Dr. Hesselink adds faith: ' "sola scriptura", "sola fide" . . . Where these phrases are more than mere slogans, one does indeed find an evangelical faith'.[14] The fact that so many find it necessary to refine our understanding of 'evangelical' is a clear indication of the slipperiness of the term.

It would be broadly true to say that most Anglican conservative evangelicals of the period 1850—1920 would have associated themselves with the traditional Reformed view. Those episcopalian Puritans who sought to reform the Church of England from within would certainly have done so, and so, in their wake, would Newton, Toplady, Venn and Grimshaw. Among their nineteenth century successors would be found Charles Simeon and Henry Martyn. Anglican evangelicals have traditionally defended the Establishment, and have been loyal to the *Book of Common Prayer*. At their best — witness the Clapham Sect — they have shouldered their responsibilities to the less fortunate in what some latter-day historians have been too ready to pronounce a patronising, paternalistic manner. A minority of conservative evangelical Anglicans has been vociferously anti-Roman. Few summed up the stance of this party so succintly as Bishop J. C. Ryle (1816–1900) of Liverpool. He defined evangelical religion both positively and negatively. Standing by the absolute authority of scripture, it affirms man's corruption in sin, maintains the penal substitutionary theory of the atonement, and emphasises the work of the Holy Spirit in regeneration and in the life of grace. It is not anti-intellectual; it does not under-value the Church, the ministry, episcopacy, the Prayer Book, good order, holiness or self-denial, though it does take a ministerial rather than a magisterial and sacerdotal view of the ministry; it denies that the sacraments convey grace *ex opere operato*; and while it believes that episcopacy is the most desirable form of church government, it does not deny the validity of non-episcopally ordained ministries.[15] It is not hard to read a case against Anglo-Catholicism between some of Ryle's lines.

Conservative evangelicalism lingered in all the main nonconformist denominations of England, Wales and Scotland, and in the Church of Scotland too. The leadership of these bodies moved increasingly towards accommodation to newer thought, both in respect of adjusting to biblical criticism, utilising the concept of evolution, heeding pressing social needs, and becoming increasingly silent on those profoundly doctrinal questions which had fuelled the older Calvinist-Arminian debates. C. H. Spurgeon was a lonely exception among the Baptists, and even he was sufficiently in accord with the predominant spirit of the age to say, 'Every century sees a marked advance in the world's condition and we shall proceed at a quicker rate when the Church wakes up to her responsibility'.[16] Some conservative Methodists who stood, whether they all realised it or not, in the tradition of evangelical Arminianism, found a focus for their interests in Cliff College, a training centre for home missionaries which grew out of the vision of Thomas Champness (1832–1905), and whose first Principal, Thomas Cook, was appointed in 1903.[17] Even so, Dr. Workman spoke for most Methodists when he said that 'Methodism is rightly undisturbed by the higher criticism of the Bible'.[18] The mention of Cliff College, noted for its class meetings, its choruses, its evangelistic treks and the like, reminds us yet again that we are dealing with ethos and not with doctrine only.

This is not in any way to minimise the importance of doctrine. Some are *confessionally* conservative and evangelical, calling themselves Reformed or Lutheran. Among the former some, saddened by the way in which some professedly confessional churches have, in their view, lapsed, have taken to themselves the term 'Orthodox'. In Scotland we find the small Reformed Presbyterian Church (1743) which stands in the covenanting tradition; the continuing Free Church (1843); and the Free Presbyterian Church (1893).[19] When the majority of the Free Church was on the point of joining with the United Presbyterians to form the United Free Church of Scotland (1900), the Free Church was congratulated on the impending union by the Assembly of the Irish Presbyterian Church. The Reverend James Hunter, however, was by no means in sympathy with his Assembly's resolution, and for many years he waged a battle in the interests of Calvinism, and against modernism. Matters came to a head when in 1927 he formally charged the Reverend J. E. Davey of the Irish Presbyterian College, Belfast, with denying *inter alia* the full inspiration of the scriptures. The Assembly found in favour of the Professor by 707 votes to 82, and Hunter felt that he could no longer remain a member of so compromised a Church. With other seceders he formed the Irish Evangelical Church, which on 26th March 1964 changed its name to the Evangelical Presbyterian Church. The Reformed Presbyterian Church of Ireland (Presbytery 1763; Synod 1811) continues in rather greater numerical strength than its Scottish Mother Church. In England Calvinistic conservatism is the continuing stance of the Strict Baptists, and of those Reformed Baptist churches which have been increasing in numbers since the 1960s, and some of which are more overtly confessional in character.[20] There are conservative evangelical individuals and groups in the mainstream denominations of Britain, and from from some of these such interdenominational bodies as the IVF and the Evangelical Alliance draw some of their support.

In America conservative evangelicalism has ever been well represented among the major Baptist denominations, and vociferous minorities have seldom been wanting who have lamented the encroachment of liberal thought, and the departure from old standards. On occasion secession has resulted, as witness, for example, the General Association of Regular Baptist Churches (1932) which came out of the Northern Baptist Convention, and which esteems the Baptist Confession of 1689; and the Conservative Baptist Association of America, which emerged from the same parent in 1947. However, the more consciously confessonal Presbyterians have experienced the greatest strategic difficulties in their desire to be open to advancing thought on the one hand, and to prevent schism on the other. The Presbyterian Church of the U.S.A. was particularly exercised in this matter. The attempts during the 1880s and 1890s of Professor Charles A. Briggs of Union Seminary New York to acquaint his Church with the *advantages* of the higher criticism led to his suspension in 1893. The General Assembly of 1892 and 1893 had meanwhile declared that the original biblical documents were devoid of error, and the 1892 Assembly refused the request of fifteen presbyteries that the Westminster Confession be revised. In time, however, the newer thought held sway within the Church until, conservative and fundamentalist opposition notwithstanding, those who felt that their Church was entering into an unholy alliance with non-Christian thought forms seceded in 1936. The leader of this secession was J. Gresham Machen (1881–1937), a Professor at Princeton Theological Seminary. Machen stood in the line of Charles and A. A. Hodge and B. B. Warfield (whose views, incidentally, of biblical authority had been attacked by T. M. Lindsay as being scholastic rather than Reformed),[21] and although schism was not his intention, he and his supporters threw down the gauntlet to their Church with the establishment in 1933 of the Independent Board of Foreign Missions. Three years later the break-away Presbyterian Church of America was formed. In 1939, on the separation of Carl McIntire's more millenarian and separatist Bible Presbyterian Church, the PCA changed its name to the Orthodox Presbyterian Church.[22] Of the other conservative American Presbyterian bodies we may mention two denominations which stand in the cov-

enanter tradition: the Reformed Presbyterian Church of
North America and the Reformed Presbyterian Church,
Evangelical Synod.

We should not do justice to American conservative evangelical confessionalism were we to fail to mention such denominations as the Reformed Church in America (1628) and the
Christian Reformed Church. These are of Dutch origin, the
latter being formed in 1890 by the union of two secessions
(1822 and 1857) from the former. To some extent the disputed issues were reflections of troubles in Holland, but the
stand against Freemasonry, which those who joined the
Christian Reformed Church took, was a further ingredient in
the strife. Both Churches adhere to the Heidelberg Cat-
echism, the Belgic Confession and the Canons of Dort.[23]
To the Missouri Synod Lutherans we have already referred,
and it hardly needs to be said that there are numerous other
conservative evangelical groups in America, concerning some
of which the casual observer may be forgiven for thinking
that they are distinct from their brethren as much because of
pride as because of principle.

We can no longer delay our attempt to unpack that most
emotive of terms, 'fundamentalist'. We have waited until now
in order first to make plain that there is much conservative
evangelicalism to which the term 'fundamentalist' in the
sense often assigned to it — aggressively evangelistic, highly
emotional, lacking in clear doctrinal emphasis, decisionist —
does not apply at all. Nor can we content ourselves by saying
that a fundamentalist is one who subscribes to the five fundamental doctrines which collectively gave their name to the
movement: the verbal inspiration of the Bible; the Virgin
Birth of Christ; his substitutionary atonement; his bodily
resurrection; and his imminent personal return. For not only
is it the case that many Roman Catholics could assent to all
five; but also, many conservative evangelicals of the confessional kind, though likewise eager to endorse these fundamental doctrines, were not able to acquiesce in the individualism, the millenarianism, and the evangelistic methodology
which were the hallmarks of many fundamentalists. We shall
proceed cautiously, therefore, by noting three strands which,
in addition to the interest in scriptural authority and regener-

ation, helped (to varying degrees in varying places) to make fundamentalism into what it became. These strands are revivalism, the scriptural holiness movements, and the prophetic and millenarian movements. After an introductory paragraph we shall treat each in turn.

Like its Old World counterpart the Calvinism of the New World was not immune to tensions.[24] There was the antinomian controversy of the 1630s associated with Mrs. Anne Hutchinson. There was the denial by William Pyncheon as early as 1650 that Christ bore the Father's wrath.[25] Rationalistic Arminianism began to make its impact as witness John Wise's *Vindication of New England Churches* (1717); and America was not bereft of 'Arians' such as Jonathan Mayhew and Thomas Barnard. In 1784 Charles Chauncy wrote on the *Salvation of all Men,* by which time the impetus in the direction of unitarian universalism had already appeared in the person of John Murray, who arrived in America in 1770, having learned his theology from James Relly in London.[26] The seeds were thus already sown for the split between liberalism and evangelical revivalism which was to follow the Great Awakening.[27] The supreme challenge laid upon Jonathan Edwards (1703–1758) was to prevent a landslide from the Calvinistic side of the ravine. He therefore staunchly upheld the view that man is morally unable to do the good, apart from regeneration by God; and that the only 'freedom' natural man enjoyed was the freedom to follow a sinful course. The efforts of Edwards's disciples Joseph Bellamy (1719–90) and Samuel Hopkins (1721–1803), who were influenced by the governmental theory of the atonement and by Leibnizian theodicy, lay in the direction of a contemporary reassertion of Calvinism. In fact both the Calvinism of Edwards and the Calvinism of the 'Old Lights' who opposed the Great Awakening were modified to some extent by the revival. The modifications were carried further by Nathanael Emmons (1745–1840), Timothy Dwight (1752–1817) and Nathanael W. Taylor (1786–1858). Taylor maintained the equality of reason and revelation, and concerning what he took to be Edwards's faulty estimation of man's natural ability he expostulated, 'It is an essential nothing'.[28] Thus emerged the New Divinity.

Charles G. Finney (1792–1875)[29] was dramatically converted on 10th October 1821, and promptly became a revivalist preacher. Perhaps the best way of summarising his
'offences' is to say that he was 'Pelagian', latterly perfectionist, and given to non-scriptural evangelistic practices — his
'new methods' which comprised appeals, the 'anxious seat'
and the like. As to the first, Finney, influenced by Taylor,
denied that God's sovereignty extended to the physical
realm. There man was free — indeed, the *a priori* intuitions
of human reason are free of error.[30] God's omnipotence is
thus limited by man's freedom. It follows that in theory
every man is open to persuasion: hence the importance of
preaching. There can be no such thing as moral inability. Man
is under an obligation to surrender to God, and he can do it if
he will. Depravity is a state of selfishness in which uncon-
verted man *voluntarily* continues. All of which leads to a
radical revision of the traditional doctrine of regeneration. By
conversion now is meant a freely-chosen new direction: 'The
fact is, sinners, that God requires you to turn, and that what
he requires of you, he cannot do for you. It must be your
own voluntary act.'[31] More strongly, he argued that conversion is not immediately by the Holy Ghost, but by argument
and persuasion.[32] None of this met with Dr. Warfield's approval: 'It is quite clear that what Finney gives us is less a
theology than a system of morals. God might be eliminated
from it entirely without essentially changing its character.
All virtue, all holiness, is made to consist in an ethical determination of will.'[33] Consistent with this is Finney's view that
election means God's foreknowledge of those who will be
converted.[34]

In later years Finney admitted that many of his converts
had lapsed, and he attributed this to the inadequate doctrine
of sanctification which, earlier in his career, he had espoused.
Now at Oberlin College, he developed his version of perfectionism, building upon his own conversion experience which,
he thought, had left him free of sin.[35] Certainly, to some of
his converts 'entire sanctification' was a real possibility — in
which connection Dr. Opie rightly remarked, 'Ironically, his
critics condemned only his Pelagianism as an awful lapse.
They would have been thunderstruck had they not missed

his Gnostic streak entirely.'[36] Finally we note those less able theologians, but considerable pragmatic revivalists, who stood in Finney's line. Pre-eminent among these was Dwight L. Moody (1837–99),[37] of whom the following sober, not to say caustic, assessment has recently been penned:

> ' "I am an Arminian up to the Cross; after the Cross, a Calvinist." By 1875 Dwight L. Moody, the foremost revivalist of his day, could make a shambles of theological controversy with hardly a murmur of dissent. Evangelicalism, once a powerful theological movement, based on revivalism, had been shattered. In its place Moody offered an enthusiastic but comfortable moralism. The sovereign God of American religious awakenings before the Civil War had become by the Gilded Age a friendly personal counselor. Sin, once a truly awful condition, Victorian gentility translated into the social improprieties of laziness, drunkenness and poverty. Grace had been a marvellous last-minute rescue from the threat of eternal suffering and had offered a vision of blessedness. Now grace provided for the pleasantries of self-confidence, comfort, and prosperity. Conversion, once the most shattering experience of man's short and harsh life, became the voter's judicious right to change his party affiliation. Moody's revivalism reached its climax not in mystical transcendence or intense piety, but in sentiment.'[38]

We turn now to the holiness element, in conservative evangelicalism. It may be contrasted with Finney's version of man's quest of holiness in that it was more traditionally evangelical than Pelagian, and there was often much less emphasis upon the mechanics of revivalism, and more on the original, and not just on the co-operative, work of God the Holy Spirit.[39] In a word, this strand of thought and experience is the heir of Wesley and of those Moravian pietists and those mystics from Tauler to Law, upon whom he drew. We may observe in passing that some pietists, horrified by the more barren tracts of Protestant scholasticism, became anti-intellectualist in rather the same way that some later fundamentalists who despised 'book learning' did. But our main concern is to indicate that the Wesleyan holiness tradition, the classic expression of which is Wesley's *A Plain Account of Christian Perfection* (1766) was far removed in spirit and in doctrine from the Oberlin perfectionism of later times. Wesley did not teach the possibility of sinless perfection in this life; to him such perfection was possible for man only in eternity. Moreover (and here he was at odds with the Calvinistic doctrine of perseverance) the sanctified may yet fall and perish. The concern for scriptural holiness was continued within the Salvation Army, founded by the ex-Methodist William Booth (1829–1912); it is the *raison d'etre* of the American Church of the Nazarene which dates from the late nineteenth century, and of its British counterpart, the Calvary Holiness Church; it fired the preaching of the Americans W. E. Boardman and Mr. and Mrs. R. Pearsall Smith; and it is the distinctive doctrinal feature of the Keswick Convention, the first of which was held in 1875, and among whose early leaders was Evan H. Hopkins.[40] Some of those associated with Keswick departed from Wesleyan perfectionism in this important respect: they separated sanctification from justification, and made the former a future prospect and the object of a second blessing.

Finally, we have the growing interest in millenial matters and prophecy. This element has been brought to the fore by Dr. Ernest Sandeen in particular.[41] Rejecting H. R. Niebuhr's sociological explanation of fundamentalism in terms of urban *versus* rural communities, he claims that the fundamentalist base of support was as bourgeois and urban as was that of liberalism.[42] Fundamentalist leadership was, however, characterised by millenarian and prophetic inclinations. Dr. Sandeen traces this interest from Daniel Whitby, Rector of Salisbury; he mentions the impetus provided by the French Revolution, and the growing concern for the fate of the Jews — a concern represented by the teaching of Lewis Way; he analyses the split between pre- and post-millenarians, the former of whom took a more pessimistic view of the world; and he provides an account of the dispensationalism of J. N. Darby and his Plymouth Brethren,[43] distinguishing this from that native American dispensationalism whose leader was William Miller: 'The Millerites did not accept the restoration of the Jews to Palestine as a part of the prophetic time-table, nor were they willing to admit that biblical prophecy had any further promises to keep so far as the Jews were concerned'.[44] In addition to all of this there was the futurism of such groups as the Mormons and the Shakers — not to mention the power of the 'American dream'. Dr. Sandeen reminds us that Jonathan Edwards himself was the first post-millenial American theologian;[45] and Professor Harland has remarked that 'Neither the American past nor the nature of her present bewilderment and frustration can be understood without taking fully into account how this strong sense of particular calling, of "destiny under God" has remained a constant aspect of the ideological structure of the nation'.[46]

Among the steps on the road to orchestrated fundamentalism was the series of Niagara Bible Conferences (1883–97). From the 1890 Conference there issued James Hall Brookes's fourteen-point statement in which scriptural inerrancy and the premillenial return of Christ were affirmed. Other leaders, drawn from a variety of denominations, included Arthur T. Pierson and William J. Erdman. In 1882 the first Bible School was founded at Nyack-on-the-Hudson, and there followed Moody's Chicago Evangelistic Society (later the Moody Bible Institute) in 1886. Many other such schools sprung up, and among their most important common features were the advocacy of interdenominational evangelism and the abhorrence of liberalism in theology. Then, between 1910 and 1915 was published that series of pamphlets to which we have already referred, whose collective title was 'The Fundamentals'. Sponsored by the layman Lyman Stewart, the series was enhanced by the contributions of such distinguished scholars as B. B. Warfield and James Orr. Advanced critical views were countered (though Orr, to the disquiet of some, gave a qualified welcome to theistic evolution as not necessarily undermining the faith); bodies such as the Mormons and the Christian Scientists were opposed; and the basic orthodox doctrines, and in particular the five fundamentals, were upheld. At the World's Bible Conference in Philadelphia in 1919, among whose leaders were R. A. Torrey and W. B. Riley, attention was focussed upon the fundamentals, and an attempt was made to place the apocalyptic element in perspective. There followed the stormy decade of fundamentalist *versus* liberal controversy. Trouble had been brewing for some years, but in May 1922 Harry Emerson Fosdick, the liberal Baptist, preached his celebrated sermon, 'Shall the Fundamentalists win?'. In the following year the New York Presbytery of the Presbyterian Church U.S.A. — that body which only thirty-one years before had rejected C. A. Brigg's position on scriptural interpretation — caused offence to conservatives with its Auburn Affirmation. Elsewhere the issues which were to come to a head in the Scopes trial were being canvassed, and for all these reasons and others the question of biblical authority came to the fore once again. We can therefore understand why Dr. James Packer characterised fundamentalism thus: 'What Scripture says, God says. This equation was the formative principle of fundamentalism, as it has been of all evangelicalism in history'.[47] On the other hand, in view of the varied assortment of available doctrinal options — revivalist, perfectionist, millenarian, holiness, prophetic — and more recently pentecostal — we can see why some have regarded fundamentalism as a distinctively modern phenomenon.[48] We can also understand why such a Reformed conservative evangelical as Dr. Machen disliked the term. To him it suggested a narrow, novel, sometimes anti-intellectualist and over-emotional movement, which was based upon an inadequate range of doctrine, and which frequently sat loosely to churchly allegiance.[49] Fundamentalism was an amalgam of old and new, and among its most acute latter-day critics have been some of the neo-evangelicals.[50]

II

We turn now from the confused and confusing situation in conservative evangelical quarters, to the equally confused and confusing liberal-modernist scene. One way of highlighting the issues is to consider P. T. Forsyth's claim to be modern, but not liberal; and then to show how very different was his modernism from Catholic and other varieties of that plant. Of Forsyth it has been said that 'He was liberal in his intellectual address and technique, and liberal, surely, in his repudiation of any authoritarianism that would coerce the judgment and conscience. But he was conservative of the Faith. And, for him, the Faith meant a theology only because it meant a gospel, *the* Gospel. If he appeared to be a Biblicist — a term which he would not have accepted — it was because he saw that Gospel and Bible were joined together and were not to be put asunder.'[51] This is well said, but it should not allow us to overlook Forsyth's mistrust of the theological labels which some were all too keen to use. He was anxious to maintain that 'the word which is employed to express the adjustments native to a positive Gospel is not "liberal" but "modern". A modern theology is one thing, theological liberalism is another.'[52] This understanding of liberalism seems at first sight to be in line with that of the Anglican Modernist H. D. A. Major, who said that 'the Modernist claims with conviction and humility that he more truly has his rightful home in the Church of Christ than has his Traditionalist brother, whose rightful home is really the Synagogue'.[53] It further reminds us of Dr. Vidler's distinction between liberality, which signifies openness, freedom of enquiry and the like, and liberalism, which in theology means a body of nineteenth century doctrines and critical stances of a negative kind.[54] But when Dr. Major defines modernism as 'the claim of the modern mind to determine what is true, right and beautiful in the light of its own experience, even though its conclusions be in contradiction to those of tradition',[55] he is defining what Forsyth shunned as liberalism:

> 'by liberalism I mean the theology that begins with some rational canon of life or nature to which Christianity has to be cut down or enlarged (as the case may be); while by a modern positivity I mean a theology that begins with God's gift of a super-logical revelation in Christ's historic person and cross, whose object was not to adjust a contradiction but to resolve a crisis and save a situation of the human soul. For positive theology Christ is the object of faith; for liberal He is but its first and greatest subject, the agent of a faith directed elsewhere than on Him. It is really an infinite difference. For only one side can be true.'[56]

Again, Forsyth's modernism not only differed from Major's; both were in some respects poles apart from the

contemporary Catholic Modernism.[57] While Major distinguished between the English Modernists and the Liberal
Protestants in that the former placed greater emphasis upon
the Church and the concept of development than the latter —
who, like Harnack, sought to locate the essence of Christianity by *going back* to a pre-Pauline gospel[58] — the Modernists stood sufficiently consciously in the Broad Church tradition not to accept Rome as the last churchly word. Many
elements went into the making of Roman Catholic Modernism — or, as Pius X said in more evaluative terms, Modernism
was 'a compendium of heresies'. In fact as Loisy, one of its
leading exponents, declared, Modernism was the concern of
'a quite limited number of persons, who share the desire to
adapt the Catholic religion to the intellectual, moral, and
social needs of the present time'.[59] The Modernists sought
institutional and societal reform, but they put forward no
commonly agreed or intellectually coherent policies, though
it may be said that their general adoption of a critical stance
towards the Bible was an important common thread uniting
them. It remains only to advert to the immanentist thrust of
Catholic Modernist thought — yet another feature which
differentiates it from Forsythian modernism. This emerges clearly in such a work as Loisy's *The Gospel and the
Church* (1902), his rejoinder to Harnack's *What is Christianity?* (1900). Loisy opposed the manner in which Harnack
minimised the eschatological, and maintained that the gospel
cannot be understood apart from the concept of development. That is, it is not static, but dynamic. Thus the gospel
cannot be considered properly in the absence of a consideration of what it has become in the life and experience of the
Church, and in relation to the Church's eschatological goal.
The immanentist thrust is clearly evident too in the philosophy of L. Laberthonnière who, notwithstanding the encyclical *Aeterni Patris* (1899), which advocated a Thomistic
basis for Christian philosophising, turned against Aristo-
telian staticism in favour of a neo-Kantian theory of knowledge and a version of post-Hegelian dynamism. Other
Modernists, such as M. Blondel, were influenced by pragmatism, and began to develop a philosophy of action which
would make Christianity much more a matter of practice

than of theory. Manifestly the Catholic Modernists were
going a fair distance farther than the Anglican Liberal Catholic Gore in revising the content of the Christian message and
not its shape only. It is also clear that in its basic immanentist
thrust the New Theology of R. J. Campbell had more in common with Catholic Modernism than with Liberal Protestantism. It remains only to add that some Catholic Modernists,
because of their immanentism and their adoption of advanced critical views, sat somewhat lightly to biblical history.
Such would take encouragement from George Tyrrell's definition of a Modernist as being 'a churchman, of any sort, who
believes in the possibility of a synthesis between the essential
truth of his religion and the essential truth of modernity'.[60]

Thus far we have Forsyth, modern (yet conservative!) in
spirit — or, as Dr. Vidler might say, manifesting liberality if
not espousing liberalism. We have English Modernists who
valued the Church whilst endorsing the critical principle and
occasionally becoming unnecessarily sceptical as a result. We
have the Catholic Modernists who imbibed the spirit of the
age and modified the Christian message to some extent.[61]
And we have Gore, a Liberal Catholic if not in all respects a
liberal man. We must next face up to the fact which has
already become plain, namely, that the terms 'liberal' and
'modernist' are sometimes used interchangeably; and we
must then consider those who added 'evangelical' to the
former label.[62]

It goes without saying that the line of theological liberals
is a long one; Origen, Erasmus, Socinus, the rationalistic
Arminians, the Latitudinarians — all these and others are to
be found in that succession. We recall, for example, Mr.
Thomas's remarks on Philip Doddridge: 'If we define a liberal
in theology in terms of advanced ideas . . . Doddridge was no
liberal . . . But if, more properly, we define a liberal in terms
of an undogmatic temper of mind, then Doddridge was one
of the most liberal Dissenters of the early eighteenth century'.[63] Modern liberalism, however, derives largely from
Kant's epistemology percolated *via* Schleiermacher or Hegel
in varying proportions; it flowers in an age in which old se-
curities are being challenged by immanentist-evolutionary
thought, and by the new historico-critical methodology; and

it takes advantage of the demise of the old theological debate, highlighted by Calvinist *versus* Arminian which, however inadequately at times, had kept the central issues of the
gospel before men's minds. Nowhere did the liberal stream
flow more strongly than in America.

Two types of dissatisfaction with the New England theology had come to be expressed. On the one hand there was
the protest of William Ellery Channing against Congregationalism's Calvinism which, he felt, both degraded God by overlooking his Fatherliness, and debased man by its doctrine of
total inability. In the wake of Channing there came the
Emersonian transcendentalists, the increasing universalist
thrust, overt unitarianism,[64] and humanitarianism. On the
other hand, there was that development of thought represented and inspired by Horace Bushnell (1802–76) whose
emphasis on the personal, rather than the moral and governmental, in respect of the God-man relation gave relief to
many. The influence upon Bushnell of Coleridge, Maurice
and F. W. Robertson was clear. In addition to their personal-
istic immanentism Bushnell and those theologians who followed him – Theodore J. Munger, Washington Gladden and
others, together with the great pulpit voices of the New
Theology, Henry Ward Beecher and Phillips Brooks – maintained the progressive nature of revelation and, consistently
with scientifically-inspired optimism, the 'American dream',
and the societal implications of Ritschlianism, sought to sub-
due the earth for God. Hence the Social Gospel, whose pre-
eminent advocate was the Baptist Walter Rauschenbusch
(1861–1918).[65] God was near to man; and man was under
an obligation to be about God's business in the world – and
that not only as an individual, but as a member of societies
and corporations of all kinds. The Kingdom was realisable on
earth, and sin comprised those remediable injusticies and
inequalities which stained society. Our brief statement of the
Social Gospel position should not mislead anyone into thinking that there were no theological differences between its
proponents. For example, Shailer Mathews (1863–1941) was
perhaps the most liberal, theologically, of the Social Gospel
men; certainly he was closer to Ritschl than the other leaders
of the movement. Rauschenbusch and Gladden were more

conservative, but the following words of the latter capture something of the spirit of them all:

'The idea of the immanence of God; the idea that God's method of creation is the method of evolution; the idea that nature in all its deepest meanings is supernatural; the idea of the constant presence of God in our lives; the idea of the universal divine Fatherhood and of the universal human Brotherhood, with all that they imply — these are ideas which are here to stay . . . [God] is in the whole world . . . but he is also over it all . . . He is working in us, but . . . his working in us never overbears our choices . . . He is helping us all he can without undermining manhood; no more . . . *He is leading Humanity into the green pastures and beside the still waters.* That is the meaning of history.'[66]

However inadequate the theology of these liberals may now seem to be, it would be indefensible to overlook their genuine evangelistic passion. Nowhere is this more clearly affirmed than by Rauschenbusch, writing from hospital: 'My life has been physically very lonely, and often beset by the consciousness of conservative antagonism. I have been upheld by the comforts of God . . . It has been my deepest satisfaction to get evidence now and then that I have been able to help men to a new spiritual birth. I have always regarded my public work as a form of evangelism, which called for a deeper repentance and a new experience of God's salvation.'[67]

By contrast, some of the writings of the harbingers of Dutch liberalism seem arid in the extreme, while some of the English authors seem relatively bloodless. As to the former, W. M. Horton has drawn attention to two rather distinct generations of modernists in holland. The older men included Opzoomer of Utrecht, an empiricist in the Schleiermacherian sense; Scholten of Leiden, an Hegelian monist; and the Mennonite Hoekstra of Amsterdam, a Neo-Kantian. These were succeeded by the ethical modernists, led by Opzoomer's pupil Allard Pierson. He concluded that the concepts of sovereignty and fatherhood could not both consistently be applied to God. While the philosophers paved the way for ethical humanism, the more extreme biblical critics such as

Loman and van Manen joined Pierson in affirming that Christianity was 'Idea' only, and that neither Jesus nor Paul ever existed.[68] In the light of such dilutions the Calvinistic revival led by Abraham Kuyper (1837–1920) is not hard to understand. Kuyper's testimony was as follows:

> 'There is no doubt . . . that Christianity is imperilled by great and serious dangers. Two life systems are wrestling with one another, in mortal combat. Modernism is bound to build a world of its own from the data of the natural man, and to construct man himself from the data of nature; while, on the other hand, all those who reverently bend the knee to Christ and worship Him as the Son of the living God, and God himself, are bent upon saving the "Christian Heritage". This is the struggle in Europe, this is the struggle in America, and this also, is the struggle for principles in which my own country is engaged, and in which I myself have been spending all my energy for nearly forty years.'[69]

Returning to England we find that, as in America, one variety of Christian liberalism issued in modern Unitarianism. If we may attempt a one-sentence summary of a fascinating story, it is this: English Unitarianism is the product of a confluence of Establishment and Dissenting Arminianism and Arianism which made out its liberal theological case on the basis of a conservative use of scriptural proof texts; that it later, not least under the influence of Channing, adopted a less coldly rationalistic approach to worship whilst becoming ever more rationalist and less biblicist in defence of its distinctive emphases; and that from time to time it attracted to itself individuals and groups of other original persuasions.

The Anglican leader *par excellence* was Theophilus Lindsey (1723–1808) who became so zealous in his justification of his newly-claimed name 'Unitarian' that some thought he must be a 'methodist'! On the failure of the Feathers Tavern petition, presented to Parliament in 1772, and designed to relax the subscription laws which were enjoined upon Anglican incumbents, Lindsey left the Church of England.[70] The term 'unitarian' had been used since 1682 to describe all who held to the unipersonality of the Godhead, but from 1774 it became the name of a distinct sect, and Lindsey's liturgy was designed in such a way that God the Father alone was worshipped. On 17th April 1774, Essex Street Chapel, London, was opened, the service on that day being attended by Benjamin Franklin and Joseph Priestley (1733–1804) – the latter representing the Dissenting strand to which we referred. Dr. Gordon informs us that Priestley was an Arminian by 1751, an Arian by 1754; that by 1768 he had accepted Lardner's view of the simple humanity of Christ; and that in 1784 – much to Lindsey's surprise – he rejected the doctrine of the Virgin Birth.[71] In his works, *History of the Corruptions of Christianity* (1782) and *History of Early Opinions concerning Jesus* (1786) he argued that the early Christians were unitarians, and that the orthodox worship of Christ was blasphemous. Meanwhile there had begun a protracted controversy with Archdeacon Samuel Horsley (1733–1805) whose general attitude to both rationalists and methodists may be gauged from the following passage from his primary charge to the Diocese of St. David's (1790). He there declared that if more sound doctrine were preached 'our churches would be thronged; while the moralising Unitarian would be left to read his dull weekly lecture to the walls of his deserted conventicle, and the field-preacher would bellow unregarded to the wilderness'.[72]

Unitarians began to take tentative organisational steps – tentative not least because their doctrinal position was illegal. A Bible commentary which advocated their views was published by the Society for Promoting Knowledge of the Scriptures (1783), but it was Thomas Belsham (1750–1829) who did more than any other to weld unitarians into a denomination. He left the Independents in 1788 and was the main inspiration of the Unitarian Society for the Promotion of Christian Knowledge and the Practice of Virtue by the Distribution of Books (1791). An *Improved Version of the New Testament* (1808) was published; two erstwhile Baptists, Richard Wright and David Eaton, were converted to unitarianism and began home missionary preaching; and in 1806 the Unitarian Fund for Promoting Unitarianism by means of Popular Preaching was established. Joseph Cooke (1775–1811) adopted unitarianism and was expelled from the Wesleyan ministry in 1806, whereupon he became the leader of Lancashire's Methodist Unitarians.[73] Later, in 1841, Joseph Barker (1806—1875) was expelled from the Methodist New Connexion, and the two hundred Christian Brethren congregations which he founded on an unsectarian basis eventually attached themselves to the Unitarian movement.[74] Meanwhile Scotland's first Unitarian building had been erected in Glasgow in 1811; on 21st July 1813 the Unitarians had been accorded civil rights, and in 1819 the Unitarian Association had been founded to safeguard them; the British and Foreign Unitarian Association came into being in 1825; the Irish Non-Subscribing Presbyterians constituted themselves a separate body holding unitarian doctrine in 1830; and there had been a number of legal battles over the tenure by Unitarians of (generally) erstwhile orthodox property.[75] Among such battles was that at Wolverhampton. There were financial wrangles too. In 1705 Lady Hewley had founded a Trust for the maintenance of 'poor and godly' ministers serving north of the Trent. Resources from this being denied to Unitarians, Robert Hibbert (1770—1849) founded the Antitrinitarian Fund (subsequently the Hibbert Trust) in 1847.

The rise of modern biblical criticism, the spirituality of Channing, and the anti-supernaturalism of Theodore Parker (1810—60) influenced English Unitarians in a new direction. In this regard the undoubted leader was James Martineau (1805—1900). Whereas Priestley and Lindsey had upheld the evidential value of the biblical miracles, for example, Martineau's followers took miracles less seriously, while not denying the supernatural. They sought a reasonable faith, not unduly reliant upon proof texts, but also a warm piety. Arianism was held in increasingly less favour; Jesus was exemplar only; and Romantic intuitionalism came to the fore.[76]

Among other English harbingers of modern theological liberalism we may note the Hegelian Congregationalist J. Baldwin Brown (1820—84), who challenged the penal substitutionary theory of the atonement in the interest of the concept of the divine Fatherhood, and John H. Godwin (1809—99) whose Congregational Lecture on *Christian Faith* (1858) gave publicity to the view that trust in Christ rather than belief in doctrines was of the essence of Christianity, and should issue in sincere discipleship. Godwin's distinction between the Jesus of history and the Christ of faith was later to be taken up by the Congregational minister Robert Roberts, whose *Hibbert Journal* article, 'Jesus or Christ? An Appeal for Consistency' led to a controversy, and to the publication of the symposium *Jesus or Christ?* (1909) to which seventeen writers of all shades of opinion contributed. Some further 'advanced' views were expressed by J. Allanson Picton (1832–1910) at the Leicester Conference of 1877. Religious fellowship should not, he thought, be determined by doctrinal or historical opinions — a view from which the Congregational Union dissociated itself in the following year.

Meanwhile the term 'Broad Churchman' was replacing 'Latitudinarian' within the Church of England. It 'has been attributed either to Arthur Hugh Clough or to W. J. Conybeare, who used it in his article on "Church Parties" in the *Edinburgh Review,* for October, 1853. By the eighteen seventies the term "Liberal Churchman" or "Liberal Clergyman" was becoming common.'[77] We should not suppose, however, that there were no differences between older Broad Churchman and later Anglican Modernist. Dr. Major has listed three ways in which their emphases differed: the Broad Churchmen were more Erastian, more inclined to a humanitarian utilitarianism, and 'flaccid and unhistorical' in regard to doctrine and exegesis.[78] Dr. A. M. Ramsey, in commenting upon the liberalism of Rashdall, which was content with a symbolic incarnation and an exemplarist atonement, indicates something of the breadth of Anglican liberal modernism as he compares Rashdall with Gore and Inge. It was a favourite theme of Rashdall's 'that the orthodoxy of teachers such as Gore presented the doctrine of the Trinity in a manner more tritheistic than S. Augustine or S. Thomas Aquinas would countenance. On the other hand, he was apart from Inge, and nearer to Gore, in a distrust of mysticism and a dislike of the appeal to religious experience.'[79] Dr. Stephenson has summed up the things the English Modernists fought for during what he calls their 'great period' thus:

'They fought, above all, for a supernatural, but non-miraculous, Christianity — or, rather, a Christianity where miracles were not *contra naturam*. They fought for a degree Christology, i.e. they believed that all men were sons of God but Christ pre-eminently so. This led them to the dangerous corollary that not simply Christ, but man, was consubstantial with the Father. They held strongly to the doctrine of the Incarnation but they were unwilling to insist that the Incarnation necessarily involved the Virgin Birth or the physical Resurrection.'[80]

The main thrust of Liberal Protestantism at large was provided by the more or less left wing disciples of Ritschl. Supreme among these was Harnack. There can be no doubt that in removing what he regarded as Pauline and Hellenistic accretions from the simple gospel he emphasised the ideas of the Fatherhood of God and the brotherhood of man. It is, however, an oft-committed error to suppose that this slogan (for that is what it became) exhausts his teaching. He was equally in earnest in propounding his view of the Kingdom of God, with all that that entailed concerning the command-ment of love. Further, as J. K. Mozley pointed out, he did recognise 'the mystery inherent in the Person of Christ' but he 'refused to accept the historic account of the Person of Christ as given in the doctrines of His divinity and incar-nation. His deep reverence for Jesus as the supreme Teacher and the Revealer of God did not lead him to the acceptance of the Pauline and Johannine Christology and to the affir-mations of the Nicene Creed.'[81] To none was Harnack's position more unsatisfactory than to the Catholic Modern-ists. We have already mentioned Loisy's reply; but Tyrrell's words were no less severe: 'The Christ that Harnack sees, looking back through nineteen centuries of Catholic dark-ness, is only the reflection of a Liberal Protestant face, seen at the bottom of a deep well'.[82] But to many the power of the Harnackian Jesus was considerable, and a prominent British exposition of this type is that of the Baptist T. R. Glover: *The Jesus of History* (1917).

Many theological liberals would have agreed with the American Leighton Parks that 'Modernism is not a body of doctrine. It is a state of mind. It is an attempt to "justify the ways of God to man", that is, to man in the twentieth century.'[83] Not the least of the liberal-conservative frictions arose because of the difficulty the latter had in persuading the former not only that their position was wrong, but that it was dogmatic! But — yet another qualification! — not all liberals were professedly undogmatic. Some were anxious that the term 'evangelical' should be added to their designation, and to these we finally turn.

Dr. Storr provides us with a definition of Liberal Evangelicalism with which many of his contemporaries would have agreed: 'Liberal Evangelicalism emphasises the primacy of spirit and idea, and is always on the watch lest any outward embodiment of organisation, or rule or order, should usurp the place which rightfully belongs to what is inward'.[84] He proceeds to show that Liberal Evangelicalism is 'suspicious of all cut and dried schemes of doctrine';[85] that it upholds belief in the progressive revelation of truth; and that it is heir to Schleiermacher in its conviction that 'the dogma should grow out of the experience, and, if necessary, be modified as the experience developed'.[86] Storr does not wish to imply, however, that liberal evangelicals do not know where they stand, and have no positive gospel; so he begs some important questions in affirming that 'Liberal Evangelicalism finds its ultimate ground of authority in the Mind and Spirit of Christ'.[87] The liberal Congregationalist C. J. Cadoux was a little more specific in averring that the use of the labels 'liberal' or 'modernist' 'presupposes belief in the existence, sovereignty, and goodness of God, in the Lordship and Saviourhood of Jesus Christ, and in the reality and power of the Christian Gospel of Salvation'.[88] The use of the terminology of orthodoxy did little to reassure some, and when Fosdick declared that *he* was a Liberal Evangelical — and not one of the unthinkingly optimistic kind either — the conservatives were appalled, and the Unitarians pressed him to shun hypocrisy and come over.[89]

We have attempted to chart troubled waters. The legacy of the nineteenth century to theology was confusion — though in fairness we must confess that that confusion was not entirely the fault of the nineteenth century. The roots of the theological predicament of the early twentieth century go a long way down the centuries. The nineteenth century is the period during which the cumulative effect of older tendencies and newer methodologies is felt with tremendous force. The legacy of that century is the question 'What *is* the heart of the gospel, and how may we best express it?'. It might be said that every age has to face that question; and this is true. But *we* have to face it in a post-Christendom period. Our situation is in certain important respects more like that of Justin Martyr, Irenaeus, Clement and Tertullian,[90] than it is like that of Augustine, Aquinas, Luther or Calvin — all of whom could easily make the assumptions of Christendom.

CHAPTER SIX

CONSERVATIVES, LIBERALS AND THE GOSPEL

Having sought to characterise conservatives and liberals as dispassionately as possible, we must now see what is to be learned from the debate between them. This we shall begin to do by reviewing a prominent, albeit popular, treatment of the question, 'What is the heart of the Christian gospel?'.

I

In his *Christianity and Liberalism* (1923),[1] J. Gresham Machen provides as provocative an expression as we have found of the conservative case against theological liberalism. Machen who, significantly, had studied in Germany under Ritschl's disciple Herrmann, was determined to defend orthodox Christianity as he conceived it, and to show that liberalism's gospel was 'another gospel'. Both sides of the equation are important, and Machen himself felt that his positive purpose had been insufficiently appreciated by those who reviewed his book. On 13th April 1923 he wrote to his mother lamenting that early reviewers had failed 'to get the "Christianity" side of *Christianity and Liberalism* — they had failed to see that the book purports to be a summary of Christian Doctrine, in the light of modern attacks, it is true, but still with a positive purpose'. Machen's biographer informs us that 'His only later regret was that he had not used the term "modernism" rather than "liberalism". The latter designation seemed to him to give greater credit to this religious phenomenon than it deserved, the former served at least to suggest that it lacked the support of the charter of Christianity and had emerged from modern thought as an innovation.'[2] Be that as it may, Machen was utterly convinced of the truth of Christianity, and of the evil of liberalism; and he would have found himself in unaccustomed agreement with the liberal journal *The Christian Century* which asserted that 'Two world-views, two moral ideals, two sets of personal attitudes, have clashed, and it is a case of ostrich-like intelligence blindly to deny and evade the searching and serious character of the issue. Christianity, according to fundamentalism, is one religion. Christianity, according to Modernism, is another religion.'[3]

In *Christianity and Liberalism* Machen aims to present the matter in the clearest possible terms. Whilst believing that liberalism is open to criticism on the ground that it is unscientific, his particular concern is to show that it is 'unChristian'.[4] 'Liberal Christianity' is a misnomer, for it overlooks many facts of the Christian case,[5] and whatever form it takes, its origins are in naturalism: 'that is, in the denial of any entrance of the creative power of God (as distinguished from the ordinary course of nature) in connection with the origin of Christianity. The word "naturalism" is here used in a sense somewhat different from its philosophical meaning.'[6] Unfortunately Machen does not spell out the precise ways in which his use of the term differs from its use in philosophy, and this can only weaken his case. Certainly we have found many varieties of liberalism — Catholic, immanentist, Platonist — which could only very confusingly be described as naturalistic. What Machen appears to have in mind is the attitude adopted by some experience-centred liberals that creeds and confessions are redundant because religion is life. Against such an attitude he properly protests, 'a creed is not a mere expression of Christian experience, but on the contrary it is a setting forth of those facts upon which the experience is based'.[7]

Here is the nub of the matter: 'the Christian movement at its inception was not just a way of life in the modern sense, but a way of life founded upon a message. It was based, not upon mere feeling, not upon a mere program of work, but upon an account of facts. In other words it was based upon doctrine.'[8] It is not that for Paul and others doctrine came temporally before life, but that logically doctrine precedes life.[9] The gospel, or 'good news', is event plus meaning — and that is doctrine: ' "Christ died" — that is history; "Christ died for our sins" — that is doctrine. Without these two elements, joined in an absolutely indissoluble union, there is no Christianity.'[10] 'Christianity depends, not upon a complex of ideas, but upon the narration of an event'.[11] The implication is that if we wish to discover what Christianity is we must return to its origins. Indeed Machen said as much elsewhere when he declared that Christianity is 'an historical phenomenon like the State of Pennsylvania'.[12] How verbally near, and yet how presuppositionally far this is from Harnack!

Christianity offers us events, facts, of which we may have knowledge. Machen is no irrationalist; he is a Christian realist: 'The Christian gospel consists in an account of how God saved man, and before that gospel can be understood something must be known (1) about God and (2) about man'.[13] Hence the inadequacy of feeling alone; for example, 'the ascription of deity to Jesus . . . is meaningless unless the word "God" has an antecedent meaning attached to it . . . Rational theism . . . is at the very root of Christianity'.[14] The element of intellectual assent to propositions cannot be removed from faith.[15] We cannot believe in someone without believing that something about him is true, that is, without having knowledge of him.[16] When attempts in the contrary direction are made the result is confusion. Men use traditional terminology, but have evacuated traditional meanings from it.[17] This last point has more recently been reaffirmed by the conservative philosopher W. C. Young:

'J. G. Machen, E. S. Brightman, H. N. Wieman, and John Dewey all use the term "God". Does this mean that all of them are theists of the same school? An examination of the writings of each will show that Machen means by "God" a Being Who is infinite, perfect, and supreme in every conceivable way; that Brightman means a Being Who is perfectly good, yet limited in power by uncreatedness within Himself; that Wieman means an impersonal, striving, creative Force wholly immanent in nature; and that Dewey means the relation between the ideal and the actual in relation to human and temporal existence.'[18]

The knowledge of God which is at the basis of Christian

faith is not, says Machen, to be acquired by the prosecution of historical analysis alone. Although God is revealed in his works of creation, by his voice within us, and through the Bible, we, sinful as we are, cannot find him by searching.[19] Knowledge of God is his gift to us; it is revealed to us by the Holy Spirit. This supernatural revelation acquaints the sinner with the saving grace of God, and of this he could have gained no knowledge at all either from nature or from his own conscience.[20] The God who thus makes himself known is both transcendent and immanent, though Machen underlines the former in face of the immanentist drift of the thought of his day:

> 'But one attribute of God is absolutely fundamental in the Bible; one attribute is absolutely necessary in order to render intelligible all the rest. That attribute is the awful transcendence of God. From beginning to end the Bible is concerned to set forth the awful gulf that separates the creature from the Creator. It is true, indeed, that according to the Bible God is immanent in the world. Not a sparrow falls to the ground without Him. But he is immanent in the world not because He is identified with the world, but because He is the free Creator and Upholder of it. Between the creature and the Creator a great gulf is fixed.'[21]

By contrast, the immanentisms which profess to bring God near serve only, when they degenerate into pantheism, to remove him further from us; for pantheism 'brings Him physically near, but at the same time makes Him spiritually remote; it conceives of Him as a sort of blind vital force, but ceases to regard Him as a Person whom a man can love and whom a man can trust'.[22]

The Christian revelation brings to such sinful men as God chooses — to men under his wrath — a word of grace and salvation. It informs them by the Spirit that God in Christ has made a vicarious atonement on their behalf, and that by it they are saved. Nor is this message true only for those who accept it. It is universally true that God has thus acted, though not all are reborn into this knowledge of God.[23] Here we observe Machen's particularism, and it is this which leads him to make his affirmation of the centre of the Christian religion in the following terms: 'the absolutely undeserved and sovereign grace of God, saving sinful men by the gift of Christ upon the cross. Condemnation comes by merit; salvation comes only by grace: condemnation is earned by man; salvation is given by God.'[24]

The contrast between his gospel and that of liberalism appalled Machen. He had been sorely tried by many liberals, and of Fosdick he wrote in a letter, 'he is dreadful! Just the pitiful modern stuff about an undogmatic Christianity . . . I should hate to think that Christianity were reduced to such insignificant proportions.'[25] Let us list the principal features of Machen's syllabus of liberal errors. Liberals find the heart of the faith in the universal Fatherhood of God. But to Machen this is but the presupposition of Christianity, not its heart: it provides the starting point in natural religion for 'the proclamation of the gospel of divine grace'.[26] Moreover, by failing to emphasise God's holy transcendence and wrath on the one hand, and man's sin on the other, the modern Church finds herself 'busily engaged in an absolutely impossible task, [that of] calling the righteous to repentance'.[27] She forgets that

> 'it was Jesus — Jesus whom modern liberals represent as a mild-mannered exponent of an indiscriminating love — it was Jesus who spoke of the outer darkness and the everlasting fire, of the sin that shall not be forgiven either in this world or in that which is to come. There is nothing in Jesus' teaching about the character of God which in itself can evoke trust. On the contrary the awful presentation can give rise, in the hearts of us sinners, only to despair. Trust arises only when we attend to God's way of salvation.'

Further, where liberals are satisfied with an exemplary Christ, true Christians know that 'their method of ridding themselves [the passive voice would surely better have become a Calvinist!] of sin was by means of Him'.[29] Real love is costly,, and of the kind of God who will necessarily forgive us whatever we do we must say that 'Such a God may deliver us from the fear of hell. But His heaven, if He has any, is full of sin'.[30] In thus refusing to accept these considerations the liberals reject the authority of Christ in favour of their own shifting, sinful emotions, they spurn his work, and reduce him to 'the Founder of Christianity because He was the first Christian'.[31] In fact Jesus offers to men far more than the liberals will accept: 'He offered, not primarily guidance, but salvation'.[32] Further, 'the example of Jesus is useful to the Christian not prior to redemption, but subsequent to it . . . that is the true order of Christian pedagogy — "trust in His redeeming blood" first, and then "try His works to do" '.[33] In a word, 'Liberalism is altogether in the imperative mood, while Christianity begins with a triumphant indicative'.[34]

Consistently with their presuppositions the liberals oppose the supernatural and are sceptical concerning miracles. But 'The truly penitent man glories in the supernatural, for he knows that nothing natural would meet his need';[35] and what price an immanent God who cannot work miraculously without means above (though not against) nature?[36] Again, and not surprisingly, liberals say little about the world to come and busy themselves with this-worldly concerns. Not indeed that the Christian should withdraw from the world; but whereas 'The liberal believes that applied Christianity is all there is of Christianity, Christianity being merely a way of life; the Christian man believes that applied Christianity is the result of an initial act of God'.[37]

Machen grants that not all liberals are affected by liberal 'heresies' to the same degree.[38] Nor does he intend to suggest that all points of doctrine are of equal importance.[39] (We recall that he himself sat more lightly to millenarianism than many in his day. This raises the question, here unresolved, of the criteria for deciding between more and less crucial doctrines — a question which becomes clamant when, as in Machen's case, the terms of Christian fellowship are at issue). Finally, Machen did not wish to deny that those who disagreed with him had the right to maintain their views; but he certainly wished to deny that, whether or not individual liberals were true Christians, their views were not Christian.[40] It remains only to add that Machen's entire position turns upon the doctrine of the plenary inspiration of the Bible.

How was *Christianity and Liberalism* received? To Lewis Browne the book was 'a broad and inclusive condemnation of any and every attempt to let light into the attic of theology'.[41] W. L. Sperry regretted the 'particular mixture of theological patronage and of theological vitriol which it offers the "liberal" '.[42] On the other hand, the reviewer in *The Journal of Religion* concluded that 'The argument is well sustained, and the book is a dignified and scholarly defense of orthodoxy';[43] and *The Independent* declared that Machen had produced 'an extremely able apologetic'.[44] A less enthusiastic second review was written for *The Journal of Religion* by G. B. Smith, who complained that no hint was given by Machen as to why so many were becoming "liberal".[45] By Unitarians Machen was applauded for upholding confessional statements which others had dishonestly set on one side;[46] and among outside observers both Walter Lippmann and H. L. Mencken praised Machen's integrity, the former adding that 'the liberals have yet to answer Dr. Machen when he says that "the Christian movement at its inception was not just a way of life in the modern sense, but a way of life founded upon a message" '.[47] For the most part British periodicals paid no attention to *Christianity and Liberalism*, though the *British Weekly* gave space to it in 1924, and *The Modern Churchman's* reviewer over-reacted in a rather snootily 'British' way:

> 'Such homilies, full of declamation and irrelevance, are not calculated to affect the realities of the situation. Yet something must be excused in those who hravely plead a lost cause; their rancour is intelligible, even though their ignorance is appalling. Yet it would seem that the zeal of these crusaders boils higher in America than in England. Can it be that owing to the lower standard of general education they have more public support?'[48]

We will waste no words on such aristocratic ignorance.

Our own conclusion, with benefit of hindsight and a more tranquil atmosphere, is that Machen's book is not scholarly, nor did it set out to be. It is true that, scholar though he himself was, he does not explain the growth of liberalism; he does not differentiate between the many different kinds of liberalism which were extant in his day; he does not — in *Christianity and Liberalism* — defend his flank adequately

against attack, especially on the criteria for the selection of
those doctrines which are said to be crucial to the Faith. On
the other hand, we do not find him generally unclear or
vitriolic; and if he is unduly assertorial, we may put this
down to the fact that guarders of the Ark have traditionally
felt that assertion and attack were the two things needful.

We endorse Machen's maintenance of the Creator-creature
distinction, and we approve of his holding together of doctrine and life. Above all, we welcome the way in which he
thrusts the question of the nature of the gospel to the fore.
Machen was not, of course, the only one to differentiate his
understanding of the gospel from the liberalism of his day.
Prominent among others in this field was P. T. Forsyth, who
wondered whether liberalism was not in fact a different
religion — a new gnosticism.[49]

II

In recalling the work of J. Gresham Machen were we simply
reviving passe polemics, or were we in touch with one expression of a perennial problem? It is our conviction that notwithstanding changing times, circumstances and modes of
expression, God's holy love does not change; the prime needs
of man concerning sin and salvation do not change; the
fundamental gospel message concerning God's redemptive
action in Christ does not change, and the ways in which that
message may be distorted display an almost monotonous
likeness through the ages. Notable among these ways are
the several varieties of Pelagianism, with which so much
of the churchly debate on the God-man relation has been
concerned; and the longstanding tendency towards unhistorical mysticisms coupled often with a blurring of the
Creator-creature distinction, to which their philosophical
commerce has led some Christians. Both tendencies posit
understandings of the nature and relations of God and man
which ill accord with the basic thrust of the gospel. We may
therefore say that although the particulars of the modern
conservative-liberal debate — the modern understanding of

history and criticism, evolutionary-immanentist thought, and so on — *were* new, the main issues in the debate were venerable indeed. We shall attempt to isolate some of these perennial themes as they emerge in the debates of the early twentieth century. We shall show that the hands of neither conservative nor liberal are entirely clean when it comes to distorting the gospel (nor are those of self-appointed adjudicators, no doubt!); and we shall enter our plea for theological balance.

We return first to the liberals — and at once we enter a caveat. We have been at some pains to point out that between those liberals who advocated a this-worldly 'get up and go' version of Christianity which took its cue from the historical Jesus *qua* exemplar, and such philosophical immanentists as T. H. Green, who sought to safeguard Christianity from historical relativities and criticism, there is a great gulf fixed. Hence any list of liberal distortions (and likewise of conservative distortions) will be generalised. So, for that matter, will be any account of liberal and conservative virtues.

It can hardly be denied that some liberal critics of the Bible adopted an unduly sceptical attitude towards the scriptural texts. Strauss eventually concluded that the only honest thing to do was to deny that he was a Christian. Many, however, anxious to love God with all their minds and to exercise responsible stewardship over their personal resources, applied themselves reverently and with the best possible motives to the sacred text:

> 'They . . . read the Bible, not merely for personal edification, like many of the older men, who put more gospel into the Book of Leviticus and the Book of Judges than some people now-a-days can find in the Epistle to the Romans; not merely for the purpose of collecting fresh materials to use for the conversion of sinners; but to discover what the Bible really meant. And that was surely admirable. The gentle — the violent — pressure which used to be put on reluctant texts by theologians and preachers of all creeds to *make* them *say* the right thing or to *prevent* them from saying the wrong, was as bad as the gentle or violent pressure put on obstinate heretics by the Inquisition with precisely the same object.'[50]

In the course of their work such men received as new light
the deliverances of the anthropologists, psychologists and
students of comparative religion — more often than not being
inspired by the thought that if they were indeed handling
God's Word, no scientific advance could undermine it, but
that if it became clear that they had been bound to supersti-
tions, the sooner they discarded them the better. In their
theologising they eagerly took a leaf out of Plato's book and
determined to follow the argument wherever it might lead.
Further, they were especially concerned to ensure that it was
a *moral* God with whom they had to do. Not for them the
God of caprice; not for them the God who required the
murder of his Son before he could be induced to forgive
(truth to tell some of them thus parodied all but the most
brazen of conservatives in making their points). Again, since
God's revelation was couched in moral terms, those who
responded to it must be moral too. Erskine of Linlathen was
among those who early emphasised this point: 'The reason-
ableness of a religion seems to me to consist in there being a
direct and natural connection between a believing of the
doctrines which it inculcates, and a being formed by these to
the character which it recommends. If the belief of the
doctrines has no tendency to train a disciple in a more exact
and more willing discharge of its moral obligations, there is
evidently a very strong probability against the truth of that
religion.'[51] This ethical emphasis was later taken up with
other than individual reference, and the idea that the Church
could sit unprophetically by whilst unjust social structures
were allowed to exploit the masses (however much private
beneficence there may have been), was severely and rightly
trounced by the men of the Social Gospel school.

Yet the very zeal with which some of these ideas were
pursued led to imbalance; and the liberal C. J. Cadoux had
to agree that there were individual modernists and groups of
modernists (however unrepresentative they were) against
whom the charges which he lists could justifiably be levelled:

'Modernism today unduly exalts man, and teaches him to
deify himself, to emancipate himself from God's authority,
and to believe that he is completely self-sufficient: it therefore largely ignores the problem of sin and evil, and has an

unwarranted confidence in the certainty of human progress. It is accused also of rejecting the authority and
witness of the Bible, dishonestly misdating its documents,
denying the Lordship, Divinity, and saving power of Jesus,
denying the Incarnation and Resurrection, having no
place for sacrifice, and in general abandoning the Christian Gospel. It is branded as individualistic, intellectual-
istic, rationalistic, humanistic, and optimistic in the wrong
senses, subjective and anarchic, proud, foolish, poisonous,
and even Satanic. It is held responsible for the decline of
the churches, and having been weighed in the balance and
found wanting, may be pronounced dead.'[52]

We shall provide evidence to show that some liberals, in their
desire to reduce the burden of belief, did threaten the gospel; and that they were encouraged in this direction by an
optimism in man inspired by evolutionary-immanentist
thought of various hues. We shall cite the Social Gospel
school as bearing clear marks of those attenuations of the
gospel which concern us, while recognising their genuine and
major challenge to Christian ethical theory. While we note
their inadequate diagnosis and prescription, we shall not fail
to applaud their proper moral concern for man in society.

Few liberals assailed the doctrinal undergrowth as zestfully
as the Dutch. Professor Bavinck of Kampen lamented thus:

> 'It is a slow process of dissolution that meets our view. It
> began with setting aside the Confession. Scripture alone
> was to be heard. Next, Scripture also is dismissed, and the
> Person of Christ is fallen back on. Of this Person, however,
> first His Divinity, next His pre-existence, finally His sinless-
> ness, are surrendered, and nothing remains but a pious
> man, a religious genius, revealing to us the love of God.
> But even the existence and love of God are not able to
> withstand criticism. Thus the moral element in man be-
> comes the last basis from which the battle against Materi-
> alism is conducted. But this basis will appear to be as
> unstable and unreliable as the others.'[53]

Undeterred by such warnings, some preachers joined the
liberal theologians in their quest of a naturalistically-honed
Ockham's razor. Frank Lenwood, pastor of a busy Leeds

Congregational church sought a principled approach to a situation in which a quiet revolution was taking place — 'so quiet that most of the congregations do not notice the alteration, and go on repeating the hackneyed arguments in a vain attempt to satisfy the restless younger minds'.[54] Lenwood was convinced that 'until we clear away the condemned building, we shall never get room for the new architecture which we plainly require.'[55]

For most liberals the new architecture was most desperately sought in relation to the doctrines of God, sin and atonement, and many thought they had found it. Thus, the Unitarian Dr. S. H. Mellone declared, 'We have now affirmed our faith in the essential humanity of God and the native divine spark in the spirit of man [no novel idea this!]. The idea of the one now helps to say what we mean when we try to define the other.'[56] Contemporaneously, across the Atlantic, Leighton Parks was rejoicing in the passage 'from the thought of the Sovereignty of God to the Fatherhood of God. As a dogma, that has always been accepted; as a living truth, it is the discovery of the nineteenth century.'[57] In the thought of Dr. A. E. Garvie we see the old struggling with the new in such a way as to raise a serious question concerning God's sovereignty:

'We now all believe in the universal Fatherhood of God, the love which wills not the death of any sinner, but wills that all should be saved, if they themselves will. But we must beware of treating that truth as though it were a doctrine of natural theology, a matter of course, a truism, a commonplace. It is revealed and realized in Jesus Christ, His redemption of man from sin, and His reconciliation of man to God. Men are not by nature the children, but only the creatures of God . . . What destiny will and can Divine love appoint for man? The doctrine of eternal punishment in its crude form is impossible for any enlightened Christian conscience. To assert that all will be saved is to ignore the possibility of the persistence of sin and unbelief in some men, and the impossibility of God saving any but by moral and religious means. For persistent defiance of grace there can be only Divine Judgment. If we are to believe in God's Fatherhood we shall believe that He will do all He can do as love, as holy love, to save all men; but should any refuse salvation, such penalty will fall on them as love, holy love, appoints.'[58]

Qualifications notwithstanding, how far is this last sentence from the view of some liberals and, oddly enough, of some fundamentalist evangelists, to the effect that 'God will save you if you let him?'. What does that imply concerning God's sovereignty? The danger is that we pass from saying that God is, strictly, pitiful, to saying that he is pitiable — because he would save, but cannot.

No doubt there were ways of speaking of God which made him appear to be an arbitrary tyrant, but in reacting against such views many liberals verged upon the sentimental, and, unlike Garvie, overlooked the *holiness* of God's love. As a chastened modernist put it, modernism's 'doctrine of God has not been big enough'.[59] In similar vein the authors of a report on 'American Congregational Theology' noted that 'The substitution of the New Testament doctrine of God as Love, in place of the Old Testament idea of Sovereignty [an inaccurate dichotomy this] . . . has been made "an occasion of the flesh" on the part of those whose only idea of love is that of a weak, indulgent sentimentalism, instead of the most searching and sincere of all passions, compassionate but never compromising, sacrificial but severe'.[60] In H. R. Niebuhr's classic phrase, 'A God without wrath brought men without sin into a Kingdom without judgment through the ministrations of a Christ without a cross'.[61] The positive point was finely put by Robert Mackintosh: 'God's love is the radiance of His righteousness; God's justice is the sternness of His love'.[62]

In the absence of the note of holiness much liberal theology devalued the doctrine of the atonement. Undeniably there had been immoral representations of that doctrine which deserved demolition, but in many quarters the pendulum swung so far that there was resumed in modern dress the Bernard *versus* Abelard dispute. If God loves all men; if he is Father of all; if all men are his children (a term which some liberals took to mean 'sons', thereby overlooking the fact that in the New Testament sonship comes by adoption); then God will so desire fellowship with men as to provide an exemplar Christ who will show men how to live; and this he has done. On this view sin is something less than radical; man is something more than unable; the atonement is an example given rather than a price paid. In fact the doctrine of sin which some liberals espoused was as atomistic as that of Pelagius. It well accorded with the contemporary anthropocentric subjectivism which some learned from such psychologists as J. B. Pratt, for whom the crucial matter was not the restoration of a right relationship with God, but 'the achievement of a new self' which it is the *individual's* task to create.[63] One of the most surprising features of some liberal theology is that for all its emphasis upon the pressing need to secure social justice and to ameliorate conditions in society at large, it entertained for the most part the most individualistic understanding of sin and atonement. The individual had only to imitate Christ, and all would be well.[64] (Not indeed that all liberals were thus at fault: Charles Gore for one neither exalted man nor minimised the importance of sin. We speak of general tendencies only).

An investigation of the several varieties of Pelagianism would show that the temptation unduly to exalt man's competence to live aright is of long standing. We find it not only in the more formal context of 'Pelagian' — 'Augustinian' debate, but also in such a one as the provocative Daniel Whitby (1638—1726) who was persuaded that man's natural ability to improve was such that his progress in this regard would continue until the millenium dawned. But it was the evolutionary-immanentist strain of nineteenth century thought which really launched latter-day optimism in man. The hellenistically inclined followed F. D. Maurice in holding that the Incarnation testifies to the fact that man is already redeemed;[65] J. R. Illingworth regarded the Incarnation as the 'guiding star' of every phase of progress;[66] and while few went as far as Bender of Bonn in holding that 'Not God but man is the central element in faith; man is the sun round which circles the world of religious thought',[67] popular lyricists did not lag far behind:

> 'I am the master of my fate
>   I am the captain of my soul'

sang W. E. Henley in his *Invictus;* while Swinburne eulogised, 'Glory to Man in the highest! for Man is the master of things'. In some quarters pulpit banality was rife, so that Mandel Creighton, writing of Dean Stanley's sermons, said, 'There was a certain amount of moral enthusiasm, to the intent that it was desirable to be good rather than bad; but I had previously gathered that from other sources'.[68] But the tide could not be held back. To Walter Rauschenbusch the 'swiftness of evolution' in America *proved* 'the immense latent perfectibility in human nature';[69] Albert Peel reassured his fellow English Congregationalists that any dismay occasioned by the higher criticism should be offset by confidence in the progress of the human race — he said that as late as 1923;[70] and Rhondda Williams stood the seventeenth century John Robinson on his head when he averred 'there is still more light and truth to break forth *through the souls of men*'.[71]

Many of the tendencies we have noted found their natural home in Social Gospel theory. Not indeed that such theory was the inevitable consequence of liberalism in theology. On the contrary, although there were echoes of Social Gospel thinking in, for example, Anglican Modernism ('The ideal ever before the Church must be that of efficient service for the bringing in of the Kingdom of God'),[72] Dr. A. M. G. Stephenson, himself a Modern Churchman, had to admit that 'Some of them were uninterested in social problems'.[73] The Social Gospel was, however, of considerable importance. It administered a much needed jolt to an American religiosity which had preached the moral values whilst ignoring the unjust social structures which threatened those very values. It stood, moreover, in the tradition of the Pilgrim Fathers, of whom it was said that 'they applied the principles of the Gospel to elevate society, to regulate education, to civilize humanity, to purify love, to reform the church and the state, to assert, to defend and to die for liberty, in short to mould and redeem by its all-transforming energy everything that belongs to man in his individual and social relations'.[74] With such declarations as this the Social Gospel movement was heralded; it gathered momentum during the 1870s and 1880s and thereafter, for three decades, it was a principal constituent of America's 'Age of Crusades'.[75]

The immanentist philosophy had taught men that God needed them and was close to them; evolutionary thought had popularised the concept of progress; and undoubted scientific and technological marvels had encouraged man to exult in his prowess. Older understandings of man's nature and lot had been shown, so it was thought, to be partial, threadbare, and even repellant. The spotlight was taken off sin as an affront to God's holy love, and turned upon sin as social injustice:

> 'It is impossible to lead a Christian life except in a Christianized society. Yet if we accept the thought of divine immanence, sin and evil cannot be quite so bad as they seem to be. Considered from the viewpoint of the Social Gospel the thought that God would damn a man because of sin is offensive.
>
> Since man is inherently good and all men are God's children, there is in modern religion no place for individual salvation . . . In a word, the social gospel addresses itself to the task to make the world a decent place to live in . . . What was formerly spoken of as religious is of value only in so far as it serves social ends.'[76]

Thus some came to speak of 'a hell frozen over or turned to innocuous ashes';[77] and of the liberal doctrine 'surround the individual or community with a good environment and salvation will result' the *Watchman Examiner* declared that 'No greater or more insidious heresy ever issued from hell than this . . .".'[78] Most Social Gospel thinkers, however, would have endorsed the Englishman John Clifford's view that the Social Order is the burden of Jesus's teaching.[79] Many too would have supported his plea for more social missionaries, and would have applauded his complaint that 'The Church has made too much of theology'.[80] Many, but not all. Dr. D. W. Forrest remained convinced that 'ministers of the Gospel should aim first at being professional theologians rather than amateur sociologists'[81] — and with him we agree. So many Social Gospel men seemed to think that they could do God's work for him: 'The strength of evil institutions need not dismay us. All that is needed for their removal, and for rearing upon their ashes the structures of a new world, is new thought and new feeling.'[82] All? But the

Kingdom is God's gift, and as far as *man's* credentials as
architect of it are concerned, we cannot but agree with D. R.
Davies that after two World Wars 'Social salvation, which was
always a chimera, is now trailing the whiskers of senility'.[83]
Many thus came to feel the inadequacy of the Social Gospel
diagnosis of man's disease — and none more acutely than
Reinhold Niebuhr:

> 'It is not moral complacency of which liberal Christianity
> stands convicted but moral superficiality . . . What is lack-
> ing is the realization that even the best human will in the
> world has the corruption of sin in it . . . Our whole diffi-
> culty in American Protestantism is in having so long
> regarded Christianity as synonymous with the simple
> command to love God and our fellow men, that we have
> forgotten that the Christian religion is really a great deal
> more than this . . . the divine mercy revealed in Christ is on
> the one hand a power which overcomes the contradiction
> between what we are and what we ought to be, and on the
> other hand a pledge of forgiveness for this sinful element
> which is never completely overcome short of the culmi-
> nation of history. Only such a faith can disclose the actual
> facts of human existence. It alone can uncover the facts
> because it alone has answers for the facts which are
> disclosed.'[84]

In saying that immanentist thought was a powerful impetus to theological liberalism, we do not overlook the fact
that some liberals so shunned philosophy as to place themselves in a positivism of experience no less constricting than
the biblical positivism which they scorned. Ritschl and
Harnack had no patience with Hegelianism, for example.
But for all their overt hostility to the immanent Absolute,
their methodological presuppositions were congenial to the
general immanentist mood if only in the negative sense that
they seldom employed the concept of transcendence, or
invoked that of the supernatural. We would go so far as to
say that most of the recoils from intellectualism that the late
nineteenth century witnessed were inspired by one variety or
another of immanentism. Where philosophy was shunned,
what was viewed with suspicion was monism rather than
immanentism, and this owing to the inadequate attention to

value, experience and history which monism was held to pay. We may thus accept Forsyth's generalisation, 'Liberal theology . . . views the course of religion as an immanent evolution accounting even for experience'.[85]

As we have seen, the climate of immanentist-evolutionary thought provided fertile soil for many fresh expressions of Spinoza's belief that 'whatever is, is in God'.[86] This soil was congenial both to those who wished to avoid the perils of historicity on the one hand, and the more mysterious reaches of theology in the interest of practical Christianity on the other: seldom had a philosophical stance proved to be so contradictorily adaptable. Of the more practical expressions we have already spoken. It remains to note, as a rider to our earlier discussion of immanentism, some further examples of the impact of that variety of thought upon theology itself. Immanentism enabled the philosopher Bosanquet to affirm, 'We are spirits, and our life is one with that of the Spirit which is the whole and the good'.[87] It enabled Rhondda Williams to sermonise thus: 'Every new discovery brings a new world, but all such discoveries pale to insignificance before the crowning discovery that man is spirit, and that the human spirit is one with God . . . In every human birth a part of God . . . is enfleshed, incarnated.'[88] H. D. A. Major could point out that 'The modern Churchman differs from the Chalcedonian Fathers by holding that the substances of Deity and of Humanity are *not two,* but one'.[89] If in Jesus the liberal Congregationalist T. Wigley saw 'the highest expression of the law of our evolution, an example of the true order of divine humanity',[90] to Lowes Dickinson the existence or non-existence of Jesus in history was immaterial.[91] Finally, immanentism gave a licence to many Incarnational theologians to remodel that doctrine so that even the Unitarian Martineau could declare, 'The Incarnation is true, not of Christ exclusively, but of Man universally, and God everlastingly'.[92]

The criticisms of the above positions are now quite familiar to us, and can simply be listed and endorsed. The first point is the ontological one. The blurring of the Creator-creature distinction which immanentism entails encourages idealism rather than religion. This is so whether we think of

monism or of experienced values. In the former case we have
'an infinite extension of our horizon or our self-consciousness'[93] but nothing of the transcendent majesty of God. In
the latter case, as Dr. Quick said of Ritschlian theology, it
'can only excuse us for treating our Lord as God on the
ground of his goodness: it cannot justify us in affirming that
He is God on the ground of His being, unless it proceeds
further to assert that all Godhead is but a quality of man'.[94]
But the most serious criticism of immanentism is that all too
often it makes theologians unable or unwilling to take adequate account of God's nature and demands, and of man's
nature and needs. In consequence it all too often leaves us
with worthy aspirations which we are impotent to realise,
with undifferentiated mysticism or humanism; or with a
religion of ungrounded charity which — especially if the
prevailing climate be optimistic — all too easily unwhole-
somely exalts man and demeans God, encourages works
and sits light to grace.

In a not untypical piece of liberalism K. C. Anderson,
having declared against ecclesiasticism and theological ob-
scurantism, waxed lyrical:

> 'What are the reports that are coming in from all parts
> of the world to-day? They all tend to one announcement,
> they all unite their voices to preach one mighty Gospel,
> the essential goodness of the world and of life: that the
> universe is cradled in love; that it is not only a unity, but a
> beneficent unity; that the life of man, the child of the uni-
> verse, lies embosomed in one great Life; that the essence of
> things is good, and the purpose and the outcome good.
> But what is this but a confirmation of the essential Gospel
> of Jesus Christ?'[95]

We can well imagine what P. T. Forsyth would have said in
reply to that question. Indeed, he said it in an article on 'The
reality of grace' which immediately precedes that of Anderson in the journal in question — never were two articles more
engagingly juxtaposed. He there castigated preachers who
'coo over the people the balmy optimisms of a natural and
unconscious Christianity which makes no call upon the will
for positive belief, but delights those who are only at the

aesthetic stage of life'.[96] As he elsewhere said, 'There is a liberalism whose badge is redemption *from* an Apostolic Gospel, and not *by* it'.[97] B. C. Plowright came to the same rueful conclusion and confessed, what is more, that the practical benefits expected of liberalism had quite failed to materialise:

> 'We believed with a *naiveté* which at this distance of time has something sadly humourous about it, that we had but to recast our theological thinking and re-phrase our theological vocabulary, and hey, presto! our church doors would be crowded once more with multitudes of men and women who had been put off religion simply because its theology was old-fashioned and had been exploded by modern science. How could the modern man trained in evolutionary thought be expected to believe in the Fall, in the literal inspiration of the Bible, in the Virgin Birth, a substitutionary theory of the Atonement, and so forth? Whereupon we proceeded to rationalize religion in the conviction that that was all that the modern man needed or desired. Religion became simple commonsense, and whether we intended to do so or not, we left the modern man with the impression that it was all plain sailing, that there neither was nor could be in it either mystery or marvel or anything before which he need bow in the woder of worship.'[98]

P. T. Forsyth put the tendency we have been discussing into historical perspective thus:

> 'The Gnosticism of the second century, the Spiritualism of the sixteenth, and the Protestant liberalism or Roman modernism of the twentieth all represent outcrops of the same pagan tendency to replace faith by insight, to make mere inspiration to do the work of revelation . . . The Reformers lived with the note of revelation, on a theology of facts; the Anabaptists with the note of inspiration, on a theology of consciousness . . . as the vice of the one was to dry into a hard orthodoxy severed from experience, the vice of the other was to deliquesce into a vagrant experience on whose bogs flitted the enticing firedrakes of subjective whim.'[99]

What now of 'hard orthodoxy'? We have said that there are conservative no less than liberal ways of distorting the gospel, and Forsyth has put his finger on one way in which conservatives are guilty. But before we proceed to investigate conservative distortions it will be instructive, by way of a bridge, to see how a recent writer, whose Reformed and conservative credentials are impeccable, has set matters down. Professor-Emeritus R. A. Finlayson enquires whether modernist belief and evangelical faith are the same — and the fact that he enquires as recently as 1973 suggests that to some at least the issue is still a live one. Mr. Finlayson's answer is, not surprisingly, negative: modernism is 'another gospel', and this for the following reasons:

> 'Evangelical Christian belief holds that true religion is from God in the sense that the initiative is with God . . . Modernism holds that . . . all religion . . . is a movement from man to God . . . Evangelical belief holds that *man has reliable authority for his faith in the Holy Scriptures.* Modernist belief holds that *a man's authority for his faith must be found in his own consciousness* . . . Evangelical faith holds that *in Jesus of Nazareth God became man.* Modernist belief holds that *in Jesus of Nazareth man became God* . . . For the evangelical Christian *the Cross of Calvary represents an act of God for the redemption of mankind.* For the modernist *the Cross points the way by which man can save himself* . . . Evangelical faith is that *moral character is the permanent quality in life and that it determines our destiny after death.* Modernist belief is that *life after death is uncertain, but that if the human soul survives, the All-loving Universal Father will treat all His children alike.'[100]

If we qualify Finlayson's 'modernists' by 'some' we can accept much of what he says. Even Machen, we recall, allowed that not all liberals were equally heretical. But there is nothing in the article to suggest that conservatives too can be guilty of reducing the gospel. We shall now make good that omission; and we shall discover that while some conservative errors are the obverse of liberal virtues, others are the peculiar contribution of the conservative mentality.

III

At the outset we must observe that if anything conservatism prevents more internally contradictory gospel-distorting possibilities than liberalism. We do not, therefore, have a straightforward conservative-liberal dichotomy on our hands; we shall often find conservative against conservative. Thus on the one hand there are conservatives who emphasise system, and who tend towards intellectualism in theology and legalism in morality and ecclesiology; on the other hand there are conservatives whose emphasis is upon heart rather than head, who suspect scholarship, sit light to churchmanship, and can become antinomian. As we look at each of these very generalised groups in turn we shall discover that each has its own way of being 'Pelagian'.

Some conservatives, Dr. G. H. Clark among them, set great store by the fact that Christianity is a system. Among others who have taken this stance are Professors Louis Berkhof and Cornelius Van Til. Invariably this position is associated with the doctrine of the plenary inspiration of the Bible — a doctrine which all the writers here named are anxious to distinguish from a 'dictation' theory of inspiration. What they seek is the happy concord of faith and reason; what they oppose is unbiblical rationalism in all its guises. In the hands of some this approach can lead to a gospel-denying scholasticism: to the view that Christianity is a philosophy before it is a religion. Thus D. B. Stevick has criticised Van Til on the ground that 'The God of [his] formulations (i.e. 'a self-complete system of coherence') is one God; the God of Abraham, Isaac, and Jacob is another . . . no one [according to the position criticised] can understand the Gospel except through skill in using the thought-forms of Western culture. This, in turn, means that the more philosophical skill a person shows, the better Christian he is — a kind of modern Gnosticism.'[101] We do not find that in fact Van Til makes so aristocratic a claim as this. But an impression of undue intellectualism can all too easily be created, even if philosophical skill is not held to be the mark of the top-grade Christian. Thus Professor Young has argued that some 'hyper-covenantists' such as Hermann Dooyeweerd, who have exploited certain strands of Kuyper's thought, have disparaged piety and vital religion.[102] It is doubtless because of similar apprehensiveness at this point that, having maintained that in the interests of rationality and of the objectivity of religious truth conservative Protestants uphold the authority of the divinely inspired Bible against ecclesiastical or subjectivist authority, Dr. Henry proceeded to say that 'Evangelical Christianity is not, however, mainly a revealed metaphysic or systematic exposition of supernatural reality; rather, it is the personal assurance of forgiveness of sins and of divine redemption through faith in Christ's mediatorial work for sinners'.[103] Our question is, 'If Christianity is the latter, can it at all (not 'mainly') be the former?' And our answer is that it cannot. The gospel implies a system, but in itself it is not a system. Systems have an educational and expository role — even if they cannot guarantee orthodoxy — but in the last resort, 'It is not mere truths or doctrines, not even if they were guaranteed by a perpetual Divine miracle, that can generate and nourish Christian life, but the personal action of the personal God, rendered possible through Christ's work and through faith in Christ'.[104] As H. R. Mackintosh said, 'Theologies from the first have perished; they wax old as doth a garment; as a vesture Time folds them up, and lays them by. Nothing save the Gospel is abiding, and its years shall not fail'.[105]

Now it is not simply that some conservative theologians emphasise system *per se;* it is that in practice they have to exalt one of a number of *competing* systems, all of which claim to be scripturally based. Thus, *within* the broadly Calvinistic position there were gospel-denying possibilities, as when some found themselves holding that since the elect alone could be saved, and since salvation was the work of God alone, there could be no general overtures, or 'free offers' of the gospel. This position is advocated by the Gospel Standard Baptists, for example, to this day.[106] It is not difficult, however, to find numerous examples to show that this is a minority view among Calvinists — indeed that one Calvinist's systematic meat is another Calvinist's systematic poison. Thus Zanchius, Calvin's younger contemporary, exhorts his readers to emulate Christ and the apostles 'who all . . . took every opportunity of preaching to sinners and enforced their ministry with proper rebukes, invitations and exhortations as occasion required'.[107] Again, the first chapter of the Second Helvetic Confession (1566), prepared by Heinrich Bullinger (1504–75), contains a classic statement of the duty of freely offering the gospel, and of the distinction between the preacher's external call to all hearers and the Holy Spirit's internal call to the elect. 'Beloved', cried Tobias Crisp to his flock, 'will you starve in a cook's shop, as they say? Is there such plenty in Christ, and will you perish for hunger?'[108] Robert Traill expounded the free offer in masterly fashion;[109] John Mason appealed to sinners, 'Come as you are; come poor, come needy, come naked ... His heart is free; His arms are open, 'tis His joy and His crown to receive you';[110] Horatius Bonar reminded his hearers that 'the Gospel is not, "Christ died for the elect"; neither is it "Christ died for all". But it is "Christ died for sinners" '.[111] Finally, in our own time, Professor John Murray and others have defended the free offer of the gospel.[112]

When the contrary position is taken numerous difficulties ensue. How does the preacher know to whom to offer the gospel? What of the perils of undue introspection to which believers are liable when they have so regularly to look within to ensure that they are indeed the 'sensible sinners' for whom Christ died? Small wonder that one of the main questions at issue in the Marrow controversy was that of assurance. Thomas Boston and his colleagues contended that men had the right to know that they had a saving interest in Christ, and they set themselves to defend the free offer of the gospel, thereby becoming the harbingers of revival and missionary zeal in Scotland. Historically, the situation was complicated by a contractual, rather than a truly covenantal theory of grace, and it was against this that McLeod Campbell protested in the nineteenth century. He claimed that the doctrine of limited atonement undermined the free offer of the gospel (whereas the orthodox distinguished between the external and the internal calls),[113] and focussed attention not upon what Christ has done, but upon the contractual duties the sinner needs to have performed — repentance, obedience — and the inward feelings he needs to have, in order to be assured of his right to the gospel. All of which is one conservative variety of 'Pelagianism': God alone elects us, but we have to fulfil certain conditions, *and keep on fulfilling them if we would be sure of it.*[114]

The resultant legalism has persisted in some conservative circles, and that long after the explanatory theology has been forgotten by many. As D. B. Stevick observed of fundamentalism, 'There is a long heritage . . . of inflamed attacks on the theater, John Barleycorn, tobacco, dancing, cardplaying, and other sinful indulgences — in other words, a long heritage of fiddling while Rome burns'.[115] On which mentality the conservative Dr. Carnell made the proper comment:

> 'Fundamentalists defend the gospel, to be sure, but they sometimes act as if the gospel read, "Believe on the Lord Jesus Christ, don't smoke, don't go to the movies, and above all don't use the Revised Standard Version — and you will be saved". Whenever fundamentalism encourages this sort of legalism it falls within the general traditon of the Galatian Judaizers.'[116]

Finally, preoccupation with system can foster that totalitarianism spirit which has caused so much anguish in Christian circles, and which has all too often disrupted the household of faith. It comes as no surprise to discover that one of the factors in giving a new lease of life to the old conservative-liberal disputes is the modern ecumenical movement as represented principally by the World Council of Churches, a body which sits far too lightly to the Bible and to doctrine for the liking of the more thoroughgoing conservative systematisers.[117]

But not all conservatives are system builders. Far from it: some of them abhor systems. Just as some liberals denigrated theology on the ground that it unnecessarily impeded social action, so some conservatives have despised 'book learning', applauded the 'old-time religion' which was good enough for Moses *et al,* and regarded theological seminaries as inventions of the devil designed to drive the last vestiges of faith out of erstwhile 'Bible-believing' ordinands. Such are the results of a *warped* pietism - of a pietism with which Spener and Wesley would by no means have felt at ease.[118] They were neither anti-intellectualist nor individualistic in the pejorative sense.

Conservative individualism shows itself in a variety of ways. It can lead to an anti-Church mentality. This may arise either because the existing churches have become so schismatic in the name of conservative confessionalism that gentler spirits cry 'We are of Christ' and resign; or because the more evangelistic members, having failed to move their fellows to mission, inaugurate separated, and often inter-denominational agencies to meet the need. On occasion both motives may jointly be present. As to the former R. W. Dale rightly advised that 'Evangelical Christians should remember that Individualism involves a suppression of half the duties and a surrender of half the blessedness of the Christian life. The children of God belong to "the household of faith".'[119] Concerning the latter Robert Mackintosh regretted that all too often 'Evangelicalism does not wish to be distracted by any wider moral outlook than the desire to save one's own soul in the first place and, secondly, to promote the salvation of the souls of other individuals . . . Infant baptism is the great rock of offence to the triumphant revival [because it places the infant individual within a covenanted fellowship]'.[120]

Next, the methodology of individualistic, broadly Arminian Christianity can carry 'Pelagian' overtones no less than the exaggerated Calvinism to which we have already referred. William Cunningham detected such overtones in the Morisonianism of his day; the Finney-influenced revivalists of the later nineteenth century further popularised the questionable approach; while the contemporary 'voice over' decision has, we may hope, carried the technique to its technological limit. The error amounts to the view that the individual's action in making a faith commitment is the truly decisive thing. Hence such appeals as, 'Only believe . . .'; 'God wishes to save you — will you let him?' 'Why not decide for Christ now?' These all fail to state (if those who employ such slogans do not fail to believe in) the priority of God's regenerative work; they make it appear that man holds the key to his salvation; and at their worst they present the pitiable, rather than the sovereign, God who cannot make a move without the sinner's permission. None of which is to deny that proper synergism in which God does all and man does all;[121] it is only to disallow that synergism which proclaims that God does part and man does part, but that the former cannot do his part until the latter has done his. Traill rightly expostulated, 'How abominable it is to Christian ears, and how much more unto Christ's, to hear a man plead thus for pardon: "Here is my repentance; where is thy pardon? Here is my faith; where is thy justification?" '[122] Toplady was nearer the mark, 'Nothing in my hand I bring, Simply to Thy cross I cling'.[123]

The emphasis upon the believer's feelings has not only encouraged anti-intellectualism in some varieties of conservatism, it has also spawned antinomianism in ethics.[124] P. T. Forsyth's warning stands against any who would easily set aside law in the supposed interests of grace: 'So many converted lives go wrong and relapse because their conversion has not given them a Sovereign but only a Saviour. And the Christian life is not only gratitude for blessing received, but absolute obedience to a claim that we must own as holy just and good, whether we feel it is our blessing or not.'[125]

Of more practical consequence has been the unfortunate inhibiting effect of conservative individualism upon Christian social ethics. Here we have the obverse of the Social Gospel. There is, of course, no necessary connection between social unconcern and theological conservatism. The Reformed tradition has had its Prime Minister Kuyper, and many of the pietists made a valiant contribution to the social welfare of their fellows: 'Few movements in church history and few schools of theological conviction have been, in proportion to population, so productive of institutional inventiveness and cultural creativity as have been the Moravians, the Methodists, and their counterparts within the larger churches'.[126] Wesley's schools, Whitefield's orphanage, the Clapham Sect, the Salvation Army, the missions of the nineteenth century, the multitude of philanthropic, sometimes quite localised, institutions — all these sought in their several ways to fufil the Christian hope of a world reconciled to God.[127]

In this last phrase we have the clue to the conservative suspicion of the Social Gospel men. The conservatives could not make any easy identification of progress in the world with the coming of the Kingdom; and many of them, since

they thought in terms of an aggregate of saved souls who
together would renew the world, could not challenge those
diseased systems which were the cause of the symptoms
against which they so zealously battled. So great had the
severance of practice from Christian thought been that some
concluded that Wesley and Jonathan Edwards were, as
regards socio-political thought 'rationalists, sons of the
Enlightenment'.[128] Dale had made a similar diagnosis sixty
years earlier:

> 'Although [the leaders of the Evangelical movement]
> insisted very earnestly on the obligation of individual
> Christian men to live a devout and godly life, they had
> very little to say about the relations of the individual
> Christian to the general order of human society, or about
> the realization of the kingdom of God in all the various
> regions of human activity. As the Revival had no great
> ideal of the Church as a Divine institution, it had no great
> ideal of the State as a Divine institution; nor had it any
> great ideal of the Divine order of the world.'[129]

When to this was added the later individualistic thrust of
revivalism and fundamentalism, the prospect of lively Christian social ethics emanating from the conservative side re-
ceded still further. Some indeed saw the need: 'if [the
Church] is to retain its ascendency over the minds of men
[it must] bring Christianity to bear as an applied power on
the life and conditions of society . . . I look to the twentieth century to be an era of Christian Ethic even more than of
Christian Theology'.[130] But the renewal was a long time
coming. Professor Jellema has accurately analysed three ways
in which conservatives rationalised their avoidance of ethical
questions: they exalted separation from the world; they over-
simplified the gospel so that it had to do only with personal
salvation; and they formally repeated the formulations of
Christian ethics of an earlier generation, thus 'evading the
problems of a contemporary society by giving a series of
irrelevant answers'.[131]

IV

With the passage of the years liberalism changed. It is fashion-

able to say that Bath's *Romans* (1919), appearing as it did in
the wake of war, was instrumental in effecting this change.
But Gore, Inge and Temple, Forsyth and Oman, were well
aware of man's sinful malaise before that catastrophe over-
took the nations. On the other hand some, like Albert
Peel, decided *not* to be unduly influenced by Barth, and
maintained their liberal optimism into the 1930s. But that
there was change cannot be denied. Many came to feel
that undue confidence in progress and in man was no
longer to be indulged in. As well as the War there were the
depressions, and the rise of modern totalitarianism. Who was
sufficient? Theologians began to rehabilitate the concept of
transcendence. Among the leading figures in this reappraisal
were Reinhold Niebuhr, W. M. Horton, and John C. Bennett.
In 1934 Horton declared with respect to liberalism that
'Disintegration is not too strong a word. The defeat of the
liberals is becoming a rout'.[132] A further sign of the times was
Fosdick's sermon of 1935, 'The Church must go beyond
Modernism'. He here argued that Modernism had failed in
being too preoccupied with the intellect, in being too sentimental, in diluting the idea of God, and in seeking a too
ready accommodation with the prevailing culture.[133] To the
same period belongs D. R. Davies's *On to Orthodoxy* (1939),
the powerful testimony of a convert from liberalism.

Conservatism too has changed, and that in two main ways.
Those in the tradition represented by Carl Henry — the neo-
evangelicals — have urged a reappraisal of older attitudes. A
catalyst in this regard was Harold J. Ockenga's negative reply
to his own question of 1947, 'Can Fundamentalism win
America?'.[134] These men are open rather than closed; systematic rather than idiosyncratic. Others, under such leaders as
Carl McIntire, have pursued the separatist path, have vehem-
ently opposed the World Council of Churches and, it would
seem, have been more than a little involved in right wing
politics.[135] As Dr. Henry said, 'By mid-century, fundamentalism obviously signified a temperament as fully as a
theology'.[136]

A contemporary debate in conservative circles is that
between those who wish to maintain the doctrine of the
plenary inspiration of the Bible, and those who wish to

advocate the modified view that it is the biblical doctrines which are inerrant.[137] We cannot yet pronounce a verdict upon this debate, though we may dare to hope that the pursuit of inerrancy will not become a world-denying hobby. It cannot yet be said that conservatives have made significant contributions to ecclesiology or to sacramental theology — still less to the question of the theological response to non-Christian religions. They are, however becoming much more ethically conscious, and herein lies hope. The year 1947 saw the publication of Carl Henry's *The Uneasy Conscience of Modern Fundamentalism.* In this book and in many since he has urged his fellow conservatives to develop a doctrine of redemption adequate to the needs of the whole man in all his personal and societal relations.The evangelicals who met in Lausanne in 1974 declared that 'Reconciliation with man is not reconciliation with God, nor is social action evangelism, nor is political liberation salvation. Nevertheless, it is our duty to be involved in socio-political action . . . For both active evangelistic and social involvement are necessary expressions not only of our doctrines of God and man . . . but also of our love for our neighbour and our obedience to Jesus Christ.'[138] Has there so far been more talk than action? Some evangelicals think so, as witness President I. J. Hesselink's diagnosis:

'one of the main reasons for this lack of progress, despite an awareness of the problem, is the unevangelical, i.e. unbiblical, view that social, political, and economic problems are of secondary importance and that these problems can be solved by redeemed individuals without attacking the structures of society which are unjust.

The real problem is that some "evangelicals", like old-time liberals, have operated with a truncated Bible, despite their formal acknowledgment of its authority. They have rung the changes of John 3:16 and Acts 16:31 — "Believe on the Lord Jesus Christ and you shall be saved" — but they have conspicuously ignored the social significance of the Magnificat and the Beatitudes. They have reveled in passages like Isaiah 1:18 — "Though your sins be like scarlet, they shall be white as snow" — but have paid little heed to a major motif in the prophets as summarized in

Amos 5:24 — "Let justice roll down like waters and righteousness like an ever-flowing stream".'[139]

All of which is an attenuation of the gospel.

Before the conservative-liberal debate in modern theology reached its height John 'Rabbi' Duncan said,

> 'Some persons preach only doctrine; that makes people all head, which is a monster. Some preach only experience; that makes people all heart, which is a monster too. Others preach only practice; that makes people all hands and feet, which is likewise a monster. But if you preach doctrine and experience and practice, by the blessing of God, you will have head, and heart, and hands, and feet — a perfect man in Christ Jesus.'[140]

Here is the balance for which we plead; and it presupposes the saving activity of the transcendent yet immanent God, in whose Son we see the truth about his holy self and our needy selves; whose Spirit deepens and challenges our experience, and is ever present with power as we live in the world for his sake. If our study of the conservative-liberal debate in modern theology stimulates us to theologise in a manner consonant with and reflective of this blance, the old disputes will have served us well.

NOTES

CHAPTER ONE

1. H. D. Aiken, *The Age of Ideology,* New York: Mentor Books, 1956, p.15.

2. Kant, *Prolegomena to any Future Metaphysic,* trans. P. G. Lucas, Manchester: Manchester U.P., 1953, p.9.

3. Kant, *Critique of Pure Reason,* trans. J. M. D. Meiklejohn, London: Dent, 1964, p.12.

4. We italicise these words in order to make plain the fact that Kant is not a straightforward idealist. In fact, as Professor H. D. Aiken reminds us, (*op. cit.,* p.33), Kant did not hold that mind is the sole reality, or that the mind creates the world it knows. Further, things-in-themselves are independently real. They are not, however, objects of knowledge, and hence 'about them the understanding has properly nothing whatever to say'. Thus Dr. Alexander is near the mark when he interprets Kant as holding that 'In the constitution of knowledge the mind contributes as much as it receives'. See *The Shaping Forces of Modern Religious Thought,* Glasgow: Maclehose, 1920, p.156. But this assertion must not be understood in such a way as to overlook Kant's powerful streak of realism, or to make him a Berkeleian phenomenalist-idealist who believes that we actually perceive things-in-themselves. Cf. the following paragraph.

5. J. V. Langmead Casserley, *The Christian in Philosophy,* London: Faber, 1949, p.125.

6. A. S. Pringle-Pattison, *The Philosophical Radicals,* Edinburgh and London: Blackwood, 1907, p.224.

7. R. Mackintosh, 'Theism', *Encyc. Brit.,* 11th edn., art. 'Theism'.

8. George Galloway, 'What do religious thinkers owe to Kant?', *The Hibbert Journal,* V, 1907, p.650.

9. C. Van Til, *A Christian Theory of Knowledge,* Philadelphia: Presbyterian and Reformed, 1969, p.153.

10. I. Kant, *Religion within the Limits of Reason Alone,* trans. T. M. Greene and H. H. Hudson, New York: Harper Torchbooks, 1960, p.157n.

11. See A. S. Pringle-Pattison, *op. cit.,* pp.266—7.

12. H. R. Mackintosh, *Types of Modern Theology*, London: Nisbet, 1937, p.23.

13. A. S. Pringle-Pattison, *op. cit.*, p.256.

14. E. Brunner, *The Mediator*, trans. Olive Wyon, Philadelphia: Westminster, n.d., p.142. Cf. H. F. Lovell Cocks, *By Faith Alone*, London: James Clarke, 1943, p.34; and D. M. Mackinnon, 'Kant's Philosophy of Religion', *Philosophy*, L, 1975, pp.131—44.

15. Kant, *Religion within the bounds of Reason Alone*, p.95. Later in the same work, however (pp.178—9), Kant does allow that the idea of grace, *though wholly transcendent*, is one which we are entitled to *assume* will effect in us what nature can not, *on condition that* we use our powers aright. We here verge upon a Pelagianising doctrine of works: in fact God's grace is unconditional, or it is not grace. Again, Kant says that apart from *hope* in grace, we have no confidence that the evil in man will be overcome. Such utilitarianism seems to make a prop out of grace. Michael Despland provides a useful discussion of Kant on grace in his *Kant on History and Religion*, Montreal & London: McGill-Queen's U.P., 1973, chap. IX.

16. Though H. J. Paton (*The Categorical Imperative*, London: Hutchinson, 1947, p.196) writes: Kant's 'Formula of Universal Law, insisting as it does on the spirit as opposed to the letter of the moral law, is his version of the Christian doctrine that we are saved by faith and not by works'. Two comments require to be made here: (i) The formula as here described is rather a plea for integrity and a denunciation of hypocrisy. (ii) The Christian doctrine, which as Professor Paton expresses it might imply that faith itself is a work, is that we are saved by grace through faith.

17. Quoted by C. Welch, *Protestant Thought in the Nineteenth Century*, New Haven and London: Yale U.P., 1972, p.63.

18. A. M. Fairbairn, *Christ in Modern Theology*, London: Hodder & Stoughton, 6th edn., 1894, p.224.

19. Schleiermacher, *The Christian Faith*, trans. and ed. H. R. Mackintosh and J. S. Stewart, Edinburgh: T. & T. Clark, 1960, p.17. For *On Religion* we use trans. J. Oman, New York: Harper Torchbooks, 1958. It is thus misleading when R. S. Franks ('Trends in Recent Theology' *The Congregational Quarterly*, XXIII, 1945, p.22) says that 'Schleiermacher found a new starting-point for theology by going back to Calvin's idea of religion as the way in which we depend upon God'; for to Calvin the dependance was upon a God supernaturally revealed in his Word; to Schleiermacher the supernatural reference is excluded. As W. P. Paterson says, 'What Schleiermacher was impressed by in Christian experience was in truth an important fact — it was the same fact which impressed Calvin when he studied the content of the believing mind and

heart, and was aware of a joyful feeling of assurance that a divine work of reconciliation and regeneration had been wrought, and that it had been wrought by the instrument of the Word of God. The difference was that while Calvin rightly interpreted the feeling as a finger-post pointing to the mine of revealed truth, the subjective school in its typical representatives has looked upon it as being itself the spiritual mine.' *The Rule of Faith*, London: Hodder & Stoughton, 1912, pp.168—9. Compare Van A. Harvey, 'A Word in Defense of Schleiermacher's Theological Method', *The Journal of Religion*, XLII, 1962, pp.151—70 with Franks; and for the alternative view see Kenneth Hamilton, 'Schleiermacher and Relational Theology', *ibid.*, XLIV, 1964, pp.29—39.

20. W. A. Brown, *The Essence of Christianity*, Edinburgh: T. & T. Clark, 1904, p.171.

21. H. R. Mackintosh, *op. cit.*, p.48. Cf. J. Macquarrie's sympathetic article, 'Schleiermacher Reconsidered', *The Expository Times*, LXXX, 1969, pp.196—200; and S. Sykes, 'God and World in Schleiermacher', *The Month*, II, 1970, pp.79—83.

22. Schleiermacher, *On Religion*, p.88.

23. *The Christian Faith*, p.183.

24. G. P. Fisher, *A History of Christian Doctrine* (1896), Edinburgh: T. & T. Clark, 1949, p.510.

25. *The Christian Faith*, p.65.

26. Donald G. Bloesch, 'The Missing Dimension', *Reformed Review*, XXVI, 1973, p.166.

27. Cf. H. R. Mackintosh, *op. cit.*, p.71n. and *On Religion*, p.89.

28. Thus, 'At the Reformation, in the Puritan upheaval, and in the Wesleyan revival, it is much clearer that the preaching of a gospel was a cause of the spiritual convulsion, than that the constituent ideas of this gospel were a description and interpretation of the emotional phenomena'. W. P. Paterson, *op. cit.*, p.128.

29. *The Christian Faith*, p.277.

30. *Ibid.* para. 98.

31. H. F. Lovell Cocks, *op. cit.*, p.98. See *The Christian Faith*, para. 100, and the perceptive comments of James B. Torrance, 'Interpretation and Understanding in Schleiermacher's Theology: Some Critical Questions', *The Scottish Journal of Theology*, XXI, 1968, pp.268—82.

32. H. R. Mackintosh, *op. cit.*, p.100.

33. See e.g. M. F. Wiles, *The Remaking of Christian Doctrine*, London: S.C.M., 1974; and for comments upon it see *inter alia* Nicholas Lash, 'The Remaking of Doctrine: Which way shall we go?', *Irish Theological Quarterly*, XLIII, 1976, pp.36—43.

34. In addition to the works on Hegel referred to below see, J. H. Stirling, *The Secret of Hegel* (1865), Edinburgh: Oliver & Boyd, 1898; Robert Mackintosh, *Hegel and Hegelianism*, Edinburgh: T. & T. Clark, 1903; W. T. Stace, *The Philosophy of Hegel* (1924), London: Macmillan, 1955; B. M. G. Reardon, *Hegel's Philosophy of Religion*, London: Macmillan, 1977.

35. Hegel, *The Phenomenology of Mind*, trans. J. B. Baillie, London: Allen & Unwin, 1931, I, pp.70ff.

36. E. Caird, *Hegel*, Edinburgh and London: Blackwood, 1891, p.124. For Fichte see R. Adamson, *Fichte*, Edinburgh and London: Blackwood, 1881; E. B. Talbot, *The Fundamental Principle of Fichte's Philosophy*, Ithaca: Cornell U.P., 1906; for Schelling see John Watson, *Schelling's Transcendental Idealism*, Chicago: Griggs, 1882.

37. G. R. G. Mure, *The Philosophy of Hegel*, London: O.U.P., 1965, p.40. Cf. W. H. Walsh, *Metaphysics*, London: Hutchinson, 1966, p.72 and chap. IX. See also J. N. Findlay, *Hegel, A Re-examination*, London: Allen & Unwin, 1958, pp.19—23 and 348—51; and Gyorgy Nádor, 'Hegel on Empiricism', *Ratio*, VI, 1964, pp.154—60. Nádor reminds us (p.159) that whereas the empiricist analyst peels the onion until the onion is no more, Hegel is concerned that we shall end up with an onion. He refers us to Hegel's *Encyc.*, II, para. 220, app.

38. G. R. G. Mure, *op. cit.*, p.35.

39. See E. Caird, *op. cit.*, chap. III.

40. E. Caird, *op. cit.*, pp.138, 140.

41. H. D. Aiken, *op. cit.*, p.71.

42. See J. C. O'Neill, 'Bultmann and Hegel', *Journal of Theological Studies*, XXI, 1970, p.400. O'Neill's earlier point to the effect that Hegel and Bultmann rejected the anti-Enlightenment romanticism which made God accessible to feeling only is well made, p.395.

43. L. Harold DeWolf, 'Liberalism: A Re-evaluation. 1 Motifs of Continuity and Discontinuity', *Religion in Life*, XXXII, 1963, p.335. Royce is quoted in support.

44. H. R. Mackintosh, *op. cit.*, p.105.

45. F. H. Bradley, *Appearance and Reality*, London: Swan Sonnenschein, 1893, p.533.

46. D. Miall Edwards, *The Philosophy of Religion*, London: Hodder & Stoughton, 1924, p.277.

47. Hegel, *The Philosophy of History*, trans. J. Sibree, 1857, p.336—7.

48. G. R. G. Mure, 'Hegel, Luther and the Owl of Minerva', *Philosophy*, XLI, 1966, p.132. In this article the question is raised as to whether Hegel really thought that his own position implied its own

supersession — and also, since the two were in his view inextricably interwoven, the supersession of Christianity. The suggestion is made that Hegel's Lutheranism prompted his moments of recoil from eternal flux, though such moments were never decisive.

49. B. Bosanquet, *The Value and Destiny of the Individual,* London: Macmillan, 1913, p.217.

50. R. Niebuhr, *The Nature and Destiny of Man,* London: Nisbet, 1941, I, p.129.

51. A. S. Pringle-Pattison, *op. cit.,* p.291.

52. J. M. E. McTaggart, *Studies in Hegelian Cosmology,* Cambridge: C.U.P., 1901 edn., p.250.

53. H. Davies, *Worship and Theology in England: From Newman to Martineau. 1850—1900,* Princeton and London: Princeton U.P. and O.U.P., 1962, pp.83, 210.

54. A. E. Garvie, *The Missionary Obligation in the light of the Changes of Modern Thought,* London: Hodder & Stoughton, 1914, pp.65—9.

55. For a lucid account of the several varieties of nineteenth-century immanentism, and one to which we are much indebted, see C. C. J. Webb, *A Study of Religious Thought in England from 1850,* Oxford: Clarendon, 1933.

56. For Feuerbach see W. B. Chamberlain, *Heaven wasn't his Destination,* London: Allen & Unwin, 1941.

57. For Comte see E. Caird, *The Social Philosophy and Religion of Comte,* Glasgow: Maclehose, 1885; R. Mackintosh, *From Comte to Benjamin Kidd,* London: Macmillan, 1899.

58. L. E. Elliott-Binns, *English Thought 1860—1900,* London: Longmans Green, 1956, p.65.

59. W. A. McKeever, *Man and the New Democracy,* New York: Doran, 1918, p.94.

60. R. W. Sellars, *The Next Step in Religion,* New York: Macmillan, 1918, p.7. This and the previous quotation are in John Horsch, *Modern Religious Liberalism,* Chicago: The Bible Institute Colportage Assocn., 2nd edn., 1924, pp.69—70.

61. In addition to the surveys of Webb and Elliott-Binns already referred to see for the whole period, John Tulloch., *Movements of Religious Thought in Britain in the Nineteenth Century* (1885) Leicester: Leicester U.P., 1971; Vernon F. Storr, *The Development of English Theology in the Nineteenth Century,* London: Longmans, 1913; B. Willey, *Nineteenth Century Studies,* 1949, and *More Nineteenth Century Studies,* 1956, London: Chatto & Windus; K. Barth, *Protestant Theology in the Nineteenth Century,* London: S.C.M., 1972: C. Welch, *Protestant Thought in the*

Nineteenth Century, I, New Haven and London: Yale U.P. 1972; for the wider scene see L. E. Elliott-Binns, *Religion in the Victorian Era*, London: Lutterworth, 1936; A. R. Vidler, *The Church in an Age of Revolution*, Harmondsworth: Penguin, 1961; Owen Chadwick, *The Victorian Church*, London: A. & C. Black, I, 1966, II, 1970; for the earlier period see B. M. G. Reardon, *From Coleridge to Gore*, London: Longmans, 1971; for the later period see A. M. Ramsey, *From Gore to Temple*, London: Longmans, 1960; J. Macquarrie, *Twentieth-Century Religious Thought*, London: S.C.M., 1963; for selected readings see ed. B. M. G. Reardon, *Religious Thought in the Nineteenth Century*, Cambridge: C.U.P., 1966.

62. V. F. Storr, *op. cit.*, pp.127–30.

63. For Coleridge see C. R. Sanders, *Coleridge and the Broad Church Movement*, Durham, N.C.: Duke U.P., 1942.

64. H. W. Clark, *Liberal Orthodoxy*, London: Chapman & Hall, 1914, p.140.

65. C.Welch, *op. cit.*, p.114.

66. Coleridge, *Aids to Reflection*, 6th edn., 1848, I, pp.168–92.

67. See Lawrence Buell, *Literary Transcendentalism*, Ithaca and London: Cornell U.P., 1973, p.4. For Channing see *Memoir* by W. H. Channing, London, 1848; for Emerson see J. E. Cabot, *A Memoir of Ralph Waldo Emerson*, 2 vols., 1887, and B. Perry, *Emerson Today*, Princeton: Princeton U.P., 1931; for Parker see J. Weiss, *Life and Correspondance of Theodore Parker*, New York, 1884; for Bushnell see M. B. Chaney, *Life and Letters of Horace Bushnell*, New York, 1880, and T. T. Munger, *Horace Bushnell, Preacher and Theologian*, Boston: 1899.

68. *Ibid.*, p.5. He further notes that 'Almost all reached Transcendentalism by way of Unitarianism before they were thirty years old; more than half were at least trained for the Unitarian ministry; almost all the men attended Harvard. Many were from backgrounds of wealth and gentility . . .' p.7. Not indeed that all Unitarians were open to new ideas. Some remained epistemologically with Locke, and R. V. Holt, commenting on the reception accorded by his fellow Unitarians to Martineau notes George Armstrong, faithful to Locke, who confessed 'to a hatred of the instinctive, transcendental and what-not German school of moral and metaphysical philosophy — the spawn of Kant's misunderstood speculations — the dreams of the half-crazed Coleridge, and the inane fancy of the Hares, Sterlings, Whewells, in loud and varied succession since'. See R. V. Holt, *The Unitarian Contribution to Social Progress in England*, London: Lindsey Press, 2nd rev. edn., 1952, p.343.

69. John McLachlan, *The Divine Image*, London: Lindsey Press, 1972,

p.158. He further quotes Martineau (*Essays* I, p.103) as saying that Channing's 'sense of the inherent greatness of man' was 'a fundamental point of faith'.

70. T. Parker, *Works* 1863, I, p.104.

71. For Campbell see ed. Donald Campbell, *Reminiscences and Reflections*, London: Macmillan, 1873, and *Memorials of the Rev. John McLeod Campbell*, 2 vols., London: Macmillan, 1877; J. B. Torrance, 'The Contribution of McLeod Campbell to Scottish Theology,' *The Scottish Journal of Theology*, XXVI, 1973, pp. 295–311.

72. For Carlyle see D. A. Wilson, *Life of Thomas Carlyle*, 6 vols., London: Kegan Paul, 1923–34.

73. Thirlwall and Hare are in *D.N.B.*, as is Maurice, for whom see also, ed. J. Frederick Maurice, *The Life of Frederick Denison Maurice*, London: Macmillan, 2 vols., 1884; A. R. Vidler, *The Theology of F. D. Maurice*, London: S.C.M. Press, 1948; A. M. Ramsey, *F. D. Maurice and the Conflict of Modern Theology*, Cambridge: C.U.P., 1951; O. J. Brose, *F. D. Maurice, Rebellious Conformist*, Ohio: Ohio U.P., 1971; F. M. McClain, *Maurice, Man and Moralist*, London: S.P.C.K., 1972.

74. In addition to the general works listed above see P. O. G. White, 'Essays and Reviews', *Theology*, LXIII, 1960, pp.46–53; Ieuan Ellis, ' "Essays and Reviews" Reconsidered', *ibid.*, LXXIV, 1971, pp.396–404.

75. H. D. A. Major in *The Modern Churchman*, XI, 1921, p.357; quoted by A. M. Ramsey, *op. cit.*, p.73.

76. For Caird see H. Jones and J. H. Muirhead, *The Life and Philosophy of Edward Caird*, Glasgow: Maclehose, 1921; for Green see W. H. Fairbrother, *The Philosophy of T. H. Green*, London: Methuen, 1896. For accounts of how Hegelianism came to England see J. H. Muirhead, *The Platonic Tradition*, chap. II, and A. M. Quinton, 'Absolute Idealism', *Proc. British Academy*, LVII, 1971, espec. pp.322–6; James Bradley, 'Hegel in Britain: a brief history of British commentary and attitudes', *The Heythrop Journal*, XX, 1979, pp.1–24, 163–82. For some theological reactions to idealism see A. P. F. Sell, 'Christian and Secular Philosophy in Britain at the Beginning of the Twentieth Century', *The Downside Review*, XCIII, 1975, pp.122–43.

77. E. Caird's preface to *Essays in Philosophical Criticism*, eds. A. Seth and R. B. Haldane, London: Longmans, 1883, p.5. Caird explains that by this remark Green meant that 'the first development of idealistic thought in Germany had in some degree anticipated what can be the *secure* result only of wider knowledge and more complete reflexion'.

78. C. C. J. Webb, *op. cit.*, pp.100, 109–11.

79. H. R. Mackintosh, 'A Philosopher's Theology', reprinted in his *Some Aspects of Christian Belief,* London: Hodder & Stoughton, 1923.

80. A. S. Pringle-Pattison, *The Idea of God in the Light of Recent Philosophy,* London: O.U.P., 2nd edn., 1920, p.157.

81. H. R. Mackintosh, *op. cit.,* p.266.

82. A. C. McGiffert, 'Divine Immanence and the Christian Purpose', *The Hibbert Journal,* V, 1907, p.777.

83. A. E. Garvie, *The Christian Certainty Amid the Modern Perplexity,* London: Hodder & Stoughton, 1910, p.138.

84. H. R. Mackintosh, *op. cit.,* p.300.

85. L. Hodgson, *The Grace of God in Faith and Philosophy,* London: Longmans, 1936, pp.110–1.

86. Quoted by H. R. Mackintosh, *op. cit.,* p.294.

87. In confining ourselves to Campbell, as being an influential because popular exponent of the New Theology, we do not deny the impact of post-Hegelian immanentism upon such Roman Catholic modernists as George Tyrrell (1861–1909). Under the influence of Gore, Campbell subsequently returned to a more orthodox position, ended his sojourn with the Congregationalists, and reverted to the Anglican Church of his youth, finally becoming Canon and Chancellor of Chichester Cathedral. While he was still in sympathy with the New Theology Campbell wrote 'The Aim of the New Theology Movement', *The Hibbert Journal,* V, 1907, pp.481–93. Into the Social Gospel aspects of the New Theology we do not here enquire; but see pp.106–7 below and our concluding chapter. Campbell is in *Who Was Who* for 1951–60, but was not in *D.N.B.* See his *A Spiritual Pilgrimage,* London: Williams and Norgate, 1916.

88. R. J. Campbell, *The New Theology,* London: Chapman & Hall, 1907, p.4.

89. *Ibid.*

90. *Ibid.,* p.18.

91. *Ibid.,* p.174.

92. Donald G. Bloesch quotes this phrase of Campbell's in the course of making the point that men otherwise as various as William Blake, T. J. Altizer, Michel Quoist, J. A. T. Robinson, R. Gregor Smith, and Campbell himself have, by reason of a 'pan-sacramentalist or pantheistic orientation' lost the distinction between 'the holy and the profane, the spiritual and the secular'. See *Reformed Review,* XXVI, 1973, p.164.

93. On the contrary, he advocated what he called '*liberal* catholicism'. His *Lux Mundi* paper on 'The Holy Spirit and Inspiration' grieved

some of the older Anglo-Catholics, notably H. P. Liddon (1829−90), who had earlier recommended the appointment of Gore to the Principalship of Pusey House.

94. C. Gore, *The Old Religion and the New Theology*, London: John Murray, 1907, pp.43−4. Professor E. A. Sonnenschein regarded the New Theology as 'The New Stoicism'. See his article of that title in *The Hibbert Journal*, V, 1907, pp.541−53. He concludes, 'Shall I misrepresent the facts if I say that any doctrine of Immanence approaches Stoicism in proportion as it regards God as transcending man only in the sense in which a whole transcends a part?'.

95. *The Baptist Times*, 8.2.1907, quoted by Keith W. Clements, 'God at Work in the World: Old Liberal and New Secular Theology', *The Baptist Quarterly*, XXIV, 1972, p.349.

CHAPTER TWO

1. The second edn., *Prolegomena zur Geschichte Israels*, appeared in 1883; E. T., 1885. *Die Komposition des Hexateuchs und der historischen Bucher des Alten Testaments* was published in 1885.

2. See his *Tractatus Theologico-Politicus*, chap. IV; especially p.94 in the 1862 E.T.

3. See especially Locke's *An Essay for the Understanding of St. Paul's Epistles by consulting St. Paul himself*, 1707.

4. Reimarus's work received fresh attention with the publication in 1906 of A. Schweitzer's *Von Reimarus zu Wrede* (E.T.: *The Quest of the Historical Jesus*, 1910).

5. Quoted by H. McLachlan, *The Unitarian Movement in the Religious Life of England*, London: Allen & Unwin, 1934, pp.14−5. All the Britons named in this para. are in *D.N.B.* See also Alexander Gordon, *Heads of English Unitarian History*, London: Green, 1895.

6. H. McLachlan, *op. cit.*, p.51. The demand had also been made by Coleridge in his posthumous *Confessions of an Enquiring Spirit*, 1840. In this work Coleridge gave conservatives a weapon: 'Whatever finds me must have proceeded from the Holy Spirit'.

7. The latter designation better accommodates the fact that Henry H. Milman (1791−1868) was of Brasenose College, Oxford, while Connop Thirlwall (1797−1875) was a Fellow of Trinity College, Cambridge. In view of our ascription of liberalising tendencies to the Noetics it is noteworthy that in 1827 Whately found John Henry Newman (1801−90), then of the later Oriel, or Tractarian school, *too* liberal for his liking. Indeed he accused him of Arian-

izing. See Newman's *Apologia pro vita sua* (1864), London: Dent, 1946, p.38. For the Noetics see John Tulloch, *Movements of Religious Thought in Britain during the Nineteenth Century* (1885), Leicester: Leicester U.P., 1971, Lect. II.

8. V. F. Storr, *The Development of English Theology in the Nineteenth Century, 1800–1860,* London: Longmans, 1913, p.119.

9. On this see chapter I above.

10. For Scott see *The Evangelical Magazine,* 1858, pp.757–61; for Clulow see *D.N.B.* For the episode referred to see K. W. Wadsworth, *Yorkshire United Independent College,* London: Independent Press, 1954, pp.113–4.

11. We recall the similar position of Erskine of Linlathen (1788–1870) who declared that the Bible's authority may only rightly be acknowledged by us 'when we discern its agreement with the testimony of the spiritual witness within us'. See his *The Doctrine of Election,* London, 1837, p.525.

12. *The Evangelical Magazine,* 1846, p.529.

13. See R. Tudor Jones, *Congregationalism in England 1662–1962,* London: Independent Press, 1962, pp.248–9.

14. Thus described in H. S. Skeats and C. S. Miall, *History of the Free Churches of England 1688–1891,* London, n.d. but preface has 1891, p.547.

15. For Lynch see *D.N.B.* and ed. William White, *Memoirs of Thomas T. Lynch,* London: Ibister, 1874.

16. Quoted by Skeats and Miall, *op. cit.,* p.547. For the controversy see *ibid.* pp.547–51; A. Peel, *These Hundred Years,* London: Independent Press, 1931, pp.142–58; R. T. Jones, *op. cit.,* pp. 249–51.

17. For Davidson see *D.N.B.* Supplement; *The Autobiography and Diary of Samuel Davidson* ed. by his daughter Anne J. Davidson, Edinburgh: T. & T. Clark, 1899; R. Allen, *The Presbyterian College Belfast 1853–1953,* Belfast: Mullan, 1954, pp.44–6, 307–8.

18. See J. Thompson, *Lancashire Independent College 1843–1893,* Manchester: Cornish, 1893, pp.127–8; R. T. Jones, *op.cit.,* pp. 254–6. John Lea, 'Historical source materials on Congregationalism in Nineteenth century Lancashire', *The Journal of the United Reformed Church History Society,* I, 1974, pp.110–1, and 'The Davidson controversy', *Durham University Journal,* LXVIII, 1975, pp.15–32. For Vaughan see his *Memorials,* 1869 and *The Congregational Year Book,* 1869. Before becoming the first Principal of Lancashire College he was Professor of Modern History at London University. For many years he edited the *British Quarterly Review.* His son, Robert Alfred Vaughan (1823–57) wrote *Hours with the Mystics* (1856) which went through

many editions; and a long essay on Schleiermacher (among the first by a Briton) appears in his *Remains* (1858, enlarged edn. 1864). And see *D.N.B.* and *Cong. Y.B.* For the entire period see W. B. Glover, *Evangelical Nonconformists and Higher Criticism in the Nineteenth Century,* London: Independent Press, 1954 and H. D. McDonald, *Theories of Revelation 1860—1960,* London: Allen & Unwin, 1960.

19. For Colenso see G. W. Cox, *The Life of John William Colenso D.D.,* 2 vols., London, 1888; Peter B. Hinchliff, *John William Colenso, Bishop of Natal,* London: Nelson, 1964. Wilberforce and Colenso are in *D.N.B.*; Burgon is in *D.N.B. Supplement. The Nonconformist* of 10th Feb. 1864 found the official judgements on both *Essays and Reviews* and Colenso to be such as to pose a serious threat to the evangelical faith.

20. D. F. Strauss, *A New Life of Jesus for the German People,* E.T., 1865, I, p.xii. Among recent studies of Strauss, Baur etc. see Claude Welch, *Protestant Thought in the Nineteenth Century,* New Haven and London: Yale U.P., 1972; see also the reissue of George Eliot's trans. of Strauss's *The Life of Jesus Critically Examined,* London: S.C.M., 1973.

21. A. M. Fairbairn, *The Place of Christ in Modern Theology,* London: Hodder & Stoughton, 1894, pp.235—7.

22. W. Dinwiddie in *Disputed Questions of Belief,* London: Hodder & Stoughton, 1874, p.108.

23. See Robert Morgan, 'F. C. Baur's lectures on New Testament theology', *The Expository Times,* LXXXVIII, 1977, p.203.

24. J. Orr, *The Bible Under Trial,* London: Marshall, 1907, p.14; cf. his more scholarly work, *The Problem of the Old Testament,* London: Nisbet, 1908, for which he won the Bross Prize for 1905.

25. J. MacLeod, *Scottish Theology in relation to Church History since the Reformation* (1943), Edinburgh: The Banner of Truth Trust, 1974, p.226. For the controversy see H. F. Henderson, *The Religious Controversies of Scotland,* Edinburgh: T. & T. Clark, 1905, chap. VI. In the previous century Semler (1725—91) had argued that there was no evidence that the compilers of the canon were specially inspired. See V. F. Storr, *op. cit.,* p.171. Haldane, Wardlaw and Irving are in *D.N.B.* It was Haldane's influence which led F. S. R. L. Gaussen (1790—1863) to the Reformed position. The latter's *Theopneusty* (1842) was very influential in conservative circles.

26. See H. F. Henderson, *op. cit.* chap. XI; J. S. Black and G. W. Chrystal, *The Life of William Robertson Smith,* London: A. & C. Black, 1912.

27. Quoted by W. J. Grier, *The Origin and Witness of the Irish Evangel-*

ical Church (now the Evangelical Presbyterian Church), Belfast: Evangelical Book Shop, [1945], p.12.

28. B. B. Warfield, *Critical Reviews,* New York: O.U.P., 1932, p.127.

29. Lewis F. Stearns, 'The present direction of theological thought in the Congregational churches of the United States', *Proceedings of the International Congregational Council,* 1891, p.83.

30. See D. H. Kromminga, *The Christian Reformed Tradition,* Grand Rapids: Ecrdmans, 1943, pp.143—7.

31. See e.g. Ernest R. Sandeen, *The Roots of Fundamentalism,* Chicago and London: Chicago U.P., 1970, chap. VIII.

32. See Loisy's *Mémoires,* 1930—1; M. D. M. Petre, *Alfred Loisy: His Religious Significance,* Cambridge: C.U.P., 1944; A. R. Vidler, *The Modernist Movement in the Roman Catholic Church,* Cambridge: C.U.P., 1934; B. M. G. Reardon, *Roman Catholic Modernism,* London: A. & C. Black, 1970.

33. William Robertson Nicholl, quoted by W. B. Glover, *op. cit.,* p.200, from T. H. Darlow, *William Robertson Nicholl,* London: Hodder & Stoughton, 1925, p.341. For a contemporary critique of the Princetonian 'scholasticism' concerning the Bible see T. M. Lindsay, 'The doctrine of Scripture. The Reformers and the Princeton school', *The Expositor,* 5th ser., I, 1895, pp.278—93.

34. For Rogers see D. N. B.; *The Congregationalist,* 1877, pp.654—64; *The Evangelical Magazine,* 1877, pp.599—602; A. P. F. Sell, 'Henry Rogers and the Eclipse of Faith', *The Journal of the United Reformed Church History Society,* II, May 1980, pp.128—43. For Cave see *D.N.B.* Supplement and *Cong. Y.B.,* 1902.

35. *Sword and Trowel,* Aug. 1887, p.397.

36. J. Clifford, 'Baptist Theology', *Contemporary Review,* LIII, 1888, p.506. For the controversy see Spurgeon's Autobiography II: *The Full Harvest,* Edinburgh: The Banner of Truth Trust, 1973, chap. XXVIII; biogs. of Spurgeon by R. Shindler, London: Passmore & Alabaster, 1892; W. Y. Fullerton, London: Williams & Norgate, 1923; J. C. Carlile, London: Kingsgate, 1933, etc. Iain Murray, *The Forgotten Spurgeon,* London: The Banner of Truth Trust, 1966; D. Kingdon, 'C. H. Spurgeon and the Down Grade controversy' in *The Good Fight of Faith,* London: Westminster Conference and Evangelical Press, 1971, pp.35—50; and refs. in W. B. Glover, *op. cit.;* John W. Grant, *Free Churchmanship in England 1870—1940,* London: Independent Press, n.d.; Baptist histories by W. T. Whitley (1923) and A. C. Underwood (1947); E. A. Payne, *The Baptist Union,* London: Carey Kingsgate, 1958, chap. VII. For Clifford see *D.N.B.*; ed. J. Marchant, *Life, Letters etc. of Dr. John Clifford,* London: Cassell, 1924; C. T. Bateman, *John Clifford,* London: National Council of the Evangelical Free Churches, n.d.

37. In a sermon on 'The Evangelical Revival' reprinted in the book of the same name, London: Hodder & Stoughton, 1880, p.21.

38. R. F. Horton, *An Autobiography*, London: Allen & Unwin, 1917, p.85.

39. C. Gore in *Lux Mundi*, London: John Murray, 15th edn., 1904, p.250.

40. D. W. Simon, 'The present direction of theological thought in the Congregational churches of Great Britain', *Proceedings of the International Congregational Council*, 1891, p.250.

41. Joseph Parker, *A Preacher's Life*, London: Hodder & Stoughton, 1903, pp.116–7.

42. G. Campbell Morgan, *Christ and the Bible*, London: Hodder & Stoughton, 1907, p.4.

43. J. C. Ryle, *Higher Criticism*, London: Thynne, n.d., pp.3, 8.

44. *The Religious Reformer*, Nov. 1883; cf. A. P. F. Sell, 'The social and literary contributions of three Unitarian ministers in nineteenth-century Walsall', *Transactions of the Unitarian History Society*, XV, 1973, p.93.

45. W. Van Mildert, *An Inquiry into the General Principles of Scripture Interpretation*, Oxford, 1815, p.190.

46. James Drummond, *Via, Veritas, Vita*, London: Williams & Norgate, 1894, p.84.

47. A. M. Fairbairn, *op. cit.*, p.502.

48. *Ibid.*, p.508.

49. Westcott, Hort, Lightfoot, Dale and Fairbairn are in *D.N.B.* (Dale is in the Supplement). See also, ed. A. Westcott, *Life and Letters of Brooke Foss Westcott*, 2 vols., London: Macmillan, 1903; ed. A. F. Hort, *Life and Letters of F. J. A. Hort*, 2 vols., London: Macmillan, 1896; attrib. to H. W. Watkins, *Bishop Lightfoot*, reprinted from *The Quarterly Review* with an introduction by B. F. Westcott, London: Macmillan, 1894; A. W. W. Dale, *Life of R. W. Dale*, London: Hodder & Stoughton, 1898; W. R. Selbie, *Life of Andrew Martin Fairbairn*, London: Hodder & Stoughton, 1914.

50. J. T. Wilkinson, *1662 and After*, London: Epworth, 1962, p.151, quoting the *Manchester Guardian*, 19th Aug. 1929. Peake himself paid tribute to the work of S. R. Driver (1846–1914) in the same connection. See L. S. Peake, *Arthur Samuel Peake*, London: Hodder & Stoughton, 1930, pp.74–5. See further *D.N.B.* 1922–30 and J. T. Wilkinson, *Arthur Samuel Peake*, London: Epworth, 1971.

51. A. S. Peake, *The Nature of Scripture*, London: Hodder & Stoughton, 1922, pp.38–9.

52. Quoted by E. J. Poole-Connor, *Evangelicalism in England*, Worthing: Henry E. Walter, rev. edn., 1966, p.251.

53. Quoted *ibid.*

54. See Harold H. Rowdon, *London Bible College: The First 25 Years*, Worthing: Henry E. Walter, 1968. The work at post-graduate level of Tyndale House, Cambridge, and of the Tyndale Fellowship for Biblical Research should not be overlooked.

55. R. W. Dale, *Essays and Addresses*, London: Hodder & Stoughton, 1899, pp.3—4.

56. *Ibid.*, p.5.

CHAPTER THREE

1. It goes without saying that the literature on Darwin and (what is by no means entirely the same thing) evolutionism is vast. Since we are concerned not so much with scientific detail as with evolution as a theme in nineteenth century thought it will suffice to mention the following works in addition to the writings of Darwin, T. H. Huxley and Spencer, and to the works to be noted later: H. F. Osborn, *From the Greeks to Darwin*, New York: Columbia U.P., 1894; A. R. Wallace, *Darwinianism*, London: Macmillan, 1909; J. Huxley, *Evolution: The Modern Synthesis*, London: Allen & Unwin, 1942; C. C. Gillespie, *Genesis and Geology*, Cambridge, Mass.: Harvard U.P., 1951; R. E. D. Clark, *Darwin, Before and After*, Exeter: Paternoster, 1966: James R. Moore, *The Post-Darwinian Controversies: A Study of the Protestant Struggle to come to terms with Darwin in Great Britain and America, 1870—1900*, Cambridge: C.U.P., 1979.

2. See chapter I above.

3. This was, of course, a spirit upon which the Oxford Movement capitalised, and it goes far towards accounting for what E. B. Pusey (1800—82) called 'ecclesiastical antiquity': 'If a Reformed Church must be a student of Scripture, a Catholic Church must add to the study of Scripture that of ecclesiastical antiquity'. See H. P. Liddon, *Life of E. B. Pusey*, 4 vols., 1893—7, London: Longmans, I, p.336.

4. James Orr, *God's Image in Man*, London: Hodder & Stoughton, 1907, p.84.

5. T. Rhondda Williams, *The Working Faith of a Liberal Theologian*, London: Williams & Norgate, 1914, p.205.

6. A. J. Balfour, *Theism and Thought*, London: Hodder & Stoughton, [1923], p.8.

7. David Young, 'The impact of Darwinianism on the concept of God in the nineteenth century', *Faith and Thought*, CI, 1972, p.25. The entire article is most illuminating, particularly on the more

strictly scientific aspects of the debate. It is amply furnished with references.

8. See his *The Relation between the Holy Scriptures and some parts of Geological Science*, 1839.

9. L. Elliott-Binns quoting Cook's *Life of Ruskin* in *English Thought 1860–1900*, London: Longmans, 1956, p.175n.

10. R. W. Dale, *The Living Christ and the Four Gospels*, London: Hodder & Stoughton, 1895, p.5.

11. Chambers's work appeared anonymously, and it was not until 1884 that the author's identity was made public. See Robert M. Young, 'The impact of Darwin on conventional thought' in ed. A. Symonndson, *The Victorian Crisis of Faith*, London: S.P.C.K., 1970, p.16. This article, though factually informative, contains some generalisations of the kind which abound in discussions of evolution, and which it is part of our purpose to modify. Thus Mr. Young says that 'what evolution took away from man's spiritual hopes by separating science and theology and making God remote from nature's laws, it gave back in the doctrine of material and social and spiritual progress' (p.27). But by no means all evolutionists adopted the *quasi*-deistic stance here implied. Idealistic-immanentist evolutionists were, as we shall see, of quite another mind.

12. Wallace's paper and Darwin's abstract appeared in 1858 in the same number of *The Journal of the Linnaean Society*.

13. E. Griffith-Jones, *Providence — Divine and Human*, London: Hodder & Stoughton, 1925, p.22.

14. Quoted by Darwin's son Francis in his *Charles Darwin*, London: John Murray, 1908, p.58.

15. Ed. F. Darwin, *The Life and Letters of Charles Darwin*, London: John Murray, 1887, II, p.289. By the same token Darwin refused to allow Marx to dedicate the English edition of *Das Kapital* to him on the ground that he did not wish to be associated with attacks on Christianity and theism. See R. M. Young in *op. cit.* p.31 and refs. Again, when Tennyson asked Darwin whether his conclusions adversely affected Christianity he replied, 'No, certainly not'. See L. Elliott-Binns, *op. cit.*, p.37.

16. Hence the celebrated 'Monkey Trial' of as late as 1925 in which William Jennings Bryan successfully prosecuted John T. Scopes for having broken the law of Tennessee by denying Biblical creationism and teaching that man had ascended from lower forms of life. For this case see e.g. Stewart G. Cole, *The History of Fundamentalism* (1931), Westport: Greenwood Press, 1971. Dr. C. F. H. Henry draws attention to the naturalistic, anti-theistic impetus of John Dewey upon American thought, and points out that whereas in the first edition of the *International Standard Bible Dictionary*,

whose General Editor was Dr. James Orr, there was an article in favour of evolution and one against, in the second edition (1929) the latter deficiency was made good. See his *Evangelical Responsibility in Contemporary Theology*, Grand Rapids: Eerdmans, 1957, p.41. With Dewey may be contrasted John Stuart Mill, who conceded that the hypothesis of a limited God was not altogether improbable, and who was anxious to maintain the mind-body distinction, and to deny that the former could be understood exclusively in naturalistic terms.

17. T. H. Huxley, *Lay Sermons, Addresses and Reviews*, London: Macmillan, 1870, p.330. He further explained: 'According to Teleology, each organism is like a rifle bullet fired straight at a mark; according to Darwin, organisms are like grapeshot of which one hits something and the rest fall wide' (p.331). For example, where Teleology says that cats exist in order to catch mice, Darwinism says that (surviving) cats exist because they catch mice well (p.332). Cf. John Oman's way of making the point in *The Natural and The Supernatural*, Cambridge: C.U.P., 1931, p.259: 'All that put Darwin's theory in motion — the purpose of the living creature, its will to live, its subjective selection from environment, its choice of partners — instead of being the positive, directive, creative elements of evolution, were regarded merely as results'.

18. J. Orr, *God's Image in Man*, p.95.

19. C. Darwin, *The Descent of Man*. London: John Murray, 1871, II, p.395. In Darwin's view the term 'chance' was used to acknowledge plainly our ignorance of the cause of each particular variation. See *The Origin of Species*, London: Dent, 1963, p.128.

20. Quoted by J. S. Bezzant, *Aspects of Belief*, London: Nisbet, 1937, p.23.

21. Quoted by J. Orr, *God's Image in Man*, p.89, n.2.

22. A. M. Fairbairn, *Studies in Religion and Theology*, New York: Macmillan, 1910, p.92.

23. Cf. e.g. James Iverach, *Theism in the Light of Present Science and Philosophy*, London: Hodder & Stoughton, 1900, p.73. The same writer provides a still useful survey of the evolution debate in his *Christianity and Evolution*, London: Hodder & Stoughton, 1894.

24. Quoted by Horton Davies, *Worship and Theology in England; From Newman to Martineau, 1850—1900*, Princeton: Princeton U.P. and O.U.P., 1962, p.173.

25. R. W. Dale, *Fellowship with Christ*, London: Hodder & Stoughton, 1900, p.186.

26. W. R. Inge, *God and the Astronomers*, London: Longmans, 1933, p.142.

27. H. G. Wood, *Belief and Unbelief since 1850*, Cambridge: C.U.P., 1955, p.53.

28. A. N. Whitehead, *Science and the Modern World*, New York: C.U.P., 1926, p.157.

29. R. Otto, *Naturalism and Religion*, London: Williams & Norgate, 1907, p.89.

30. B. Powell, *Essays on the Spirit of the Inductive Philosophy*, 1855, p.168.

31. A. J. Balfour, *op. cit.*, pp.237—8. We prefer Balfour's destruction to his construction — or, in the more homiletic tones of R. W. Dale: 'Let us stand erect, and scorn ourselves for the baseness which would acknowledge the supremacy of the unintelligent and unconscious forces of physical nature. Reason, memory, speculation — these raise us to a nobler rank.' *Fellowship with Christ*, p.176. Among the msot celebrated philosophical refutations of naturalism is G. H. Howison's 'The limits of evolution', reprinted in W. G. Muelder and L. Sears (eds.), *The Development of American Philosophy*, Boston: Houghton Mifflin, 1940, pp.262—77.

32. H. Spencer, *First Principles*, 1862, p.46.

33. J. Iverach, *Christianity and Evolution*, p.208.

34. J. Iverach, *Theism in the Light of Present Science and Philosophy*, pp.94—5.

35. H. R. Mackintosh, *Some Aspects of Christian Belief*, London: Hodder & Stoughton, [1923], pp.284—5.

36. J. Orr, *God's Image in Man*, p.96.

37. A. E. Garvie, *The Christian Doctrine of the Godhead*, London: Hodder & Stoughton, 1925, p.14.

38. *Ibid.*, p.184. Cf. *id.*, *A Handbook of Christian Apologetics*, London: Duckworth, 1913, p.214.

39. Kingsley wrote, 'My doctrine has been for years . . . that below all natural phenomena, we come to a transcendental — in plain English, a miraculous ground'. See his *Letters and Memories of His Life*, ed. by his wife, 9th edn. London: Kegan Paul, 1877, II, p.67.

40. E. Griffith-Jones, *op. cit.*, pp.125—6.

41. D. M. Emmet, *The Nature of Metaphysical Thinking* (1945), London: Macmillan, 1966, p.84.

42. For Ward see *D.N.B.*, 1941—50; for Bergson see *inter alia* H. W. Carr, *Henri Bergson*, London: T. C. & E. Jack, 1912; A. D. Lindsay, *The Philosophy of Bergson*, London: Dent, 1911; B. Russell, *The Philosophy of Bergson*, Cambridge: C.U.P., 1914; J. McK. Stewart, *A Critical Examination of Bergson's Philosophy*, London: Macmillan, 1912.

43. W. R. Inge, *op. cit.*, pp.137–8.

44. D. M. Baillie, *Faith in God and its Christian Consummation* (1927), London: Faber, 1964, p.276.

45. For these philosophers see J. W. McCarthy, *The Naturalism of Samuel Alexander*, New York: King's Crown Press, 1948; William McDougall, *Modern Materialism and Emergent Evolution*, London: Methuen, 1929; D. M. Emmet, *Whitehead's Philosophy of Organism*, London: Macmillan, 1932; W. Mays, *The Philosophy of Whitehead*, London: Allen & Unwin, 1959.

46. J. Scott Lidgett, *The Christian Religion*, London: Culley, [1907], p.59. Among numerous books designed to relate evolutionary theory to Christian doctrine we note, S. A. McDowall, *Evolution and the Need of Atonement*, Cambridge: C.U.P., 1912; F. Hastings and A. F. Muir (eds.) *Christianity and Evolution*, London: Nisbet, 1887.

47. A. E. Garvie, *The Christian Doctrine of the Godhead*, p.318. He here echoes many others, e.g. A. M. Fairbairn, *The City of God*, London: Hodder & Stoughton, 1903, p.60.

48. A. E. Garvie, *A Handbook of Christian Apologetics*, pp.58–9. Cf. A. C. Fraser, *Philosophy of Theism*, Edinburgh and London: Blackwood, 1899, p.210.

49. A. E. Garvie, *A Handbook*, p.209.

50. A. C. Fraser, *op. cit.*, p.281.

51. O. C. Quick, *The Ground of Faith and the Chaos of Thought*, London: Nisbet, 1931, p.132.

52. Quoted by Gordon Harland, *The Thought of Reinhold Niebuhr*, New York: O.U.P., 1960, p.99. Cf. the similar view of Condorcet (1743–94) and the Encyclopaedists.

53. J. Martineau, *The Seat of Authority in Religion*, London: Longmans, 1890, p.17.

54. A. E. Garvie, *The Christian Doctrine of the Godhead*, p.214.

55. A. E. Garvie, *A Handbook*, pp.116–7.

56. W. R. Inge, *op. cit.*, p.154.

57. C. Darwin, *The Origin of Species*, London: Dent, 1963, p.462.

58. L. F. Stearns, 'The present direction of theological thought in the Congregational churches of the United States', *Proceedings of the International Congregational Council*, 1891, p.81.

59. J. Iverach, *Christianity and Evolution*, p.207.

60. H. Scott Holland, *Personal Studies*, London: Wells Gardner, Darton, 1905, p.173.

61. J. Dickie, *The Organism of Christian Truth*, London: James Clarke, [1930], p.154.

62. J. Orr, *Sin as a Problem of Today,* London: Hodder & Stoughton, 1910, p.139.

63. J. Orr, *Sidelights on Christian Doctrine,* London: Marshall, [1909], p.94.

64. J. Orr, *The Progress of Dogma,* London: James Clarke, [1901], p.328.

65. Professor Robert Watts attacked the relativism of Henry Drummond's *Ascent of Man* (1894) in his *Professor Drummond's 'Ascent of Man' and Principal Fairbairn's 'Place of Christ in Modern Theology', Examined in the Light of Science and Revelation,* Edinburgh: Hunter, n.d. For Watts see A. P. F. Sell, 'An Englishman, An Irishman and a Scotsman', *The Scottish Journal of Theology,* XXXVIII, 1985, pp.41—83.

66. Robin Gill, *The Social Context of Theology,* London: Mowbrays, 1975, p.116.

67. E. C. Moore, *An Outline of the History of Christian Thought since Kant,* London: Duckworth, 1912, p.175.

68. The Calvinist James McCosh is an interesting exception here. In his *The Religious Aspect of Evolution,* London: Nisbet, 1888, he utilised natural selection as an analogy of that gracious election of God whereby men are saved. This view did not command widespread support, not least because by now all things Calvinistic were under a cloud.

69. R. W. Dale, *The Ten Commandments,* London: Hodder & Stoughton, n.d. p.159: 'If it be said that this scientific history of our physical organization constitutes a theory of human nature, that it explains our position in the universe, that it solves those questions concerning our destiny by which the hearts of the wisest men in all ages have been perplexed, I can only reply that it explains nothing that I am most anxious to understand. My moral life remains a mystery still.'

70. F. E. Hamilton, *The Basis of Evolutionary Faith,* London: James Clarke, n.d. but preface has 1931, pp.58—60.

71. R. W. Dale, *Fellowship with Christ,* p.187.

72. Robert Mackintosh, *From Comte to Benjamin Kidd,* London: Macmillan, 1899, p.281.

CHAPTER FOUR

1. R. S. Franks, 'Trends in recent theology,' *The Congregational Quarterly,* XXIII, 1945, p.23.

2. A. E. Garvie, 'Fifty years' retrospect,' *The Congregational Quarterly,* VII, 1929, p.21.

3. For Ritschl and Ritschlianism see e.g. James Orr, *The Ritschlian Theology and the Evangelical Faith*, London: Hodder & Stoughton, 1898, and *Ritschlianism, Expository and Critical Essays*, London: Hodder & Stoughton, 1903; A. E. Garvie, *The Ritschlian Theology*, Edinburgh: T. & T. Clark, 1899; A. T. Swing, *The Theology of Albrecht Ritschl*, London: Longmans, 1901; K. K. Mozley, *Ritschlianism*, London: Nisbet, 1909; R. Mackintosh, *Albrecht Ritschl and His School*, London: Chapman & Hall, 1915; H. R. Mackintosh, *Some Aspects of Christian Belief*, London: Hodder & Stoughton, 1923, chaps. VII and VIII; *id. Types of Modern Theology*, London: Nisbet, 1937, chap.V. Briefer comments may be found in R. Mackintosh, *Essays Towards a New Theology*, Glasgow: Maclehose, 1889; J. Orr, *The Christian View of God and the World*, Edinburgh: Elliot, 1897; James Denney, *Studies in Theology*, London: Hodder & Stoughton, 1902. Of these Orr and Denney are the least favourably disposed towards Ritschl, A. T. Swing at times borders on the eulogistic, while the remainder are more positively appreciative, though with reservations. R. M. Wenley earned Swing's displeasure with his adversely critical remarks on Ritschl in *Contemporary Theology and Theism*, Edinburgh: T. & T. Clark, 1897. See also K. Barth, *Protestant Thought in the Nineteenth Century*, London: S.C.M. Press, 1972. Among recent writings on Ritschl see James Richmond (also a Glasgow graduate), *Ritschl: A Reappraisal*, London: Collins, 1978.

4. A. E. Garvie, *The Ritschlian Theology* p.26. See pp.26–30 for those who were among the first to adopt positions *vis a vis* Ritschl.

5. J. K. Mozley, *op. cit.*, p.5. Despite this last point he could say, 'It is noticeable how much of the best work on Ritschlianism has been done by members of the non-Episcopal churches' (p.viii). On the other hand A. M. Fairbairn, who absorbed most of the available theology, does not mention Ritschl in his *The Place of Christ in Modern Theology*, London: Hodder & Stoughton, 1894.

6. A. T. Swing, *op. cit.*, p.1.

7. J. Orr, *The Christian View*, p.407.

8. H. R. Mackintosh, *Some Aspects of Christian Belief*, p.152.

9. A. Ritschl, *The Christian Doctrine of Justification and Reconciliation*, III, trans. H. R. Mackintosh and A. B. Macaulay, Edinburgh: T. & T. Clark, 1900, p.210.

10. W. Herrmann, *The Communion of the Christian with God*, London: Williams & Norgate, 1895, p.30.

11. A. E. Garvie, *The Ritschlian Theology*, p.152.

12. Quoted by J. Orr, *The Ritschlian Theology*, p.42.

13. Cf. A. Ritschl, *Justification and Reconciliation*, p.8: 'If anyone

builds Christian theology on a substructure of pretended Natural Theology, the rationalistic arguments of Augustine about original sin, and those of Anselm about the nature of redemption, he thereby takes his stand outside the sphere of regeneration, which is coterminous with the community of believers.' Again, 'Theology has performed its task when . . . it exhibits completely and clearly . . . the Christian view of the world and of human life . . . It is incompetent for it to enter upon either a direct or an indirect proof of the truth of the Christian Revelation by seeking to show that it agrees with some philosophical or juridical view of the world; for to such Christianity simply stands opposed' (p.24).

14. So Garvie, *The Ritschlian Theology*, p.46, following O. Pfleiderer's *The Development of Theology*, London: Sonnenschein, 1890, p.183.

15. *Theologie und Metaphysik*, p.40, quoted by J. Orr, *The Ritschlian Theology*, p.60.

16. A. S. Pringle-Pattison, *The Idea of God in the Light of Recent Philosophy*, New York: O.U.P., 1920, p.57.

17. Dr. Orr was not so sure; Garvie doubted whether Ritschlians were *entitled* to avoid the trap of the double truth without positing the Absolute; Robert Mackintosh thought they were within their rights, and well advised.

18. E. Brunner, *The Mediator*, Philadelphia: Westminster Press, 1947, p.59. Cf. H. R. Mackintosh, *Types of Modern Theology*, p.143: 'Ritschl's aim was not so much to expel metaphysic as to keep it firmly in its right place'. Orr rightly reminds us that the intellectualism against which Ritschlians protested was older and wider than Hegelianism: even the early Church had succumbed. See *The Ritschlian Theology*, p.2 and notes.

19. See A. E. Garvie, *The Ritschlian Theology*, chap. II.

20. See e.g. J. Orr, *The Ritschlian Theology*, chap. III.

21. K. Barth, *op. cit.*, p.655.

22. J. Orr's translation of *Justification and Reconciliation*, III, first German edn., 1874, p.14 in *The Ritschlian Theology*, p.23.

23. See O. Ritschl, *Leben*, Frieburg: Mohr, 1892, I, p.346.

24. *Op. cit.*, pp.32ff.

25. A. E. Garvie, *The Ritschlian Theology*, p.45.

26. J. Orr, *The Ritschlian Theology*, pp.6, 7.

27. R. Mackintosh notes that the phrase 'Jesus has for the Christian consciousness the religious value of God' occurs in A. B. Bruce's *Apologetics* (1892) as his own *credo*, and that Ritschl never used that precise form of words. He further notes that Bruce's formula was utilised by some as 'a rallying-cry for positive Christian unity'.

See *Albrecht Ritschl and His School*, pp.274—7, 276. A. T. Swing makes Ritschl a faithful son of Luther and Calvin in his elucidation of the idea of value, *op. cit.*, chap. II.

28. A. Ritschl, *Justification and Reconciliation*, III, p.212.

29. J. King-Farlow and W. N. Christensen, *Faith and the Life of Reason*, Dordrecht: Reidel, 1972, p.143.

30. A. Ritschl, *Justification and Reconciliation*, III, pp.204—5.

31. Cf. e.g. D. Miall Edwards, *Christianity and Philosophy*, Edinburgh: T. & T. Clark, 1932, pp.50—1.

32. W. P. Paterson, *The Rule of Faith*, London: Hodder & Stoughton, 1912, p.155.

33. See *Justification and Reconciliation*, III, p.165.

34. A. E. Garvie, *The Ritschlian Theology*, p.192, quoting J. R. Illing-worth, *The Divine Immanence*, London: Macmillan, 1903, p.53.

35. W. A. Brown, *Christian Theology in Outline*, Edinburgh: T. & T. Clark, 1923, p.21.

36. W. A. Brown, *The Essence of Christianity*, Edinburgh: T. & T. Clark, 1904, p.259.

37. J. Orr, *The Ritschlian Theology*, p.53.

38. J. Orr, *The Christian View of God and the World*, p.26 and n.4.

39. A. B. D. Alexander, *The Shaping Forces of Modern Religious Thought*, Glasgow: Maclehose, 1920, p.300.

40. A. S. Pringle-Pattison, *op. cit.*, p.58.

41. A. T. Swing, *op. cit.*, p.83.

42. J. K. Mozley, *op. cit.*, pp.28, 94ff.

43. H. R. Mackintosh, *Some Aspects*, pp.148—9. Cf. his *Types*, p.155. He observes that such a later Ritschlian as Reischle emphasised the character of faith as a mode of apprehension, thereby making plain the objective reality of spiritual values. See *Some Aspects*, p.121n.

44. *Justification and Reconciliation*, III, p.13.

45. *Ibid.*, p.11.

46. *Ibid.*, p.9. Cf. A. E. Garvie, 'Ritschlianism' in ed. J. Hastings, *The Encyclopaedia of Religion and Ethics*, Edinburgh: T. & T. Clark, 1918, X, p.816b.

47. *Ibid.*, I, p.466.

48. *Ibid.*, III, pp.205—6. It is interesting to observe in this connection that Ritschl's influence was greater in America than in Britain. H. H. C. King (1858—1934), author of *The Ethics of Jesus*, New York: Macmillan, 1910, and *Reconstruction in Theology*, New York: Macmillan, 1901, was among those who found Ritschl's

practical bent congenial. It would, however, be wrong to say that Ritschl was more than one of the factors behind the Social Gospel theology. The idea of the Kingdom, associated with 'the American dream' has a long history in America. See H. R. Niebuhr, *The Kingdom of God in America*, Hamden: Shoe String Press, 1956. There was, too, the growing appeal of pragmatism. A. C. McGiffert is, nevertheless, by no means unique in thinking that although Ritschl's theology 'is full of defects, and has been made worse rather than better by his followers', yet by reason of its 'interpretation of God in terms of purpose, and . . . its interpretation of the divine message in terms of Christ's ethical method, it points the way along which Christian thinkers who seek a theology that shall support the modern social gospel will do well to travel'. See 'Divine Immanence and the Christian purpose', *The Hibbert Journal*, V, 1907, pp.779—80. Barth reminds us (*op. cit.* p.658) that Ritschl can speak, as a *quasi*-Pelagian, of man's activity in the Kingdom as being the condition of forgiveness; and, as a *quasi*-Augustinian, of the impulse to good conduct as being the effect of grace.

49. See A. E. Garvie, *The Ritschlian Theology*, pp.253—63.

50. *Justification and Reconciliation*, III, p.130.

51. R. Mackintosh, *Essays Towards a New Theology*, pp.140—1.

52. E. Brunner, *op. cit.*, pp.61—2.

53. See *Justification and Reconciliation*, III, pp.273ff. It is only fair to add that such Ritschlians as Kaftan and Haering made considerable improvements at this point.

54. See E. Brunner, *op. cit.*, pp.62, 282n.1; cf. J. Orr, *Sin as a Problem of Today*, London: Hodder & Stoughton, 1910, p.115.

55. W. P. Paterson, *op. cit.*, p.384.

56. See *Justification and Reconciliation*, III, pp.469ff.

57. *Ibid.*, p.387.

58. See *ibid.* pp.451—2 for an expression of it.

59. It was not long before some Ritschlians were making concessions at this point. See J. Orr, *The Christian View of God and the World*, pp.393—5.

60. *Ibid.*, p.238.

61. W. P. Paterson, *op. cit.*, p.385.

62. O. C. Quick, *Liberalism, Modernism and Tradition*, London: Longmans, 1922, p.19.

63. A. E. Garvie, *The Ritschlian Theology*, p.267.

64. *Justification and Reconciliation*, III, p.446.

65. *Ibid.*, p.447.

66. Some have heard echoes of Paul of Samosata at this point.

67. P. T. Forsyth, *The Work of Christ* (1910), London: Independent Press, 1958, pp.228—9.

68. T. F. Torrance, *God and Rationality*, London: O.U.P., 1971, p.63.

69. Daniel L. Deegan, 'Albrecht Ritschl on the historical Jesus', *The Scottish Journal of Theology*, XV, 1962, pp.149—50.

70. H. R. Mackintosh, *Some Aspects*, p.176.

71. A. E. Garvie in *E.R.E.*, X, p.819a.

72. A. Richardson, *Christian Apologetics*, London: S.C.M., 1947, p.148.

73. Robert Mackintosh, 'Recent philosophy and Christian truth', *Proceedings of the International Congregational Council*, 1908, pp.79—80.

74. P. T. Forsyth, *The Principle of Authority* (1913), London: Independent Press, 1952, p.384.

CHAPTER FIVE

1. To this extent we agree with Professor Welch. But when he says, 'No significant theological programme is *as such* an attempt to be liberal or conservative, to go left or right (or to stay in the center)' we pause. If by 'significant' is meant 'widely influential' agreement becomes easier; but such a definition strikes oddly on the ear of those who do not employ a *quasi*-quantitative criterion of significance. Certain it is that some 'Old Lights' in every generation have set out to be conservative, and they have often said highly significant, though not generally accepted, things. On the other hand kite-flying liberals who take a devilish glee in disturbing the faithful are not unknown either — they, however, are not usually significant. See Claude Welch, *Protestant Thought in the Nineteenth Century*, New Haven and London: Yale U.P., 1972, I, p.20. For the Calvinist-Arminian debate to which reference has just been made see A. P. F. Sell, *The Great Debate: Calvinism, Arminianism and Salvation*, Worthing: H. E. Walter, 1982, Grand Rapids: Baker Book House, 1983.

2. William P. Merrill, *Liberal Christianity*, New York: Macmillan, 1925, p.36.

3. For whom see E. Jorstad, *The Politics of Doomsday*, Nashville and New York: Abingdon, 1970; and from whom Ronald Reagan seems to have benefited in the 1980 and 1984 Presidential elections.

4. J. K. Mozley, *Some Tendencies in British Theology*, London: S.P.C.K., 1951, p.70.

5. E. W. Barnes, 'The future of the evangelical movement' in *Liberal Evangelicalism*, London: Hodder & Stoughton, n.d., p.288.

6. Professor R. J. Mouw, to whom we are indebted for this point, further notes that in eds. David Wells and John D. Woodbridge, *The Evangelicals: What They Believe, Who They Are, Where They are Changing*, Nashville: Abingdon, 1975, 'no attention is given . . . to the fact that the Missouri Synod Lutherans, and to a lesser degree the Christian Reformed Church, have been recently having their own "fundamentalist-modernist" debates, fifty years later than the traumas of the more Anglo-American groups'. See his review in *Calvin Theological Journal*, XI, 1976, p.263.

7. B. L. Manning, *The Making of Modern English Religion* (1929), London: Independent Press, 1967, p.78.

8. A. E. Garvie, 'Fifty Years' Retrospect', *The Congregational Quarterly*, VII, 1929, p.18.

9. D. R. Davies, 'The essence of Christianity', *The World Christian Digest*, Nov. 1953, p.41.

10. P. T. Forsyth, *Positive Preaching and the Modern Mind* (1907), London: Independent Press, 1964, p.139.

11. On this point contrast the positions of John H. Gerstner and Sydney Ahlstrom in eds. Wells and Woodbridge, *op. cit.* And see James A. Hedstrom, 'A bibliography for evangelical reform', *Journal of the Evangelical Theological Society*, XIX, 1976, pp. 225–38.

12. In eds. Wells and Woodbridge, *op. cit.*, p.38.

13. G. H. Clark, 'Evangelicalism', *The Encyclopaedia of Christianity*, Marshallton: National Foundation for Christian Education, 1972, IV, p.121.

14. I. John Hesselink, 'Toward a seminary that is Catholic, Evangelical and Reformed', *Reformed Review*, XXVII, 1974, p.107.

15. See J. C. Ryle, *Knots Untied* (1877), Cambridge: James Clarke, 1977, pp.3–12. For Anglican evangelicalism see G. R. Balleine, *A History of the Evangelical Party in the Church of England*, London: Church Book Room Press, 1903; D. N. Samuel (ed.), *The Evangelical Succession in the Church of England*, Cambridge: James Clarke, 1979. For Anglican evangelicals of the preceding period see Peter Toon, *Evangelical Theology, 1833–1856: A Response to Tractarianism*, London: Marshall, Morgan and Scott, 1979.

16. Quoted by A. R. Vidler, *Essays in Liberality*, London: S.C.M., 1957, p.13.

17. See Amos Cresswell, *The Story of Cliff*, Culver, Sheffield: Joyful News Bookroom, 1965.

18. H. B. Workman, 'The place of Methodism in the life and thought
of the Christian Church' in eds. W. J. Townsend *et al.*, *A New
History of Methodism*, London: Hodder & Stoughton, 1909, I,
p.30.

19. The Free Presbyterian Church denies that the Free Church of
Scotland is in truth the continuation of the 1943 Disruption:
'That the present Free Church, which we can never allow to be
the Church of the Disruption, is very much on the down-grade,
can easily be proved'. In evidence a writer quotes Kenneth A.
MacRae of the Free Church, Stornoway, who criticised some of
the younger ministers of his Church on the ground that 'a robust
Calvinism has given place to a colourless presentation of the
doctrines of grace, which will neither satisfy a Calvinist nor offend
an Arminian'. See John Colquhoun, 'The present position and
prospects of the Reformed Church in Scotland', in *Papers Com-
memorating the Quarter-Centenary of the Scottish Reformation*,
read to the F. P. Synod at Edinburgh, May 1960, p.66.

20. Since about 1960 some interesting developments towards increasing confessional consciousness have taken place amongst this
sturdily independent group of churches. In 1966 they published
We Believe, an affirmation of faith, and in 1974 there appeared
A Guide for Church Fellowship which set down 'biblical standards for the help and guidance of the local church in the ordering
of its Worship, Discipline and Witness'. *Grace Magazine*, the suc-
cessor of *Gospel Herald* (1833—1970) and *Free Grace Record*
(1920—70) is widely read among Strict Baptists. Again, since 1960
a number of Reformed Baptist churches have been founded either
de novo or as a result of secession from the Baptist Union. Many of
these honour the Particular Baptist Confession of 1689, and
Reformation Today circulates among them. The Gospel Standard
Baptists, who stand in the line of William Gadsby, continue to
maintain their distinctive witness on such matters as the gospel
offer. Their medium is *The Gospel Standard* (1835—   ). In an
editorial in this magazine (XCII, 1926, pp.5—19) the status of the
G. S. Baptists as a *distinct* denomination was clearly argued. See
also S. F. Paul, *Historical Sketch of the Gospel Standard Baptists*,
Gospel Standard Publications, 1961; P. Toon, 'English Strict
Baptists', *The Baptist Quarterly*, XXI, 1965, pp.30—6. For the
other Churches mentioned in this para. see J. H. S. Burleigh, *A
Church History of Scotland*, London: O.U.P., 1960; M. Hutchison,
The Reformed Presbyterian Church in Scotland, Paisley: Parlane,
1893; W. J. Coupar, *The Reformed Presbyterian Church in Scot-
land. Its Congregations, Ministers and Students*, Edinburgh, 1925;
G. N. M. Collins, *The Heritage of Our Fathers*, Edinburgh: Knox
Press, 1974; ed. A. McPherson, *History of the Free Presbyterian
Church of Scotland*, Publications Committee of the F.P. Church,
1975; W. J. Grier, *The Origin and Witness of the Irish Evangelical
Church*, Belfast: Evangelical Book Shop, n.d. but preface has 1945;

Austin Fulton, *J. Ernest Davey*, Belfast: Presbyterian Church in Ireland, 1970.

21. T. M. Lindsay, 'The doctrine of Scripture. The Reformers and the Princeton School', *The Expositor*, 5th Series, I, 1895, pp.278—93.

22. See E. H. Rian, *The Presbyterian Conflict*, Grand Rapids: Eerdmans, 1940; L. A. Loetscher, *The Broadening Church*, Pittsburgh: U. Pennsylvania Press, 1954; N. B. Stonehouse *J. Gresham Machen, A Biographical Memoir*, Grand Rapids: Eerdmans, 2nd edn., 1955; *Collected Writings of John Murray*, Edinburgh: The Banner of Truth Trust, 1976, I, chs. XI—XV. Machen, Stonehouse and Murray all served on the faculty of Westminster Theological Seminary, as did R. D. Wilson, O. T. Allis, C. Van Til, R. B. Kuiper and E. J. Young.

23. See D. H. Kromminga, *The Christian Reformed Tradition*, Grand Rapids: Eerdmans, 1943; Peter Y. De Jong, *The Christian Reformed Church*, Grand Rapids: Baker Book House, 1967. For the outworking of Dutch tensions in South Africa see Peter Hinchliff, *The Church in South Africa*, London: S.P.C.K., 1968, chap. IX.

24. See H. F. Foster, *A Genetic History of New England Theology*, 1907; G. N. Boardman, *A History of New England Theology*, New York: Randolph, 1899; J. Haroutunian, *Piety Versus Moralism*, New York: Holt, 1932. The contention of these books that a line can be drawn from Edwards to Bushnell has been questioned by Sidney E. Mead. He holds that 'the line can be drawn from Puritanism to Old Calvinism [i.e. that Calvinism which *opposed* the Great Awakening] to Taylorism, each the system of the dominant party of its era. It is possible, in brief, that the Edwardeanism or Consistent Calvinism was never *the* New England Theology.' See his *Nathanael William Taylor*, Chicago: Chicago U.P., 1942, p.ix.

25. See W. Pyncheon, *The Meritorious Price of our Redemption*, 1650.

26. See the works on New England Theology at n.24.

27. See James W. Jones, *The Shattered Synthesis*, New Haven and London: Yale U.P., 1973.

28. N. Taylor, *Lectures on the Moral Government of God*, New York, 1859, II, p.134.

29. For American revivalism see e.g. Bernard A. Weisberger, *They Gathered at the River*, Boston: Quadrangle, 1958; William G. McLoughlin Jr., *Modern Revivalism: Charles Grandison Finney to Billy Graham*, New York: Ronald Press, 1959; Perry Miller, *The Life of the Mind in America: From the Revolution to the Civil War*, New York: Harcourt Brace, 1965; George M. Marsden, *The Evangelical Mind and the New School Presbyterian Experience*, New Haven: Yale U.P., 1970; for Finney see his *Memoirs*, New York, 1876. For a critique of Finney's theology see B. B. Warfield,

Perfectionism, Philadelphia: Presbyterian and Reformed, 1958. We have found the following articles illuminating on the theological issues: D. M. Lloyd-Jones, 'Revival: an historical and theological survey' in *How Shall They Hear?* London: Puritan and Reformed Studies Conference, 1960, pp.38–56; Melvin L. Vulgamore, 'Charles G. Finney: catalyst in the dissolution of American Calvinism', *The Reformed Review,* XVIII, 1963–4, pp.33–42; R. E. G. Cook, 'Finney on revival' in *One Steadfast High Intent,* London: Puritan and Reformed Studies Conference, 1966, pp.4–16; James E. Johnson, 'Charles G. Finney and a theology of revivalism', *Church History,* XXXVIII, 1969, pp.338–58; John Opie, 'Finney's failure of nerve: The untimely demise of evangelical theology', *Journal of Presbyterian History,* LI, 1973, pp.155–73; D. M. Lloyd-Jones, 'Living the Christian Life. 5. New developments in the eighteenth and nineteenth century teaching' in *Living the Christian Life,* London: The Westminster Conference, 1974, pp. 82–99; Clive Tyler, 'Charles Finney and the disappearance of revival'. *Reformation Today,* 18, 1974, pp.16–27. For contemporary reactions to Finney's methods see e.g. A. A. Bonar's edn. of Bennet Tyler's *Memoirs* of Asahel Nettleton, reprinted Edinburgh: The Banner of Truth Trust, 1975; and J. F. Thornbury, *God Sent Revival,* Welwyn: Evangelical Press, 1977. The latter is a sympathetic and informed account of the life and ministry of Nettleton (1783–1844). For revivalism in Britain see John Kent, *Holding the Fort: Studies in Victorian Revivalism,* London: Epworth, 1978. For the influence of Finney and James Caughey in Britain see Richard Carwardine, *Transatlantic Revivalism: Popular Evangelicalism in Britain and America,* Westport and London: Greenwood Press, 1978.

30. C. G. Finney, *Systematic Theology,* London, 1851, p.3.

31. C. G. Finney, *Sermons on Important Subjects,* New York, 1836, p.28.

32. C. G. Finney, *Lectures on Revivals of Religion,* London, 1838, p.153.

33. B. B. Warfield, *op. cit.,* p.193. From the other side Finney was criticised by the Unitarians for his lurid descriptions of hell, and for his methods of evangelism. See Johnson, *art. cit.* pp.345–6. Among Finney's defenders was George F. Wright, 'Dr. Hodge's misrepresentation of President Finney's system of Theology' in *Bibliotheca Sacra,* XVI, 1876, pp.381–92.

34. See e.g. his sermon on 'The doctrine of election'.

35. C. G. Finney, *Memoirs,* p.23.

36. J. Opie, *art. cit.* p.160. These critics were to be even more stunned by the counterblast to revivalism in Bushnell's *Christian Nurture* (1847). Bushnell argued that a child should grow up a Christian and never know himself to be anything other than a Christian.

37. For Moody see James F. Findlay Jr., *Dwight L. Moody: American Evangelist*, Chicago: Chicago U.P., 1969.

38. J. Opie, *art. cit.*, p.155. Among Moody's contemporaries John Kennedy of Dingwall, ever loyal to Calvinism, and Robert Mackintosh, a refugee from Calvinism, criticised revivalism trenchantly. Kennedy complained that 'this proud resolve to make a manageable business of conversion-work, is intolerant of any recognition of the sovereignty of God'; quoted in Ergatees, *Arminianism — Another Gospel*, Gisborne N.Z.: The Westminster Standard, 1965, p.11. For Mackintosh's views see *The Insufficiency of Revivalism as a Religious System*, bound with *Essays Towards a New Theology*, Glasgow: Maclehose, 1889. For his spiritual pilgrimage see A. P. F. Sell, *Robert Mackintosh: Theologian of Integrity*, Bern: Peter Lang, 1977.

39. A. M. Hills criticised the Oberlin theology on the following grounds *inter alia:* it locates all sin in the attitude of the will; it confounds consecration and sanctification, making the latter a matter of growth. See his *Holiness and Power*, Manchester: Star Hall, 1913. For the American Holiness movement see D. W. Dayton, *The American Holiness Movement: A Bibliographic Introduction*, Wilmore, Kentucky: Asbury Theological Seminary, 1971.

40. For Booth see (Edward) H. Begbie, *Life of William Booth*, 2 vols., London: Macmillan, 1920; Richard Collier, *The General Next to God*, London: Collins Fontana, 1970. For the Church of the Nazarene see T. L. Smith, *Called Unto Holiness*, Kansas City: Nazarene Publishing House, 1962. In 1954 the Calvary Holiness Church joined the Church of the Nazarene. See Jack Ford, *In the Steps of John Wesley, The Church of the Nazarene in Britain*, Kansas City: Nazarene Publishing House, 1968. For Keswick see W. B. Sloan, *These Sixty Years*, London: Pickering & Inglis, n.d. but 1935. For a somewhat fuller treatment of the material in this para. see D. M. Lloyd-Jones, 'New developments', *op. cit.* He points out that Bishop Ryle never addressed the Keswick Convention, and that his book *Holiness* was a rebuttal of Keswick teaching. Likewise Spurgeon never spoke at Keswick, and Campbell Morgan gave Bible readings only. See also E. R. Sandeen, *The Roots of Fundamentalism*, Chicago: Chicago U.P., 1970, pp.178–81; D. D. Bundy, *Keswick: A Bibliographic Introduction to the Higher Life Movements*, Wilmore, Kentucky: Asbury Theological Seminary, 1975.

41. See E. R. Sandeen, *op. cit.* He has been criticised by some, however, for attaching too much significance to these themes. Donald Bloesch, for example, has fundamentalism sired by latter-day pietism (rather than dispensationalism) out of Reformed and Lutheran scholastic orthodoxy. See his *The Evangelical Renaissance*, London: Hodder & Stoughton, 1974.

42. E. R. Sandeen, *op. cit.*, p.xii. For Niebuhr's opinion see his art.

'Fundamentalism' in the *Encyclopaedia of Social Sciences,* New
York, 1937. Among many other studies of fundamentalism see
Stewart G. Cole, *The History of Fundamentalism* (1931),
Westport: Greenwood Press, 1971, Edwin H. Rian, *The Presby-
terian Conflict,* Grand Rapids: Eerdmans, 1940; Norman F. Furniss,
The Fundamentalist Controversy, 1918–1931, New Haven: Yale
U.P., 1954; Louis Gasper, *The Fundamentalist Movement,* The
Hague: Mouton, 1963; Daniel B. Stevick, *Beyond Fundamentalism,*
Richmond Va.: John Knox Press, 1964; George M. Marsden,
*Fundamentalism and Arminian Culture: The Shaping of Twentieth-
Century Evangelicalism, 1870–1925,* New York and Oxford,
1980. For a British view see James Barr, *Fundamentalism,* London:
S.C.M. Press, 1977 (2nd rev. edn., 1981). For a lively brief critique
see the editorial 'Fundamentalism Barred', *The Monthly Record of
the Free Church of Scotland,* Dec. 1977, pp.191–3. For a more
extended treatment see P. R. Wells, *James Barr and the Bible:
Critique of a New Liberalism,* Philipsburg: Presbyterian and
Reformed, 1980. In *Escaping from Fundamentalism,* London:
S.C.M. Press, 1984, James Barr sets out to be non-contreversial
and is pastorally inspired. We suspect that controversy will continue, and that not all will receive his counsel.

43. For whom see also F. R. Coad, *A History of the Brethren Move-
    ment,* Exeter: Paternoster, 1968; H. H. Rowdon, *The Origins of
    the Brethren, 1825–1850,* London: Pickering & Inglis, 1967.

44. E. R. Sandeen, *op. cit.,* p.52.

45. *Ibid.,* p.43, referring *inter alia* to C. C. Goen, 'Jonathan Edwards,
    A new departure in eschatology', *Church History,* XXVIII, 1959,
    pp.25–40.

46. Gordon Harland, 'The American religious heritage and the tragic
    dimension', *Studies in Religion,* II, 1973, p.279. It is interesting to
    observe how this aspect has influenced such people, so otherwise
    different, as conservative millenarians and Social Gospel liberals.

47. J. I. Packer in *The Word of God and Fundamentalism,* (The ad-
    dresses given at the Oxford Conference of Evangelical Churchmen,
    1960,) London: Church Book Room Press, 1961, p.115.

48. J. Opie, Jr. writes in *The Christian Century,* LXXXII, 1965, pp.
    608–11 on 'The modernity of fundamentalism'. But to him its
    modernity lies in its rationalistic scholasticism. Carl F. H. Henry
    criticised Dr. Opie in *Catholic World,* June 1967, pp.145–50, and
    Opie responded in the same issue, pp.151–6.

49. For Machen's own words on the subject see C. Allyn Russell,
    'J. Gresham Machen, scholarly fundamentalist', *The Journal of
    Presbyterian History,* LI, 1973, pp.49–50.

50. E.g. E. J. Carnell, *The Case for Orthodox Theology,* London:
    Marshall, Morgan & Scott, 1961; C. F. H. Henry, *Evangelical Res-*

ponsibility in Contemporary Theology, Grand Rapids: Eerdmans, 1957, chap. II. The latter claims that fundamentalism became reactionary, it unthinkingly blended Arminianism and Calvinism, it neglected thorough exegesis, it veered towards anti-denomination-alism, it neglected the doctrine of the Church, it frequently identified Christianity with premillenarianism, and it overlooked the cultural mandate.

51. G. O. Griffith, *The Theology of P. T. Forsyth*, London: Lutter-worth, 1948, p.15.

52. P. T. Forsyth, *Positive Preaching and the Modern Mind*, p.142.

53. H. D. A. Major, *English Modernism*, Cambridge Mass.: Harvard U. P., 1927, p.53. Dr. Major had earlier made this point when he provided a modernist's answer to those, both within and without the Church of England, who felt that the modernists should 'come clean', secede, and join the Unitarians. See his 'Modern Churchmen or Unitarians?', *The Hibbert Journal*, XX, 1922, pp.208–19.

54. A. R. Vidler, *Essays in Liberality*, p.21. Cf. I. T. Ramsey's opening sermon in *Liberal Christianity in History*, Modern Churchmen's Union, 1969. A similar plea in face of 'that wholesale condem-nation of liberalism in theology which is now in vogue' was earlier entered by W. B. Selbie, *Freedom in the Faith*, London: Indepen-dent Press, 1944, preface. Selbie said that his work was 'not an attempt to defend the liberal Protestant theology of the nineteenth century, but rather to distinguish between the liberal spirit and that particular form of its application', *ibid.*

55. H. D. A. Major, *op. cit.*, p.8.

56. P. T. Forsyth, *Positive Preaching and the Modern Mind*, p.143.

57. Though at this distance we can see some justice in B. M. G. Rear-don's remark concerning Liberal Protestantism and Catholic Modernism: 'viewed in the perspective of our age they show up as only slightly differing aspects of a unitary tendency away from traditional Christianity altogether and towards the Christianized humanism to which theology has now largely succumbed'. See his 'Liberal Protestantism and Roman Catholic Modernism' in *Liberal Christianity in History*, p.72; cf. of his *Liberalism and Tradition*, Cambridge: C.U.P., 1975.

58. H. D. A. Major, *op. cit.*, pp.30, 31. See Harnack's *What is Christi-anity?* (1900), E.T., 1901.

59. Quoted by B. M. G. Reardon, *art. cit.*, p.81.

60. G. Tyrrell, *Christianity at the Crossroads*, London: Longmans, 1901, p.5.

61. Among other works on Roman Catholic modernism see A. R. Vidler, *The Modernist Movement in the Roman Church*, Cambridge:

C.U.P., 1934; B. M. G. Reardon, *Roman Catholic Modernism*, London: A. & C. Black, 1970.

62. On this aspect of Gore see A. R. Vidler, 'Bishop Gore and Liberal Catholicism' in his *Essays in Liberality*, pp.126—51. Dr. Vidler finds that whereas Gore's beliefs qualify him for the liberal catholic name — he accepted the principles of modern biblical criticism, he was alive to the social implications of Christianity, and he was advanced in his view of the eternal destiny of those outside the Church — his temperament was aristocratic rather than liberal. Dr. Vidler has lucid chapters on liberal protestantism, Roman Catholic Modernism and English Liberal Catholicism in his *20th Century Defenders of the Faith*, London: S.C.M., 1965.

63. R. Thomas, 'Philip Doddridge and liberalism in religion' in ed. G. F. Nuttall, *Philip Doddridge*, London: Independent Press, 1951, p.122.

64. Boston was the liberal town *par excellence*. In 1804 only one out of nine Congregational churches there remained trinitarian. See Conrad Wright,*The Beginning of Unitarianism in America*, Hamden: Shoe String Press, 1976, p.253.

65. For Beecher see L. Abbott, *Henry Ward Beecher*, London: Hodder & Stoughton, 1903; W. C. Beecher and G. Scoville, *Biography of Henry Ward Beecher*, London: Sampson & Low, 1888; Clifford E. Clark, Jr., *Henry Ward Beecher; Spokesman for a Middle-Class America*, London: University of Illinois Press, 1978; for Brooks see A. V. G. Allen, *Life and Letters of Phillips Brooks*, 2 vols., London: Macmillan, 1901; R. W. Albright, *Focus on Infinity: A Life of Phillips Brooks*, New York: Macmillan, 1961; for Gladden see J. H. Dorn, *Washington Gladden: Prophet of the Social Gospel*, Ohio State U.P., 1968; R. D. Knudten, *Systematic Thought of Washington Gladden*, Atlantic Highlands N.J.: Humanities, 1968.

66. W. Gladden, *A Modern Man's Theology*, London: James Clarke, 1914, pp.6—7, 14, 15.

67. Letter to L. C. Barnes in D. R. Sharpe, *Walter Rauschenbusch*, New York: Macmillan, 1942, pp.434f. Cf. R. T. Handy, 'Walter Rauschenbusch in historical perspective', *The Baptist Quarterly*, XX, 1964, pp.313—21; Ernest F. Clipsham, 'An Englishman looks at Rauschenbusch', *ibid.*, XXIX, 1981, pp.113—21.

68. See W. M. Horton, *Contemporary Continental Theology*, London: S.C.M., 1938, pp.174—5.

69. A. Kuyper, *Lectures on Calvinism*, Grand Rapids: Associated Publishers, n.d. p.8.

70. In 1865 the law was finally amended in such a way as to require assent to the articles, rather than to *all* the articles. William Robertson (1705—1783) had resigned his Irish living in 1764, but did not continue in the ministry. For fuller accounts of the matters briefly

referred to here see Alexander Gordon, *Heads of English Unitarian History*, London: Green, 1895; C. G. Bolam *et al.*, *The English Presbyterians*, London: Allen & Unwin, 1968. For the impact of English Unitarianism on society see R. V. Holt, *The Unitarian Contribution to Social Progress in England*, London: Lindsey Press, 1952; for an example of the impact of Unitarians on one town in the nineteenth century — and for material unmentioned by Holt — see A. P. F. Sell, 'The social and literary contribution of thee Unitarian ministers in nineteenth century Walsall', *Trans. of the Unitarian Historical Society*, XV, 1973, pp.77—97.

71. A. Gordon, *op. cit.*, pp.39—40.

72. Quoted by V. F. Storr, *The Development of English Theology in the Nineteenth Century*, London: Longmans, 1913, p.41n. As he reflected on the rationalistic age H. R. Mackintosh wrote, 'It is easy to imagine how on these terms the majesty and power of the Christian Gospel vanished. There is little to produce "joy un-speakable and full of glory" in a form of Christianity which, with half a sheet of notepaper and a spare hour, the average man can construct for himself . . . It is by no means surprising that the clergy who proclaimed such a message frequently exhibited a keener interest in sport or agriculture than in the cure of souls.' See his *Types of Modern Theology*, London: Nisbet, 1937, p.15.

73. See H. McLachlan, *The Methodist Unitarian Movement*, Manchester: Manchester U.P., 1919.

74. Dr. Gordon (*op. cit.* p.49) says that Barker 'originated several congregations in the North of England'. Indeed he did, but his causes were to be found as far south as the West Midlands. After adventures in radical politics Barker went to America, eventually returning to the Methodist fold. See *D.N.B.*

75. We say 'generally' because it has been argued that at least one congregation, that at Kendal, was only doubtfully orthodox in the first place. See F. Nicholson and E. Axon, *The Older Noncon-formity of Kendal*, Kendal: Titus Wilson, 1915, chap. XXIV.

76. It is not without significance that Coleridge joined the Unitarians for a time, and contemplated entering their ministry.

77. A. M. G. Stephenson, 'Liberal Anglicanism in the nineteenth century' in *Liberal Christianity in History*, p.87. Cf. J. Tulloch, *Movements of Religious Thought in Britain during the Nineteenth Century* (1885), Leicester: Leicester U.P., 1971, pp.260—1.

78. H. D. A. Major, *op. cit.*, pp.25—8.

79. A. M. Ramsey, *From Gore to Temple*, London: Longmans, 1960, p.67. Dr. Ramsey also points out with respect to modernism that 'Where there is an underlying philosophy it is commonly that of the identity of the natures of God and Man, and where there is an underlying assumption it is commonly that of the uniformity of

nature'. (p.74). With further reference to the difficulty of labelling theologians, and with reference to Dr. Inge, J. K. Mozley writes, 'One who can say that he has "a great admiration for the old Catholic philosophy of religion, of which St. Thomas Aquinas is the most learned exponent", is at that point, which is not situated on the circumference of religious belief, as far removed from some who would claim the name of "modernist" as he is from Karl Barth'. See his *Some Tendencies in British Theology*, London: S.P.C.K., 1951, p.57.

80. A. M. G. Stephenson, 'English modernism' in *Liberal Christianity in History*, p.148. Although, like Harnack, the English modernists tended to minimise the miraculous they were not generally, like some liberal protestants, anti-supernaturalists. However, Gore felt that B. J. Streeter's paper on 'The historic Christ' in *Foundations* (1912) and J. M. Thompson's *The Miracles of the New Testament* (1911) were so sceptical concerning miracles that they came near to undermining the Faith.

81. J. K. Mozley, *op. cit.*, p.29.

82. G. Tyrrell, *op. cit.*, p.44.

83. L. Parks, *What is Modernism?*, New York: Scribners, 1924, p.5.

84. V. F. Storr, *Freedom and Tradition*, London: Nisbet, 1940, p.159.

85. *Ibid.*, p.169.

86. *Ibid.*

87. *Ibid.*, p.172. Cf. the Anglican symposium, *Liberal Evangelicalism*, London: Hodder & Stoughton, n.d., pp.vi–vii.

88. C. J. Cadoux, *The Case for Evangelical Modernism*, London: Hodder & Stoughton, 1938, p.10. Elsewhere Cadoux confessed, 'it is doubtless true that some theological thinkers are infected with a desire resembling the political habit of which Cromwell complained: "Nothing was in the hearts of these men except Overturn, overturn". The temptation to abandon beliefs because they are traditional is pernicious; and modernists must, of course, resist it, if it arises.' See his 'A defence of Christian modernism', *The Congregational Quarterly*, V, 1927, pp.164–5. Albert Peel's reflections on the 1928 Assembly of the Congregational Union of England and Wales are not without interest: 'It is clear that, so far as the Chair is concerned, Modernism, for the moment, has its hand on the helm. Mr. Wrigley's address . . . was, in itself, the best possible denial that there is any necessary or congruous connexion between a modern outlook and cold or destructive intellectualism.' See his editorial, *The Congregational Quarterly*, VI, 1928, p.273.

89. See C. F. H. Henry, *Evangelical Responsibility in Contemporary Theology*, pp.21–2. We recognise that the growth of the *Religionsgeschichtliche schule* led by Ernst Troeltsch (1865–1923)

fostered the spirit of relativism among some, and we are aware of the continuing naturalism of some of the new psychologists which was, on occasion, turned against religion. But to most of those who participated in the conservative-liberal debates between, say, 1870–1930, these were not the immediate foci of attention. More crucial ingredients were immanentism, modern biblical criticism, evolutionary thought, and Ritschlianism.

90. See A. P. F. Sell, 'Theology and the philosophical climate: Case-studies from the second century A.D.', *Vox Evangelica*, XIII, 1983, pp.41–66; XIV, 1984, pp.53–64.

CHAPTER SIX

1. Reprinted London: The Victory Press, n.d. For Machen see L. A. Loetscher in *D.A.B.*, XI, Supp. ii; N. B. Stonehouse, *J. Gresham Machen, a Biographical Memoir*, Grand Rapids: Eerdmans, 2nd edn., 1955; Paul Woolley, *The Significance of J. Gresham Machen Today*, Philadelphia: Presbyterian and Reformed, 1977; D. M. Roark, 'J. Gresham Machen', *Journal of Presbyterian History*, XLIII, 1965, pp.124–38, 174–81; G. Allyn Russell, 'J. Gresham Machen, scholarly fundamentalist', *Journal of Presbyterian History*, LI, 1973, pp.41–69; and the standard works on fundamentalism by S. G. Cole, N. F. Furniss, L. Gaspar and E. R. Sandeen; and on Presbyterian troubles by E. H. Rian, L. A. Loetscher, etc. Fuel was added to the contemporary debate by Machen's separatism (actual if not desired), for which he was later criticised by *inter alia* E. J. Carnell, *The Case for Orthodox Theology*, London: Marshall, Morgan & Scott, 1961, pp.114–7, and defended by C. Van Til. See Ronald H. Nash, *The New Evangelicalism*, Grand Rapids: Zondervan, 1963, p.83ff. Into the question of separatism we shall not here enquire.

2. N. B. Stonehouse, *op. cit.*, p.343. Cf. Machen's declaration of purpose in *Christianity and Liberalism*, p.16.

3. Quoted from *The Christian Century*, 3.1.1924 by N. B. Stonehouse, *op. cit.*, p.366.

4. J. G. Machen, *Christianity and Liberalism*, p.7.

5. *Ibid.*, p.2.

6. *Ibid.*

7. *Ibid.*, p.19.

8. *Ibid.*, p.21.

9. *Ibid.*, p.23. Cf. J. G. Machen, *What is Faith?*, London: Hodder & Stoughton, 1925, p.93f.

10. *Ibid.*, p.27.

11. *Ibid.*, p.70.

12. J. G. Machen, *What is Christianity?*, Grand Rapids: Eerdmans, 1951, p.18.

13. *Christianity and Liberalism*, p.54.

14. *Ibid.*, p.56.

15. *Ibid.*, p.142; cf. *What is Faith?*, p.48.

16. See *What is Faith?*, chap. II.

17. *Christianity and Liberalism*, pp.2, 109.

18. Warren C. Young, *A Christian Approach to Philosophy* (1954), Grand Rapids: Baker Book House, 1973, pp.46–7. Cf: 'It is a nice question whether the use of God's name is not misleading when it is applied by modernists to ideas so remote from the God men have worshipped'. W. Lippmann, *A Preface to Morals*, London: Allen & Unwin, 1929, p.27.

19. See *What is Faith?*, pp.51, 76–7..

20. J. G. Machen, *The Christian View of Man* (1937), Edinburgh: The Banner of Truth Trust, 1965, pp.16–7.

21. *Christianity and Liberalism*, pp.62–3; cf. *What is Faith?*, p.71.

22. *What is Faith?*, p.53.

23. *Ibid.*, p.135.

24. *Ibid.*, p.194.

25. Quoted by N. B. Stonehouse, *op. cit.*, pp.230–1.

26. *What is Faith?*, p.86.

27. *Christianity and Liberalism*, p.68.

28. *Ibid.*, p.84.

29. *Ibid.*, p.90.

30. *Ibid.*, p.133.

31. *Ibid.*, p.85.

32. *Ibid.*, p.95; cf. *What is Faith?*, p.98.

33. *What is Faith?*, pp.111, 113. The reference is to the hymn, 'There is a green hill far away'.

34. *Christianity and Liberalism*, p.47.

35. *Ibid.*, p.106; cf. p.136.

36. *Ibid.*, pp.99ff. Cf. C. Van Til, *The Case for Calvinism*, Philadelphia: Presbyterian and Reformed, 1963, pp.18–9, where he distinguishes between Machen's view of miracle and that of William

Hordern for whom 'natural law is something that is independent of God'. For Machen it is not.

37. *Ibid.*, p.155.

38. *Ibid.*, p.172.

39. *Ibid.*, p.48.

40. *Ibid.*, p.160. Is Dr. Bloesch quite fair in saying that Machen 'did not take adequate recognition of the fact that liberals can still be men of deep personal faith despite the errors in their thinking'? See his *The Evangelical Renaissance*, London: Hodder & Stoughton, 1973, p.149. It all depends on what is meant by 'adequate'.

44. L. Browne, *The Nation*, 27.6.1923, p.753.

42. W. L. Sperry, *Literary Review*, 14.7.1923, p.828.

43. *The Journal of Religion*, III, 1923, p.335.

44. I.e. *The Independent*, 21.7.1923, p.18.

45. *The Journal of Religion*, III, 1923, p.544.

46. See *The Pacific Unitarian*, June–July 1923, quoted by N. B. Stonehouse, *op. cit.*, pp.347–8; A. C. Dieffenbach in *Boston Evening Transcript*, 9.1.1937, quoted by E. H. Rian, *The Presbyterian Conflict*, Grand Rapids: Eerdmans, 1940, p.215.

47. W. Lippmann, *A Preface to Morals*, p.33. Mencken's comments are quoted by E. H. Rian, *op: cit.*, pp.214–5.

48. J. C. H. in *The Modern Churchman*, XIV, 1924–5, p.39.

49. See P. T. Forsyth, 'Immanence and Incarnation' in ed. Charles H. Vine, *The Old Faith and the New Theology*, London: Sampson Low & Marston, 1907, pp.57–9.

50. R. W. Dale, *The Old Evangelicalism and the New*, London: Hodder & Stoughton, 1889, pp.25–6.

51. T. Erskine, *Remarks on the Internal Evidence for the Truth of Revealed Religion*, 1820, p.59.

52. C. J. Cadoux, *The Case for Evangelical Modernism*, London: Hodder & Stoughton, 1938, pp.8–9.

53. Quoted by James Orr, *The Christian View of God and the World*, Edinburgh: Elliot, 1897, p.399. From the many contemporary analyses of liberal reductionism we note C. Gore, *The New Theology and the Old Religion*, London: John Murray, 1907, and W. L. Walker, *What About the New Theology?*, Edinburgh: T. & T. Clark, 1907.

54. Frank Lenwood, *Jesus — Lord or Leader?*, London: Constable, 1930, p.21.

55. *Ibid.*, p.29.

56. S. H. Mellone, *Liberty and Religion*, London: Lindsey Press, 1925, p.231.

57. L. Parks, *What is Modernism?*, New York: Scribners, 1924, p.138.

58. A. E. Garvie, 'Fifty Years' Retrospect', *The Congregational Quarterly*, VII, 1929, p.22.

59. B. C. Plowright, 'The misgivings of a modernist', *The Congregational Quarterly*, IX, 1931, p.293.

60. See *Proceedings of the International Congregational Council*, 1920, p.255. A. E. Garvie was concerned that the idea that all men were God's children should not be allowed to dampen missionary enthusiasm. See his *The Missionary Obligation in the light of the Changes of Modern Thought*, London: Hodder & Stoughton, 1914, p.34.

61. H. Richard Niebuhr, *The Kingdom of God in America*, Hamden: The Shoe String Press, 1956, p.193.

62. R. Mackintosh, *Essays Towards a New Theology*, Glasgow: Maclehose, 1889, p.426. See also Charles S. Braden, 'How liberal Christianity conceives of salvation', *The Journal of Religion*, VII, 1937, pp.12—29.

63. See J. B. Pratt, *The Religious Consciousness*, New York: Macmillan, 1920, p.123.

64. Thus in his book *The Strangest Thing in the World*, London: Home Words, 1891, Charles Bullock criticised Henry Drummond's *The Greatest Thing in the World* (1890 and many edns.) for being 'The Gospel with the Gospel omitted'. C. H. Spurgeon opined that Bullock 'has done grand service by laying bare the device of deleting the atonement with the idea of promoting the imitation of Jesus'. See *Sword and Trowel*, 1891, p.340.

65. F. D. Maurice, *Theological Essays*, Cambridge, 1853, p.162.

66. For A. M. Ramsey's comments on this see his *From Gore to Temple*, London: Longmans, 1960, p.5.

67. Quoted by H. R. Mackintosh, *Some Aspects of Christian Belief*, London: Hodder & Stoughton, [1923], p.131.

68. Quoted by L. E. Elliott-Binns, *Religion in the Victorian Era*, London: Lutterworth, 1936, p.280.

69. W. Rauschenbusch, *Christianity and the Social Crisis*, New York: Macmillan, 1907, p.422.

70. A. Peel, *The Congregational Quarterly* I, 1923, p.230.

71. T. Rhondda Williams, *The Working Faith of a Liberal Theologian*, London: Williams & Norgate, 1914, p.xiii, our italics. Robinson, it

will be recalled, believed that the fresh light and truth would break forth out of God's holy Word.

72. H. D. A. Major, *Basic Christianity* Oxford: Blackwell, 1944, p.57.

73. A. M. G. Stephenson, 'English Modernism' in *Liberal Christianity in History*, The Modern Churchmen's Union, 1969, p.150.

74. The second report on a Declaration of Faith submitted to the National Congregational Council of 1865.

75. G. G. Atkins, *Religion in our Times*, New York: Round Table Press, 1932, p.156.

76. Quoted by John Horsch, *Modern Religious Liberalism*, Chicago: The Bible Institute Colportage Association, 1920, pp.127–8.

77. *Proceedings of the International Congregational Council*, 1920, p.255.

78. Quoted by S. G. Cole, *History of Fundamentalism* (1921), Westport: Greenwood Press, 1971, p.83. It was interesting to hear Baroness Wootton confess in a radio broadcast on 11.6.1977 that whereas in her earlier days she would have subscribed to the doctrine here castigated, she now saw the point of the idea of original sin — or at any rate, of ineradicable human nastiness. Cf. R. Niebuhr, *The Children of Light and the Children of Darkness*, London: Nisbet, 1945, p.10.

79. J. Clifford's numerous writings on this theme are listed by J. Marchant, see next note.

80. James Marchant, *Dr. John Clifford*, London: Cassell, 1924, p.81.

81. Ed. J. H. Leckie, *Professor D. W. Forrest, Memoirs and Discourses*, London: Hodder & Stoughton, 1919, p.85.

82. T. R. Williams, *op. cit.*, p.147.

83. D. R. Davies, 'The essence of Christianity', *World Christian Digest*, 55, Nov. 1953, p.45. His book *On to Orthodoxy*, London: Hodder & Stoughton, 1939 is also very much to the point. For earlier hesitations see P. T. Forsyth, 'The insufficiency of social righteousness as a moral ideal', *The Hibbert Journal*, VII, 1909, pp.596–613.

84. Quoted by Gordon Harland, *The Thought of Reinhold Niebuhr*, New York: O.U.P., 1960, pp.45–6.

85. P. T. Forsyth, *Positive Preaching and the Modern Mind* (1901), London: Independent Press, 1964, p.150. The saying comes to mind, 'the rationalist blows cold, the mystic hot; warm up a rationalist and you get a mystic; cool down a mystic and you get a rationalist'. For this we are indebted to S. G. Craig, *Christianity Rightly So Called*, Philadelphia: Presbyterian and Reformed, 1976, p.248.

86. B. Spinoza, *Ethica*, London: Dent, 1925, p.11.

87. B. Bosanquet, *What Religion Is*, London: Macmillan, 1920, p.25.

88. T. R. Williams, *op. cit.*, pp.140, 142.

89. H. D. A. Major, *The Modern Churchman*, Sept. 1921, p.196, quoted by O. C. Quick, *Liberalism, Modernism and Tradition*, London: Longmans, 1922, p.18; italics his.

90. T. Wigley in *A Re-statement of Christian Thought*, reprinted from *The Christian World*, 1934, p.7.

91. See E. M. Forster, *G. Lowes Dickinson*, London: Arnold, 1938, p.212; cf. H. G. Wood, *Belief and Unbelief since 1850*, Cambridge: C.U.P., 1955, pp.72—4. The *criticism* of this view by the Unitarian James Drummond is revealing: to the great mass of believers 'a Christianity without Christ would be something fundamentally different from that by which they have lived. He is bound up in their religious affections, and his is the quickening breath which turns into living creatures the cold forms of truth . . . Nor have they seen in him only Man ascending to the pinnacle of human goodness, but the grace and love of God coming down to reconcile and save an estranged and sorrowful world.' See his Hibbert Lectures, *Via, Veritas, Vita*, London: Williams & Norgate, 1894, pp.291—2.

92. J. Martineau, *Essays, Reviews and Addresses*, London: Longmans, 1891, II, p.443. Into the ecclesiological implications of immanentism, and in particular into the view of the Church as being the extension of the Incarnation, we cannot now enquire.

93. P. T. Forsyth, *The Principle of Authority* (1913), London: Independent Press, 1952, p.171.

94. O. C. Quick, *op. cit.*, p.18.

95. K. C. Anderson, 'Why not face the facts?', *The Hibbert Journal*, IV, 1906, p.860.

96. P. T. Forsyth, 'A rallying ground for the Free Churches. The reality of grace', *The Hibbert Journal*, IV, 1906, p.825.

97. P. T. Forsyth, *The Principle of Authority*, p.177.

98. B. C. Plowright, *art. cit.*, p.290.

99. P. T. Forsyth, *Faith, Freedom and the Future* (1912), London: Independent Press, 1955, p.96.

100. R. A. Finlayson, 'Modernist belief and evangelical faith: Are they the same?', *The Monthly Record of the Free Church of Scotland*, Sept. 1973, pp.142—4.

101. D. B. Stevick, *Beyond Fundamentalism*, Richmond Va.: John Knox Press, 1964, p.173.

102. William Young, 'Historic Calvinism and neo-Calvinism', *The Westminster Theological Journal*, XXXVI, 1973—4, pp.48—64, 156—73.

For clear evidence that Mr. Young's criticism could not be levelled against all earlier Dutch Calvinists see M. Eugene Osterhaven, 'The experimental theology of early Dutch Calvinism', *Reformed Review*, XXVII, 1974, pp.180—9. Cf. George Brown, Jr., 'Pietism and the Reformed tradition', *Reformed Review*, XXIII, Spring 1970, pp.143—52.

103. C. F. H. Henry, 'Fundamentalism', *Catholic World*, June, 1967, p.149.

104. D. W. Simon, 'The present direction of theological thought in the Congregational churches of Great Britain', *Proceedings of the International Congregational Council*, 1891, p.79. We do not stay to consider the ecclesiological-catholic equivalent of conservative intellectualism. It is, of course, that the gospel requires the protection of orders, sacraments, or what not. We simply side with Bernard Manning: 'The grace of God . . . needs no legal machinery to protect it . . . What is it that makes the Church different from all other societies, that makes the preaching of the Word different from all other speech, that makes the sacramental rites different from all other significant acts? It is grace. Then it is not episcopacy or the lack of episcopacy.' *Essays in Orthodox Dissent*, London: Independent Press, 1953, pp.114—5.

105. H. R. Mackintosh, *Some Aspects of Christian Belief*, London: Hodder & Stoughton, [1923], p.176.

106. For the Gospel Standard Baptist position see B. Honeysett, 'The ill-fated articles', *Reformation Today*, no. 2, summer 1970, pp.23—30; reprinted under the title *How to Address Unbelievers*. The four anti-free offer articles were added to the G.S. trust deeds in 1878. See further William Wileman, 'The *secret* history of the four "added" articles; 32, 33, 34, 35', *The Christian's Pathway*, XXVI, Nov. 1921, pp.206—10. These articles have recently been discussed by David Engelsma in his series on ' "Hyper-Calvinism" and the call of the gospel' which commenced in *The Standard Bearer* in April 1974. He argues that the G.S. articles *are* hyper-Calvinistic, but that the testimony of the Protestant Reformed Church which, led by H. Hoeksema, came out of the Christian Reformed Church in 1924, is not. On the contrary, he maintains that his Church upholds the free offer, while the position approved by the Christian Reformed Church in 1924 in respect of common grace threatens the doctrine of particular redemption and therefore denies the sovereignty of grace. The C.R. Church adopted a view of common grace according to which there is 'a certain favor or grace of God which He shows to His creatures in general' and this grace includes 'the general offer of the gospel'. See also D. Engelsma, *Hyper-Calvinism and the Call of the Gospel*, Grand Rapids: Reformed Free Publishing Assocation (Kregel Publications), 1980.

107. J. Zanchius, *Absolute Predestination*, Grand Rapids: Sovereign Grace Publications, 1971, p.87.

108. T. Crisp, *Christ's Pre-eminence*, reprinted Sheffield: Zoar Publications, c.1974, pp.13—4.

109. R. Traill, *Works*, Edinburgh: The Banner of Truth Trust, 1975, I, sermon II.

110. J. Mason, *Mason's Sayings*, reprinted Sheffield: Zoar Publications, c.1974, p.14.

111. H. Bonar, 'God's will, man's will and free will', Wilmington: Sovereign Grace Publications, 1972, p.30.

112. J. Murray, *Collected Writings of John Murray*, Edinburgh: The Banner of Truth Trust, 1976, I, chap. XVII.

113. See J. Calvin, *Institutes*, III, xxiv, 8.

114. See further, J. B. Torrance, 'The contribution of McLeod Campbell to Scottish theology', *The Scottish Journal of Theology*, XXVI, 1973, pp.295—311. Writing of conversion under the Puritans R. Mackintosh said that although the convert 'had nothing to do with the law as the source of "justifying righteousness", he was bidden to use the law as the "rule of his life". Doctrinally and emotionally he was to live by grace; but his conduct was to be exactly the same *as if he expected to be justified by works.'* See *The Insufficiency of Revivalism as a Religious System*, p.8; bound with *Essays Towards a New Theology*. For the view that covenant theology *need* not become a new legalism see Donald Macleod, 'Federal theology — An oppressive legalism?', *The Banner of Truth*, no. 125, Feb. 1974, pp.21—8. The historian of the Brethren movement has detected a 'hint of Pelagianism' in J. N. Darby's view that 'unity is not seen as the result of God's work in the death of Christ, so much as a result of the Christian's conforming to that death'. See F. R. Coad, *A History of the Brethren Movement*, Exeter: Paternoster, 1964, p.33.

115. D. B. Stevick, *op. cit.*, p.59.

116. E. J. Carnell, *The Case for Orthodox Theology*, London: Marshall, Morgan & Scott, 1961, p.121.

117. Carnell and Stevick have chapters on separation. The Reformed Presbyterian Church, Evangelical Synod, has given detailed consideration to the matter. See *Minutes* of the 153rd General Synod, 1975, pp.59—80. Among many conservative evangelical critiques of modern ecumenism see David Hedegard, *Ecumenism and the Bible*, London: The Banner of Truth Trust, 1964.

118. See Donald G. Bloesch's illuminating chap. V, 'The legacy of pietism' in his *The Evangelical Renaissance*, London: Hodder & Stoughton, 1974.

119. R. W. Dale, *The Evangelical Revival*, London: Hodder & Stoughton, 1880, p.33.

120. Robert Mackintosh, *The Insufficiency of Revivalism*, pp.13, 27. Cf. D. B. Stevick, *op. cit.*, pp.25—6.

121. Cf. John 'Rabbi' Duncan: 'There is a true and a false synergia. That God works half, and man the other half, is false; that God works all and man does all, is true'. See ed. W. Knight, *Colloquia Peripatetica*, Edinburgh: Oliphant, 1907, p.30.

122. R. Traill, *op. cit.*, p.31.

123. From the hymn, 'Rock of Ages, cleft for me'.

124. For a review of the position see M. Eugene Osterhaven, *The Spirit of the Reformed Tradition*, Grand Rapids: Eerdmans, 1971, pp.132—7.

125. P. T. Forsyth, *The Principle of Authority*, pp.389—90.

126. John H. Yoder, *The Christian Witness to the State*, Newton, Kansas: Faith and Life, 1964, p.85; quoted by D. G. Bloesch, *op. cit.*, p.124.

127. For social contributions of American conservatives see e.g. G. H. Barnes, *The Anti-Slavery Impulse 1830—1844*, New York: Harcourt, Brace & World, new edn., 1964; John R. Bodo, *The Protestant Clergy and Public Issues, 1812—1848*, Princeton: Princeton U.P., 1954; C. C. Cole, *The Social Ideas of the Northern Evangelists 1826—1860*, New York: Columbia U.P., 1954; Timothy L. Smith, *Revivalism and Social Reform in Mid-Nineteenth Century America*, New York: Abingdon, 1957; Charles I. Foster, *An Errand of Mercy*, Chapel Hill: North Carolina U.P., 1960; Louis Filler, *The Crusade Against Slavery 1830—1860*, London: Hamish Hamilton, 1960; Clifford S. Griffin, *Their Brothers' Keepers*, New Brunswick N.J.: Rutgers U.P., 1960; E. Brooks Holifield, 'Thomas Smyth: The social ideas of a southern evangelist', *Journal of Presbyterian History*, LI, 1973, pp.24—39.

128. *Democracy and the Churches*, Philadelphia: Westminster, 1951; quoted by M. E. Osterhaven, *op. cit.*, p.153.

129. R. W. Dale, *The Old Evangelicalism and the New*, pp.18—9.

130. J. Orr, *The Progress of Dogma*, London: James Clarke, n.d. but preface has 1901, p.353.

131. Dirk Jellema, 'Ethics' in ed. C. F. H. Henry, *Contemporary Evangelical Thought*, Grand Rapids: Baker Book House, 1968, p.111.

132. Quoted by W. M. Horton, *Realistic Theology*, New York and London: Harper, 1934, p.2. Cf. H. P. Van Dusen, 'The sickness of liberal religion', *The World Tomorrow*, no. 14, Aug. 1931, pp.256—9; John C. Bennett, 'After liberalism — what?', *The Christian Century*, no. 50, 8.11.1933, pp.1403—6; G. G. Atkins, 'Whither liberalism?', *Religion in Life*, III, 1934, pp.335—9; Wilhelm Pauck, 'What is wrong with liberalism?', *The Journal of Religion*, XV,

1935, pp.146–60; H. S. Coffin, 'Can liberalism survive?', *Religion in Life*, IV, 1935, pp.194–203. See too the 1939 series in *The Christian Century* on 'How my mind has changed'. For this list of references we are indebted to Dennis N. Voskuil, 'The emergence of American neo-orthodoxy', *Reformed Review*, XXX, 1976, pp.35–8; and see his unpublished doctoral dissertation, *From Liberalism to Neo-Orthodoxy: The History of a Theological Transition, 1925–1935*, Harvard University, 1974. .For a critique of what he calls neo-liberalism see Robert Lightner, *Neo-Liberalism*, Nutley: The Craig Press, 1970. We have already referred to B. C. Plowright's contemporary 'Misgivings'.

133. See W. M. Horton, *op. cit.*, p.4n. Dr. Horton says of liberal concepts that 'it must now be announced, as an accomplished fact, regrettable but duly certified, that their vital sap has departed from them' (p.8).

134. *Christian Life*, June 1947, pp.13–5.

135. See Erling Jorstad, *The Politics of Doomsday*, Nashville and New York: Abingdon, 1970. For developments within conservativism see e.g. Louis Gasper, *The Fundamentalist Movement*, The Hague: Mouton, 1963; Ronald H. Nash, *The New Evangelicalism*, Grand Rapids: Zondervan, 1963; Millard Erickson, *The New Evangelical Theology*, London: Marshall, Morgan & Scott, 1969; George Dollar, *A History of Fundamentalism in America*, Greenville: Bob Jones U.P., 1973; D. G. Bloesch, *op. cit.*; eds. D. F. Wells and J. D. Woodbridge, *The Evangelicals*, Nashville and New York: Abingdon, 1975.

136. C. F. H. Henry, *Evangelical Responsibility in Contemporary Theology*, Grand Rapids: Eerdmans, 1957, p.45.

137. Thus, for example, in *The Battle for the Bible*, Grand Rapids: Zondervan, 1976, Harold Lindsell laments that such conservatives as Daniel P. Fuller, George E. Ladd and Paul King Jewett no longer defend the inerrancy of scripture. For recent defences thereof see e.g. Clark H. Pinnock, *A Defense of Biblical Infallibility*, Philadelphia: Presbyterian and Reformed, 1967, and ed. J. W. Montgomery, *God's Inerrant Word*, Minneapolis: Bethany Fellowship, 1974. The journal *Foundations*, sponsored by the British Evangelical Council and committed to inerrancy, was founded in 1978. The [American] Evangelical Theological Society (1949) and the International Council on Biblical Inerrancy are similarly committed. The following is a small sample of the mass of material on the continuing debate: Stanley N. Grundy, 'Evangelical Theology: where should we be going?', *Journal of the Evangelical Theological Society*, XXII, 1979, pp.3–13; Robert K. Johnston, *Evangelicals at an Impasse: Biblical Authority in Practice*, Atlanta: John Knox Press, 1979; Norman L. Geisler, *Inerrancy*, Grand Rapids: Zondervan, 1979; Roger R. Nicole and

J. Ramsey Michaels (eds.) *Inerrancy and Common Sense*, Grand Rapids: Baker Book House, 1980; Harold Lindsell, *The Bible in the Balance*, Grand Rapids: Zondervan, 1979. For the historical context of the debate see Jack B. Rogers and Donald K. McKim, *The Authority and Interpretation of the Bible: An Historical Approach*, San Francisco: Harper & Row, 1979.

138. As expounded by John Stott, *The Lausanne Covenant*, Minneapolis: World Wide Publications, 1975, pp.27—8. Cf. also articles by Elton M. Eenigenburg, Robert A. Coughenour and Hugh A. Koops in *Reformed Review*, XXVIII, autumn 1974. This issue also includes 'A declaration of evangelical social concern' (1973) among whose signatories was C. F. H. Henry. For further illustrations of the changing mood see e.g. Richard J. Coleman, *Issues of Theological Warfare*, Grand Rapids: Eerdmans, 1972, chap. V. R. J. Sider (ed.), *Evangelicals and Development: Toward a Theology of Social Change*, Exeter: Paternoster Press, 1981; David F. Wright (ed.), *Essays in Evangelical Social Ethics*, Exeter: Paternoster Press, 1981; Frank E. Gabelein, 'Evangelicals and social concern', *Journal of the Evangelical Theological Society*, XXV, 1982, pp. 17—22.

139. I. John Hesselink, 'Toward a seminary that is Catholic, Evangelical and Reformed', *Reformed Review*, XXVII, 1974, pp.108—9; cf. Eugene P. Heidman, 'Toward Renewed Evangelical Unity', *ibid.*, XXXIII, 1980, pp.158—63.

140. *Op. cit.*, p.167.

INDEX OF PERSONS